CONTEXTUAL SAFEGUARDING
The Next Chapter

Edited by
Carlene Firmin and Jenny Lloyd

With a foreword by
Claudia Bernard

First published in Great Britain in 2023 by

Policy Press, an imprint of
Bristol University Press
University of Bristol
1–9 Old Park Hill
Bristol
BS2 8BB
UK
t: +44 (0)117 374 6645
e: bup-info@bristol.ac.uk

Details of international sales and distribution partners are available at
policy.bristoluniversitypress.co.uk

© Bristol University Press 2023

British Library Cataloguing in Publication Data
A catalogue record for this book is available from the British Library

ISBN 978-1-4473-6642-3 hardcover
ISBN 978-1-4473-6643-0 paperback
ISBN 978-1-4473-6644-7 ePub
ISBN 978-1-4473-6645-4 ePdf

The right of Carlene Firmin and Jenny Lloyd to be identified as editors of this work has been asserted by them in accordance with the Copyright, Designs and Patents Act 1988.

All rights reserved: no part of this publication may be reproduced, stored in a retrieval system, or transmitted in any form or by any means, electronic, mechanical, photocopying, recording, or otherwise without the prior permission of Bristol University Press.

Every reasonable effort has been made to obtain permission to reproduce copyrighted material. If, however, anyone knows of an oversight, please contact the publisher.

The statements and opinions contained within this publication are solely those of the editors and contributors and not of the University of Bristol or Bristol University Press. The University of Bristol and Bristol University Press disclaim responsibility for any injury to persons or property resulting from any material published in this publication.

Bristol University Press and Policy Press work to counter discrimination on grounds of gender, race, disability, age and sexuality.

Cover design: Robin Hawes
Front cover image: iStockphoto/littleclie
Bristol University Press and Policy Press use environmentally responsible print partners.
Printed and bound in Great Britain by CPI Group (UK) Ltd, Croydon, CR0 4YY

This book is dedicated to the young people, families and practitioners whose experiences, ideas and trust have made this next chapter possible.

Contents

List of figures and tables — vii
List of abbreviations — viii
Notes on contributors — ix
Acknowledgements — xiii
Foreword by Claudia Bernard — xiv

1   Introduction: Contextual Safeguarding but not as you know it — 1
       Carlene Firmin and Jenny Lloyd

PART I   Domain 1: The target of the system

2   From peers and parks to patriarchy and poverty: inequalities in young people's experiences of extra-familial harm and the child protection system — 17
       Lauren Wroe, Jenny Lloyd and Molly Manister

3   Identifying and responding to structural and system drivers of extra-familial harm using a Contextual Safeguarding approach — 30
       Molly Manister, Lauren Wroe and Carly Adams Elias

4   Value-informed approaches to peer mapping and assessment: learning from test sites — 44
       Carly Adams Elias, Lisa Marie Thornhill and Hannah Millar

PART II   Domain 2: The legislative basis of the system

5   Reimagining Community Safety as community safeguarding in response to extra-familial harm — 61
       Joanne Walker and Carlene Firmin

6   Contextual Safeguarding beyond the UK — 77
       Delphine Peace

7   Decolonising practice: 'doing' Contextual Safeguarding with an ethics of care — 89
       Vanessa Bradbury-Leather and Sue Rayment-McHugh

PART III   Domain 3: The partnerships that characterise the system

8   "If you want to help us, you need to hear us" — 105
       Hannah Millar, Joanne Walker and Elsie Whittington

9   Parents as partners: destigmatising the role of parents of children affected by extra-familial harm — 121
       Lisa Marie Thornhill

10   What can we learn from multi-agency meetings to address extra-familial harm to young people? — 132
       Lisa Bostock

PART IV Domain 4: The outcomes the system produces and measures

11	Developing outcomes measurements in Contextual Safeguarding: explorations of theory and practice *Jenny Lloyd and Rachael Owens*	147
12	Counting children and chip shops: dilemmas and challenges in evaluating the impact of Contextual Safeguarding *Michelle Lefevre, Paula Skidmore and Carlene Firmin*	160
13	Gather round: stories that expand the possibilities of Contextual Safeguarding practice *Rachael Owens*	175
14	Conclusion: Creating societies where children can know love *Jenny Lloyd and Carlene Firmin*	188
References		196
Index		216

List of figures and tables

Figures

1.1	School assessment triangle	5
1.2	Neighbourhood assessment triangle	6
2.1	Intersectional inequalities and young people's experiences of child protection	26
3.1	Assessment to incorporate context	39
3.2	Assessment to incorporate context and structural and systemic considerations	42
4.1	Peer assessment framework	49
5.1	Legislative and governance arrangements for safeguarding and Community Safety Partnerships	63
7.1	Practising with an ethics of care	99
8.1	Young Researcher's Advisory Panel group developing work and thinking through safeguarding	112
11.1	Contextual Safeguarding neighbourhood assessment triangle	153
12.1	The theory of change for Contextual Safeguarding in Hackney	163
12.2	System Review red, amber, green rating tool for Domain 1	166

Tables

5.1	Remit of Community Safety against the Contextual Safeguarding domains	66
5.2	Community Safety Partnership pilot and future activity against Contextual Safeguarding domains	75
8.1	Breakdown of the focus group and interview activity and themes per site	110
8.2	Consultation activities with the Young Researcher's Advisory Panel	111
10.1	Number of meeting observations by site	134
10.2	Site red, amber or green rating by Contextual Safeguarding domain	136
12.1	Red, amber or green rating of Site X in 2019	169
12.2	Red, amber or green rating of Site X in 2021	169

List of abbreviations

ASB	antisocial behaviour
CCE	child criminal exploitation
CS	Contextual Safeguarding
CSE	child sexual exploitation
CSP	Community Safety Partnership
EFH	extra-familial harm
FGC	Family Group Conference
VCS	voluntary and community sector
VRU	Violence Reduction Unit
YRAP	Young Researcher's Advisory Panel

Notes on contributors

Carly Adams Elias is Head of Development at Safer London. She was the Youth Work Practice Advisor for the Contextual Safeguarding (CS) Scale-Up Project, supporting London sites to test and embed contextual approaches to safeguarding. She was seconded from Safer London, a voluntary sector organisation supporting young Londoners, families and communities affected by exploitation and violence. As Head of Development, she supports the development of CS approaches within the organisation. Carly is an experienced social worker and manager within the voluntary sector and has held roles designing, delivering, managing and developing services for children and young people affected by harm outside of the family context.

Lisa Bostock is Principal Research Fellow in the Institute of Applied Social Research (IASR) at the University of Bedfordshire. Her research focuses on effective multi-disciplinary working and the role of reflective supervision in building resilience across the helping professions to improve outcomes for people using services. She has specialised in developing 'close-to-practice' evaluative methods based on direct observations of practice to design new ways of assessing the impact of supervision on direct practice with children and families. During the pandemic, she worked with the CS programme to support local authorities in implementing contextually informed approaches to safeguarding young people in the community.

Vanessa Bradbury-Leather is Research Assistant with the CS programme at Durham University, currently working across *Contextual Safeguarding and Youth Justice* and *Contextual Safeguarding: The Next Chapter*. She is Filipina-English, and as an anti-colonial scholar and advocate, her background has focused on decolonisation, Indigenous rights and wellbeing. She is particularly interested in community-led responses to young people's experiences of structural harm, as well as the potential of critical reflexive learning in social and organisational change, starting a PhD in October 2022 to explore this.

Carlene Firmin is Professor of Social Work at Durham University, where she is the professorial convener of the Communities and Social Justice research group. Carlene has researched young people's experiences of community and group-based violence since 2008 and has advocated for comprehensive approaches that keep them safe in public places, schools and peer groups. Carlene coined the term 'Contextual Safeguarding' in 2015 and has since led a research programme to test, adapt and implement the approach into policy, research and service design. Carlene is co-convener of a special interest group on Social Work and Adolescents for the European Social Work Research Association, Associate Editor of *Child Abuse Review*, a Global Ashoka Fellow and also a member of the Churchill Fellowship Advisory Council. She has written in the national newspaper *The Guardian* since 2010 and is widely published in the area of child welfare, including through two sole-authored books. In 2011, Carlene became the youngest Black woman to receive an MBE for her seminal work on gang-affected young women in the UK.

Michelle Lefevre is Professor of Social Work at the University of Sussex, where she is also Director of the Centre for Innovation and Research in Childhood and Youth. Prior to her academic career, Michelle practised as a social worker and psychotherapist with children and families in the context of child protection concerns. Her research and teaching reflect this experience, largely focusing on the development of practice methods, interventions and systems to improve the lives of vulnerable children, young people and families. Michelle currently leads the Innovate Project (www.the innovateproject.co.uk), exploring how social care innovation might address extra-familial risks facing young people.

Jenny Lloyd is Assistant Professor at Durham University. Working within the CS team, her research focuses on harm to young people during adolescence. Jenny cares passionately about working with practitioners to improve system responses. As an embedded researcher, she works within child protection services to improve responses to harm, including serious youth violence, child criminal exploitation (CCE) and child sexual abuse. Jenny spends most of her time outside of work getting excited about new hobbies and pursuits.

Molly Manister is Research Assistant at Durham University. Her research interests include system responses to the exploitation of young people – in particular, radicalisation, structural and systems harm in child protection, intersectional feminism, social policy analysis and human rights in practice. She is particularly interested in how safeguarding policy and practice operates in perpetrating structural harm and the ethics of intervening in young people's lives, including how policy and practice aimed at addressing exploitation and abuse can be gendered, racialised and classist.

Hannah Millar is Research Assistant at the University of Bedfordshire, bringing over ten years' experience working in practice with young people to her research role. As part of the London Scale-Up Project, she co-led on the development of the Contextual Safeguarding Young People's podcast series and worked closely with the Young Researchers' Advisory Panel who produced a CS resource. Hannah continues to engage with and critically develop participatory practice research methods, ensuring that young people, particularly those from diverse and lesser-heard groups, have meaningful and ethical experiences within the research process, contributing to influential change.

Rachael Owens is Assistant Professor at Durham University. She has over 20 years' practice experience in social work and social care. Rachael was Practice Development Manager at Hackney Children's Services (2017–19), working alongside the CS research team. Following this, she was Social Work Practice Advisor (2019–22) with the University of Bedfordshire, working on the Scale-Up Project. As part of this, she facilitated and researched CS system change with five local authority children's safeguarding services, and managed the London strand of the project, overseeing parallel work in an additional four boroughs. Rachael is now Co-Investigator on 'Sustaining Social Work', a research project looking at social workers' experiences of CS practice.

Delphine Peace is Research Fellow at Durham University and has been part of the CS research programme since 2018. Her research has two broad areas of focus: challenges and innovations in how child protection systems respond to adolescent extra-familial harm (EFH) in the UK and internationally, and how participatory research and practice can help us better understand adolescents' experiences of harm and safety to inform safeguarding responses.

Sue Rayment-McHugh is Senior Lecturer and Co-Leader of the Sexual Violence Research and Prevention Unit at the University of the Sunshine Coast (UniSC), Australia. She has a PhD in Criminology, a master's degree in Psychology (Forensic) and is a registered psychologist. Her research and professional practice have focused on the prevention of sexual violence and abuse, with a particular interest in contextual models of prevention, including in First Nations communities.

Paula Skidmore was Senior Research Fellow based within the CS team at the University of Bedfordshire from 2019 to 2022. Previous to that, she worked for over 12 years within academia, conducting qualitative and evaluation research related to child/youth sexual exploitation and was on secondment to Barnardo's (Research and Development) from 2003 to 2007. She has an MA in Crime, Deviance and Social Policy (Lancaster University) and an academic background in lecturing and tutoring Critical Criminology at undergraduate and postgraduate level from 1988 to 2014, in Liverpool, Glasgow, Nottingham, London and Manchester. She is now semi-retired and happily resides in north-west England with her daughter and their little dog, Wolfie.

Lisa Marie Thornhill was a postdoctoral researcher in the CS team at Durham University during the Scale-Up Project. She worked with parents and young people engagement across the national Scale-Up test sites. Lisa has worked with adults and young people affected by abuse online and offline for over a decade.

Joanne Walker is Assistant Professor at Durham University. She is an applied social researcher with experience covering issues of engagement and participation, safeguarding in education and universal youth settings, child protection processes and legal arrangements underpinning these, EFH and intersectionality. She has developed methods to engage young people in discussions about both CS approaches and the harm they may experience in extra-familial contexts, and has theorised about service and structural challenges in engaging young people in offers of support. Historically, she has undertaken work on definitions of, and policy frameworks that respond to, exploitation across public health and social care.

Elsie Whittington is a youth researcher at the University of Bedfordshire. She holds an Honorary Knowledge Exchange Fellowship at the University of Manchester. Elsie was formerly a Research Fellow at the Safer Young Lives Research Centre at the University of Bedfordshire. Her research focuses on understanding the complexity of sexual consent and possibilities for a more ethical understanding of competence building and sexual negotiation. Elsie prioritises youth-led and participatory research methods and advocates the importance of informal education and youth work.

Lauren Wroe is Assistant Professor at Durham University. Lauren has led several research projects for the CS programme since 2018. This research has generated knowledge about young people's experiences of harm in extra-familial contexts, and specifically the role that policy and practice plays in creating safety and/or reproducing harm in the lives of young people.

Acknowledgements

There are so many people that have made this book possible. Firstly, to all the young people and families that have shared their time and stories. To the young people whose experiences have informed this work – thank you for making us laugh, sometimes cry, and always motivated to keep on going to make change.

Our thanks go to all the practitioners and sites that have allowed us to learn from you. Special thanks go to all those sites that have worked with us to test and develop Contextual Safeguarding (CS); your faith in us has allowed us to learn so much and this work would not be possible without your insights – this book is yours really.

Thank you to all our colleagues at the Safer Young Lives Research Centre at the University of Bedfordshire; you gave CS a home, and without the support and passion of colleagues there, we would not have developed our ideas or ensured such an ethically informed approach. Thank you also to our new home in the Sociology Department at Durham University for helping us to grow this work.

A huge thank you to all of the authors in this book, many of whom were new to academic writing and worked so hard to craft these chapters and bring the stories of research to life. Developing CS has been a team pursuit; each member inspires us every day.

Thank you to our funders for allowing us to develop our ideas – we hope that this work can impact many beyond ourselves.

Final thanks to our families for their love and support. The road to CS has been far smoother with you along for the ride.

Foreword

Claudia Bernard
Goldsmiths, University of London

During the 30 or so years that I have been active as a social work practitioner, educator and researcher, the landscape of child protection has become considerably more complex, so much so that we may consider it something of a minefield. I have observed how problems arising in safeguarding have increased as the changing ethnic and racial demographic of children in the child welfare system has become more diverse, and that the issues that bring them into the child protection system have become more complex and multi-layered. All told, we know that families from low-income backgrounds living in neighbourhoods with high levels of youth violence, gang activities and peer-on-peer violence find it much more challenging to protect their children from extra-familial harm (EFH). Conversely, there has been an underappreciation of the role of structural inequalities in extra-familial contexts and its impact on the risks and harms experienced by young people, which has critical safeguarding implications. In this sense, in the multi-racial, multi-cultural and multi-faith social contexts of contemporary Britain, how to effectively safeguard the diverse population of children and young people that come to the attention of child protection systems is an ongoing concern.

Additionally, amid the debates about the need to recognise and understand the social determinants of harm, there is resistance to the notion that structural and institutional racism is both within child welfare systems and part of society at large, which contributes to the over-representation of racially minoritised children and young people in the child welfare and criminal justice systems. Furthermore, the shifting landscape of inequality and disadvantage, exacerbated by the pandemic, will no doubt play a significant role in children and young people's subsequent psychosocial development. Thus, in many ways, for children's services, improving the lives of vulnerable and disadvantaged children and young people and their families is more challenging than ever.

Nevertheless, although I do not seek to deny that responding to EFH is challenging, I argue that marginalised populations are typically underserved and over-policed. In particular, I posit that Black children are usually underserved, under-supported and over-policed (Bernard and Harris, 2019). They frequently experience adultification, the subtle and unconscious race-based bias that negatively affects the treatment of Black children in the child welfare and justice systems (Bernard, 2019). Therefore, Black children are often perceived as less innocent than white children and thus less in need of protection. This was demonstrated most powerfully in the case of Child Q, a vulnerable child who was strip-searched by the police in her school. Child Q was thus failed by two of the key safeguarding partners, namely, the police and her school. It has been shown that safeguarding strategies and practices can sometimes pathologise, criminalise and harm children from marginalised communities (Johnston and Akay, 2022). We are therefore constantly reminded that the current child protection system is not working very well for racially minoritised children and can actually cause harm to some children. Indeed, I would posit that racially minoritised children are often seriously let down, and, in some instances, services may pose more of a risk to children and become part of the problem instead of the solution.

Furthermore, although practitioners in children's services are increasingly employing different child protection practice frameworks and practice tools, such as those trauma-informed, Signs of Safety and other strengths-based and systemic ways of working, most frequently, they continue to experience challenges in effectively meeting the needs of young people from marginalised backgrounds.

In *Contextual Safeguarding: The Next Chapter*, the authors present compelling evidence to show why it is important to centre the environmental and social risk factors for effective interventions to safeguard in extra-familial contexts. Contextual Safeguarding (CS) is an innovative approach to safeguarding that is all about being trauma-aware and recognising vulnerable young people exposed to extra-familial risks. In this edited collection, the authors have been developing and testing ways to advance child protection systems and multi-agency safeguarding practices to better respond to the EFHs experienced by young people. A widely adopted approach in UK child protection systems, CS's starting point is from a strengths-based and social justice perspective, thus providing an ideal framework for interventions into EFHs because it encourages practitioners to confront critical questions about the structural inequities that increase risks of harm for disadvantaged children and young people.

This innovative book explores how CS can help shift the locus of individual responsibility away from families to broader structures that create social contexts that heighten and shape extra-familial risks and harms experienced by young people. Thus, it focuses on the necessity of a deeper and more nuanced understanding from a social harm perspective. Above all, CS is underpinned by a clear theory and research grounding, giving us tools to engage critically with key issues. What I value most about CS approaches is that they shift attention away from ascribing blame to parents, especially mothers, and do not rest on assumptions that they can protect their children from all harms but encourage an appreciation of how structural inequalities impact young people's lived experiences of EFH. I concur with the central argument that there must be a critical interrogation of the institutional cultures and organisational structures of child welfare delivery through an intersectional lens, not least because intersectionality helps us to understand how contextual considerations coalesce with intra-familial and extra-familial factors to create the harms and risks disadvantaged children are exposed to. As an overall approach, it can help to navigate the complex issues that are at the root causes of the harm experienced by young people from disadvantaged backgrounds. Thus, how we understand the heterogeneity of children's experiences in unsafe neighbourhoods has been an important focus of the CS approach.

Contextual Safeguarding: The Next Chapter is essentially concerned with supporting families and empowering youth. This edited collection is especially important as it is grounded in alternative discourses that understand how structural inequalities and EFH contribute to the over-representation of racially minoritised children in the child welfare and youth justice systems. It therefore forces us to have transformative discussions about marginalised voices and experiences, and to critically engage with the everyday experiences of children and young people in their neighbourhoods and social environments. The authors importantly note, however, that contextual approaches call on us to cultivate visionary spaces to engage in effective interagency working. In this way, this book engages very well with the challenges of how we might do things differently in our safeguarding practices.

The book is fundamentally calling for a complete system change to improve the effectiveness of interventions. It offers hands-on and conceptual tools to show how a contextual approach can be used to effectively safeguard children at risk of EFH in contexts of systemic racism. In many ways, this book fills an important gap in the knowledge base and will undoubtedly play an essential role in expanding contextual research in EFHs. It offers important new insights into social issues that impact the experiences of children needing safeguarding in extra-familial contexts. The scholars in this collection have thus provided a compelling guide, inviting us to see the ways in which safeguarding partners and practice responses need to work to effectively meet the needs of young people experiencing EFHs. In this regard, the book's greatest promise is the solution it offers for navigating the multi-layered factors that foster extra-familial abuse and exploitation that are experienced by children who are intersectionally marginalised. Therefore, this is clearly essential reading for guiding policy and practice for collective solutions to support children living in environments with heightened risk of EFH.

1

Introduction: Contextual Safeguarding but not as you know it

Carlene Firmin and Jenny Lloyd

Some might think of it as a 'buzzword'. Others consider it a term to describe what they have known for some time. While some practitioners, policy makers and academics see it as a term that has revolutionised child protection responses to young people who come to harm beyond their front doors. Whichever way you describe it, one thing is true: the term 'Contextual Safeguarding' (CS) has become part of the child protection lexicon in the UK:

> 'There needs to be a shift towards a model of Contextual Safeguarding where the risks are identified in different areas of the child's life and there's a coherent multi-agency response.' (Parent participant in study on social care responses to exploitation by PACE, 2020)

> It is not enough to work with individuals when a whole peer group is participating in harmful behaviour. Contextual safeguarding promotes awareness of vulnerability in the context ... where adolescents spend their time, for example online, in parks or at school. (Triennial review of Serious Case Reviews, Brandon et al, 2020: 113)

It still strikes us as strange when we hear people reference or use 'Contextual Safeguarding', particularly when it appears in job titles. Like it's always been around. As if it is established to a point where everyone knows what it means, in theory and in practice. And to an extent, these quotes suggest that some people have 'got it'. They have understood the essence of the idea, what those of us who work with it are trying to achieve and the potential that is yet to be realised. So too do many practitioners and young people who have engaged with our work in recent years:

> 'The kids know what is safe these days and where they feel unsafe. So if adults listen, they can do something about unsafe places because they have the power to do that and to make things happen. Kids can't make the changes but know where is bad.' (Young person, Scale-Up Project)

'Because the ripple effect will work out. So if we deal with that issue as a community, with services, bang smack in the middle, the positive ripples will go all the way to the edge to where all of the young people and elderly members of the family and all the individual hub families [are] on the outside. ... So that's why I think it could be so powerful.' (Family group conferencing coordinator, Scale-Up Project)

However, at the point of editing this book, the notion of CS is seven years young. It was introduced as a concept into the field of UK social work in 2015, and offered a vision for how safeguarding partnerships, and children's social care specifically, could respond to harms young people faced beyond their family homes. We, the editors of this book, have worked together since 2016 to incrementally document how that vision has been converted into practice. We have come a long way on that journey – and the things we understand about CS have evolved over that time. We have not been alone in developing this understanding. It was just the two of us in 2016. By the summer of 2021, our research team was 17 people strong; and research in CS was also underway in other UK universities and being discussed in international academic networks. In this book, therefore, we share what that growing body of thinkers have to say about CS – the good, the bad and the yet to be worked out. Their combined efforts illustrate what the next chapter of the CS programme will consider, and why such considerations are imperative for the sustained implementation of the idea.

The foundations of our work: 2011–16

The impetus for CS has been well documented. Over a three-year period – starting in 2011 – it became evident that England's child protection system had not been designed to respond to the harm young people experienced beyond their family homes – but it was being increasingly used for this purpose. Although most young people were safe, many were at risk of significant harm in contexts and relationships beyond their family homes. Some were being exploited, both sexually and criminally, by both adults in their communities and their peers. Others experienced abuse in their first romantic or intimate relationships or were exposed to street-based violence (often from peers), sometimes coming to severe or fatal harm. Social care services, and the social workers within them, struggled to mount an effective response due to numerous, well-documented, system challenges (Gorin and Jobe, 2013; Hanson and Holmes, 2014; Firmin, 2017; Firmin and Knowles, 2020). They were using approaches, and working upon a legislative/policy basis, that:

- framed abuse in respect of (in)actions of parents/carers, rather than factors beyond parental influence;

- assessed family relationships and a child's living situation to reach conclusions about risk, and identify issues to target through intervention rather than through assessment of extra-familial contexts/relationships where this harm often occurred;
- were better designed to work with young children as opposed to those going through adolescent development; and
- assumed clear water between those who instigated harm and those who experienced it, rather than a blurry boundary between the two often found in situations of extra-familial harm (EFH).

The concept of CS was built upon a recognition of these challenges. And while it was not intended to resolve them all, it was introduced with the explicit intention of creating approaches that increased safety for young people in extra-familial contexts and relationships.

Contextual approaches were trialled over an 18-month period in 11 areas, designed and tracked through partnerships between researchers and practitioners. Work undertaken during this time evidenced that the vision of CS – responses that built safety in extra-familial contexts/relationships – could not be realised through system tweaks or appendages to services. CS was not a discrete intervention or set of practices. It required the systems in which interventions/practices were delivered to be aligned with that same vision. The systems which social workers, and their partners, drew upon to safeguard young people from harm needed to be able to engage with the contextual dynamics of that harm in every root and branch of its design.

To better articulate what such a system change required, the vision of CS was converted into a conceptual framework. The CS framework is comprised of four domains. In 2016, these were described as:

- Domain 1: The target of the system. This should be the contexts in which EFH occurs (and change the social conditions of those contexts to increase safety), not solely the young people and families impacted by it.
- Domain 2: The legislative basis of the system. This must be principally guided by a child protection, rather than a criminal justice, legislative framework.
- Domain 3: The partnerships that characterise the system. These need to feature people and organisations who can influence extra-familial contexts (and not solely those who intervene with individuals), including young people, their families and communities.
- Domain 4: The outcomes the system produces and measures. These need to be contextual as well as individual, noting whether contexts are safer as a result of responses offered, and contextualising any behaviour change young people display.

Since 2017, we have led research teams at the University of Bedfordshire (until 2021) and Durham University (since 2021) to track the operationalisation of this four-part conceptual framework, using it to guide local and national system change in respect of social work responses to EFH.

Where the last book left off: 2017–20

The last book on CS (authored by the first editor of this book and published in 2020) documented our initial learning during the first two years of testing. For the most part, this test work had occurred in one local authority area in England, but we were also ten months into testing in a further five areas – four in England and one in Wales. At that stage, we had identified four key features of CS when the framework was operationalised.

Two levels of CS

Firstly, CS is implemented at two levels within a system: we now refer to these as *Level 1* and *Level 2 CS*.

Level 1 saw practitioners contextualise their responses to young people and families impacted by EFH. For example, when social workers took a CS approach to assess young people's needs, some introduced a safety mapping activity. This activity supported young people to identify locations where they felt safe or unsafe, and social workers took the findings of the activity into consideration when developing a plan of support. For example, some social workers took care to ensure that any interventions offered to a young person were not taking place in an area where they felt unsafe; or if a young person had to travel through an unsafe area to get to college, their support plan might have identified a safe person they could turn to for their journey if needed.

Level 2 involved practitioners and managers developing responses to contexts themselves – any context where EFH was occurring. Continuing with the earlier example, when the same unsafe area was identified during assessments, social workers and their partners may have undertaken a welfare-based assessment of that context. These assessments sought to understand the needs of young people in that context, the capacity of adults who were there to provide guardianship and any environmental or community factors that may have been relevant to safety there. Such assessments were used whether a peer group, school environment or public place was the focus of an assessment, and a plan was developed and agreed to address any factors identified. As we tracked these early assessments, we converted our findings into 'context assessment triangles' (Figures 1.1 and 1.2).

These triangles communicated the focus points of an assessment when the subject was a context and not a person, and provided a framework that other social workers could use to support them in contextualising their practice.

Figure 1.1: School assessment triangle

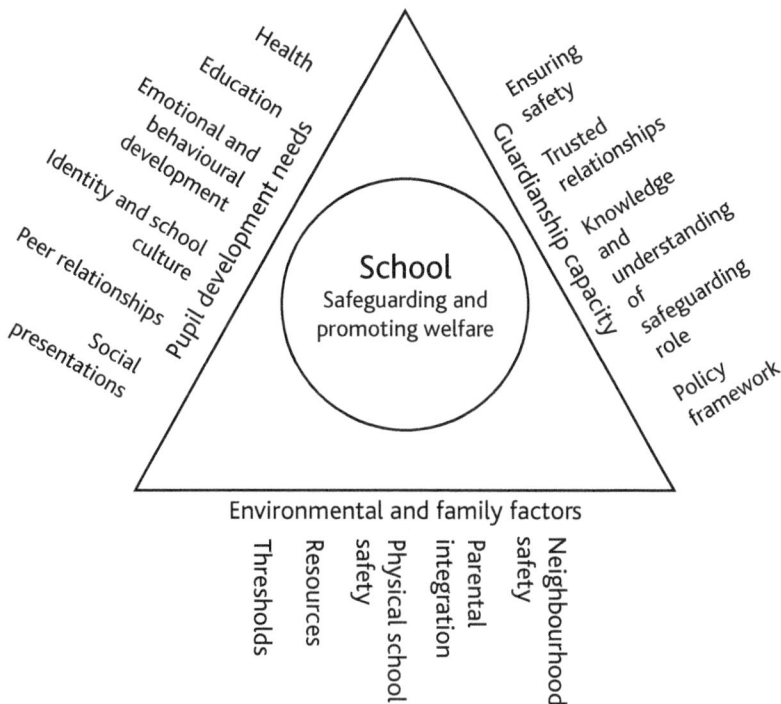

Collective capacity to safeguard

The second common feature of these early-stage efforts at CS were ambitions to build a collective capacity to safeguard young people, rather than solely focus on parental or carer capacity to keep young people safe. The notion of guardianship was particularly important in this respect. For both Level 1 and Level 2 aspects of implementation, social workers were seeking protective adults in extra-familial contexts, as well as looking at the protective capacity of their own services (and those of their partners). Attempts to shift thinking in this direction proved hard to sustain. While the intention was often there in revised assessment tools or local policies, practices often remained centred on changing the actions of parents in order to protect young people in extra-familial contexts. Child protection systems specifically, as well as child and family social work more generally, are hardwired to associate care and protection with parental (in)action. Moreover, if we accept that the risks to a child – including a risk to life – may sit with us (our services, organisations, resources, any steps we take), that might increase professional anxiety in situations often already fraught with worry. If we can locate blame for EFH with a young person's parents, it eases the burden and is aligned with wider social work practices in England and Wales. We could sense that the idea

Figure 1.2: Neighbourhood assessment triangle

of 'collective capacity to safeguard' made sense in theory and may prove more challenging in practice. Much of what we will share in this book demonstrates the steps that have been taken to gradually build and sustain collective capacity to safeguard as a core feature of CS systems.

Everybody's responsibility

The notion of 'collective capacity' to safeguard young people was associated with the third feature of CS implementation: a change in how partner agencies were asked to interpret the idea that safeguarding was 'everybody's responsibility'. This terminology is commonplace in UK safeguarding policies. All sectors, particularly statutory ones such as policing, health, education, probation and housing for example, have duties in respect of safeguarding young people. This duty is enshrined in legislation (Children Act 1989 and 2004). Its interpretation in policies and practices has largely focused on information sharing and the provision of services to children and families. In respect of EFH, therefore, all agencies have a duty to share information about young people impacted by EFH and, where relevant, provide services to those young people. In the early stages of testing, many areas had invested in training a range of partner agencies to 'spot the signs' of exploitation, for example, so that if they saw any of those signs, they could raise concerns with children's social care. When attending multi-agency meetings to discuss EFH, professionals from a range of agencies shared whether a young person, or their family, had had contact with their service, or anything else they knew about this young person, to inform a plan of support.

CS required areas to reimagine this interpretation of safeguarding being everybody's responsibility. If an organisation such as a school or a transport provider identified young people experiencing EFH within their setting, then, in addition to any information sharing, they had a responsibility to create safety for and around those young people. They had influence over the context where these young people were unsafe and so they also had a duty to contribute to any 'Level 2' plans to address risks, and increase safety, in that context. If agencies attended planning meetings for a young person affected by EFH, they might be asked to share information about the context they were responsible for, and not just the young person who was the subject of that meeting. For example, if a school attended a meeting, they might be asked about safety in the school environment and not solely about the attendance and attainment of the young person who the meeting was about; such information allowed others to put a young person's attendance at school in the context of wider trends and cultures in that school environment. During this early period of testing, partner organisations had started to understand the changing nature of their role, particularly when Level 2 assessments were underway. Yet there was much more to learn about their ability to sustain such an approach, and what the implications might be for future service and policy development.

Context weighting

All of the activities mentioned earlier served to reinforce one of the earliest identified features of CS: the practice of 'context weighting'. Across all areas of tracked implementation, practitioners used assessments to a) understand which context carried the most weight in respect of young people's safety, and b) ask whether the plans being developed targeted those contexts. For example, at Level 1, had an assessment clearly shown that a young person's peers were most influential in terms of the risks they were facing while the plan to safeguard this young person focused on their parents? Or at Level 2, professionals might ask whether a peer group was the most influential in terms of violence in a local area, or whether it was the nature of the park where that peer group were spending their time. Did violence occur wherever the peer group spent their time, in which case the peer group would be most influential? Or did they display violent behaviour in the park but less so in the youth club, in which case the dynamics of the park may need to be prioritised in terms of intervention. In all of these ways, context weighting was used to identify (mis)alignment between the findings of an assessment and the focus of the plan, and galvanise a partnership to focus their response in the context most in need of attention.

The next chapter: 2020–22 and beyond

As well as identifying the previously mentioned four features of CS, testing from 2017 to 2019 helped us surface new questions about the ethics and sustainability of the approach. It was clear that to implement the four domains of the CS framework, children's social care departments needed to implement the approach at two levels, build a collective capacity to safeguard young people, reformulate what it meant for safeguarding to be 'everybody's responsibility' and build context weighting activities into various parts of their response to EFH. But to what extent was this feasible with child protection systems in England and Wales? Moreover, would efforts to implement these features of CS produce what was intended if wider approaches to child protection cultures were not aligned?

These questions had foundations. As interest in CS increased, so too did examples of implementation that did not reflect the original intentions of the concept. We saw CS used to map, monitor and disrupt young people's friendships, rather than seek to safeguard, and build safety within, them. Young people were dispersed from contexts where they were spending their time, or professionals increased use of CCTV or police presence in public places where EFH had occurred. Some practitioners were concerned that CS would unhelpfully increase the numbers of young people subject to state intervention, with all those mapped in a peer group or identified in a public place where EFH was occurring referred into children's social care, rather than the context itself being the subject of intervention. And the widening partnerships involved in CS tests rarely involved young people and families. Local businesses, licencing departments, sports and leisure services, among others, were being drawn into safeguarding assessments and meetings, but often without the informed consent of young people and families who would likely be impacted by those assessments.

None of these practices reflected what we had in mind when we thought about CS. They did, however, reflect challenges within wider child protection systems, such as the inconsistent involvement of children and families in decisions about them (Thoburn et al, 1995; van Bijleveld et al, 2020) and a tendency to monitor risk rather than provide support (Featherstone et al, 2016; Seddon, 2008. And so, as an expanded team, in 2019, we developed and published a set of values that underpinned CS in a bid to ensure that efforts at implementation remained aligned with the original intentions of the framework (Firmin, 2020; Wroe, 2020).

The values of CS

Five values provide a foundation to CS. They ask that when implementing the four domains of the CS framework, practitioners and service leaders ask whether they are doing so in a way that is:

1. Collaborative: works with, rather than does to, young people, their families and wider communities when responding to EFH.
2. Rights-based: engages with the full range of young people's rights when developing responses to EFH. This would not only include rights to protection but a right to have their views heard and considered, a right to privacy and a right to spend time with others and so on. Directly engaging with, rather than ignoring, any tensions that might emerge when trying to protect all those rights in safeguarding processes is critical.
3. Ecological: sees young people in the contexts of their familial and peer relationships, but also sees those relationships in the contexts of school, community and online public spaces, and views those spaces in the context of wider structural drivers of harm such as poverty and racism.
4. Strengths-based: seeks to build safety, and not solely disrupt risk, for young people affected by EFH, and does this by building on the assets in their families, peer relationships and communities rather than solely profiling any risks within them.
5. Rooted in an understanding of young people's lived reality: speaks and works directly with young people to understand where they feel/are safe or unsafe, and why, rather than relying on professional perspectives or data sets to reach conclusions.

So if a service is seeking to change the social conditions of a park where peer sexual abuse is occurring (Domain 1), or trying to work in partnership with those who can influence a high street where young people have been groomed into drug distribution (Domain 3), they would need to sense-check whether their efforts to do so a) involved the young people who spent time in that context, their families and other residents who were there; b) recognised young people's rights to spend time in those public places and sought to protect those rights while also safeguarding them from harm; c) saw what was happening in the park or high street in the context of other local factors such as overcrowded housing, poverty or racist views of the young people affected; d) looked for evidence of safety in these places and tried to build on these; and e) worked with young people to understand what would help them to feel safe, or might decrease safety, in these contexts.

Applying the values and domains through the Scale-Up Project

While some of the chapters in this book draw from a range of projects to test and examine CS, over half use data from the Scale-Up Project. As such, we summarise the methodology for that project here to avoid repetition in the chapters that follow. The Scale-Up Project ran from 2019 to 2022 in five local areas in England and Wales outside of London, and a further four local areas in London from 2020 to 2022. A project team of eight researchers, working across two universities as embedded researchers, captured the process of implementing CS in these nine areas. They worked over three phases to collaboratively develop and implement system-change activities aligned with the CS framework. In the first phase, researchers and local professionals built an understanding of the site's current response to EFH and used this to develop a plan that adapted the existing response to better align with the CS framework. In the second phase, sites ran focused pilots to test an element of system change. Researchers documented that process and assessed the alignment of the system change with the CS framework. In the third phase, reflecting on feedback from young people and parents, researchers worked with site representatives to embed the pilot results into their system and disseminate learning both within the site and to children's services departments across the UK.

Researchers used a range of methods to document the design and pilot phases. These included:

- Observations of 88 meetings and practice related to cases of EFH.
- A file review of 122 cases and assessments.
- System mapping (n=18), to understand the journey of children and contexts through the system.
- Participation in 532 meetings to inform developing work.
- 61 interviews and 65 focus groups with practitioners.
- Six focus groups, two interviews and 78 surveys with parents and young people to capture their experiences and perspectives on new approaches to EFH.
- Documentary review of 154 new and existing policies and documents relating to EFH.

At two to three points in the project, researchers drew together all the data collected in the intervening period and analysed it against an RAG rating (red, amber, green) system created for the CS framework. This process helped sites to zoom out of individual activities and consider their collective impact of the system change they were seeking to create. For the purposes of various chapters in this book, this data set, or subsets of it, has been subjected to additional analysis to explore specific elements of the Scale-Up process and/or their relevance to certain domains of the CS framework.

Introduction

Mapping the next chapter of CS in this book

The chapters of this book draw upon the findings of the Scale-Up Project, and other projects undertaken within and external to the CS team since 2020, to deepen and extend how the domains and values of the approach have been used and understood.

We have organised the chapters into four parts – each focused on one of the four domains that make up the CS framework. In their own way, each chapter demonstrates how our understanding of one or all four domains of the CS framework has deepened in the five years since they were first published, and the implications of this for future efforts at implementation. In particular, each chapter individually, and as a collective contribution, does more to consider how the values of a CS approach sharpen how we communicate what each domain requires of systems, organisations and practices.

The chapters in Part I of the book further our thinking on the first domain of the CS framework: the need for responses to EFH to target the contexts in which it occurs in order to change the social conditions of those contexts. Both Chapters 2 and 3 consider the impact of structural harm on the social conditions of neighbourhood, school and peer contexts. In Chapter 2, Lauren Wroe, Jenny Lloyd and Molly Manister offer a macro account of why structural drivers of harm need to be foregrounded when assessing contexts associated with EFH and deciding upon the focus of intervention. Molly Manister, along with Lauren Wroe and Carly Adams Elias, explore this argument further in Chapter 3 by outlining the practical opportunities and challenges of responding to structural harm when Scale-Up sites piloted assessments of locations impacted by EFH. In Chapter 4, Carly Adams Elias drills down further to illuminate how assessments of peer groups require constant consideration of the values of CS to ensure they address, rather than cause, harm. In particular, she draws upon the views of young people shared during the Scale-Up Project, in addition to data collected by Scale-Up sites who attempted peer assessments, to illustrate why alignment with the values of collaboration and being rights-based ensures that peer assessments are used to target the social conditions in which young people come to harm, and not the individuals who make up peer groups. Collectively, these chapters emphasise that Domain 1 of the CS framework must be used to target the social conditions of contexts, and not solely the people within contexts (or the behaviour they display within them). The values of CS assist in maintaining this focus; however, wider system pressures may continue to limit how feasible this is.

The second part of the book is dedicated to Domain 2 of the CS framework: the need for responses to EFH to be underpinned by child protection, and not criminal justice, legislative and practice frameworks. In Chapter 5, Joanne Walker and Carlene Firmin consider a largely neglected policy framework that, like criminal justice approaches, has dominated responses to EFH in recent years: Community Safety. Using data from Scale-Up sites where Community Safety Partnerships (CSPs) were involved in CS pilots, this chapter asks whether Community Safety interventions can ever feature in a CS approach and what changes are required to facilitate this. In particular, can child protection frameworks accommodate a Community Safety perspective, or will the rub be such that such a hybrid would undermine this domain of the CS framework? Zooming out from the UK, in Chapter 6, Delphine Peace explores the relevance of CS for international child protection systems, and the extent to which these may offer more or less favourable conditions for future efforts at implementation. Chapter 7 rounds off this part by reflecting on the challenge that Domain 2 child protection frameworks built upon colonial legacies, and what the potential implications of this may be for CS in the future. In one sense, the approach seeks to return to community-based knowledge and collaboration to create safety, and yet it is trying to achieve this by changing a system that has devalued such methods. Collectively, these chapters both trouble and add depth to how Domain 2 is understood: what we, the developers of CS, mean by child protection frameworks, and what further work is required to maintain that stance in unfavourable historical and political contexts.

In Part III of the book, chapters focus on the partnerships required to implement CS (as per Domain 3 of the framework). We prioritise consideration of how young people (Chapter 8 by Hannah Millar, Joanne Walker and Elsie Whittington) and parents (Chapter 9 by Lisa Marie Thornhill) could, and on occasion have, been partners in the implementation and analysis of the approach. Each chapter offers insights into the conditions required for CS to be viewed as a benefit to young people and parents, and both promote the value of collaboration as being at the heart of such benefit. It is motivating to hear from young people and parents how CS could improve how they experience service support. These chapters also provide a stark reminder of why the values of CS, and not just the domains of the framework, are required to implement the approach. They rightly identify how, without careful consideration, CS could be used in ways to maintain state oversight of their decisions, without increasing any sense of safety they may experience. This part closes by returning to what we learnt about multi-agency working during the latest round of testing (Chapter 10). Lisa Bostock shares how multi-agency meetings have become a focal point for partnership efforts to implement CS, and the opportunities and challenges that emerge in this context. She uses the chapter to identify features of multi-agency meetings that best facilitate an alignment with the four domains of the CS framework and point to where work is needed to ensure young people and parents are afforded routes to participate in this element of safeguarding systems.

Work to understand the fourth domain of the CS framework – the need to measure impacts on contexts as well as individual young people – remains the most underdeveloped. To an extent, this is a reflection of wider system design, from local authority outcome frameworks to evaluation methods for commissioned evaluations: everyone is focused on what happens for individual young people and families – and less on what happens in the contexts where they came to harm. The chapters in the fourth and final part of this book therefore make some critical contributions to furthering how we begin to build outcome frameworks that measure not only the impact of CS but the contextual impact of child protection systems. The part begins with Chapter 11, written by Jenny Lloyd and Rachael Owens, which documents efforts to measure the contextual impact of responses designed in Scale-Up sites. They focus on efforts on one site to build the green shoots of a contextual outcome framework, which could be used at a service level, and also caution against efforts to develop outcome frameworks that undermine the overall relational principles of CS. In Chapter 12, Michelle Lefevre, Paula Skidmore and Carlene Firmin reflect on how contextual outcome measures were created and applied to three different projects that used CS. One was focused on system capability to intervene with contexts, one attempted to measure individual and contextual impacts of a CS and the other sought to design ways to monitor the contextual impacts of discrete interventions. All three illustrate the long road left to travel before a sufficient outcome framework can be utilised in either research or practice. In Chapter 13, Rachael Owens documents a range of case study responses from Scale-Up sites to help illustrate why contextual outcome measures are important. At this level, it is possible to illustrate the perceived outcomes for individual young people, peer groups and neighbourhoods when CS guides responses. The task now is to convert these case studies into a set of standardised measures that can be used across a system.

The book concludes by reflecting on what each of these sections tells us, separately and collectively, about the future of CS, both the challenges the approach has to overcome and the potential yet to be realised. Centring the values of CS, and the extent to which they call for us to love as much as the domains call for us to be evidenced, it serves as a helpful ending point for this chapter of the CS journey.

So what are you waiting for? Dive in! We hope you enjoy the journey the next 12 chapters will take you on as much as we did when we compiled them. For us, they illustrate the collective endeavour that CS has become. Not from a group of academics but as a network of practitioners, service leaders, young people, their families and communities, who have all played a role in shaping what we now understand about what Contextual Safeguard is, isn't, could be and shouldn't become. In doing so, this book provides the next set of blocks, upon the foundations of the 2020 publication, to build child protection systems that create safety for young people beyond, and not solely behind, their front doors.

PART I

Domain 1: The target of the system

# 2

From peers and parks to patriarchy and poverty: inequalities in young people's experiences of extra-familial harm and the child protection system

Lauren Wroe, Jenny Lloyd and Molly Manister

Tackling the social conditions of abuse

Many myths have circulated about the COVID-19 pandemic, a novel flu pandemic that, at the time of writing, has had a global impact for two years. One of those myths, now well documented, was that 'we are all in this together'. This was a phrase adopted by the current British Conservative politician and Chancellor of the Exchequer, Rishi Sunak. Intending to acknowledge that the virus does not discriminate, Sunak, who was announcing his first economic budget for the country at the start of the first UK national 'lockdown', wanted to let the public know that the British government wouldn't either. Over the past two years, a polyphony of voices have pointed out that, actually, we weren't all in this together. People living in poorer areas of the UK were nearly four times more likely to die from the virus than people living in affluent areas (Suleman et al, 2021). British Black Africans and British Pakistanis were two and a half times more likely to die from the virus than white British people (Platt and Warwick, 2020). These figures revealed huge disparities in how the virus impacted communities across the UK, dependent on social class, ethnicity or disability.

They also revealed something else: many driving forces of this disparity were *structural* and *systemic* in nature (we will return to a definition of these terms). People living in poorer areas were not simply dying at higher rates because they were poor but because they were more likely to be exposed to the virus, working in essential jobs that continued through the most virulent stages of the pandemic. British Black Africans and Pakistanis account for a significant proportion of the British working class, and many were essential workers and are frontline health and social care workers (ONS, 2020). Those living in poorer areas had fewer options for self-isolation, with lower household incomes and overcrowded housing making staying home from work, or isolating from family members, harder. Many did stay at home despite these additional challenges (Joseph Rowntree Foundation, 2021: 21).

These structural inequalities determined who was most exposed to the virus and least protected from getting sick, and also who was least protected from getting sacked (Joseph Rowntree Foundation, 2021: 36), or, on top of that, from being charged with a litany of new 'COVID' offences introduced through a series of emergency parliamentary measures. A report published in 2021 by the Institute of Race Relations (IRR) revealed how the government's response to the pandemic, the policies it prioritised and chose to pursue as part of its public health strategy, disproportionately impacted racially minoritised, working-class people. Discussing specifically the prioritisation of emergency measures, policing and enforcement as a response to the risks posed by the virus, the report documents that: 'whilst Asian people make up 7.5% of the population, they represent 13% of those issued with Fixed Penalty Notices (FPN), and where Black people constitute 3.3% of the population, they represent 8% of those fined', noting that 'there are disparities too in terms of social class, with those from deprived areas being more likely to be issued with FPNs. Already more likely to live in poverty, racially minoritised people have been at the sharp end of pandemic-induced economic hardship' and, the report notes, increased rates of criminalisation (Williams et al, 2021: 6).

The way society is *structured* on the basis of social class, ethnicity, disability, immigration status and so on, and the way the *system* responded to the pandemic based on this social stratification, meant that, in fact, *some people were more in it than others*. Some people were more likely to die, to lose their jobs, to have to go to work, less likely to receive adequate healthcare, more likely to get arrested for 'COVID breaches', and to experience harm at the hands of the system (not just the virus), than others. For some, the COVID-19 pandemic response meant safety; for others, it compounded or created new harms. Reflecting this, the IRR report concluded that

> in the vast majority of cases, participants were also seeking safety from the violence and harassment posed by police, often painfully aware of the risk not just of injury, but also of death. What does it mean then, for the police to play a central role in protecting the public from the dangers of Coronavirus, when the history and present of policing is defined by profound harm – a lack of safety – for certain communities? (Harris et al, 2021: 4)

What has this got to do with adolescents and their experiences of abuse beyond their families? It is common to hear that any child can be abused or exploited; but some children are less likely to receive help when they are abused, more likely to be viewed as responsible for the harm they have encountered, less likely to have access to protective structures that can reduce their chances of being harmed in their communities and more likely to be criminalised than to receive support (Davis and Marsh, 2020). Some young people are more likely to come under the radar of child protection services, some are less likely than others to receive early-help support and some are more likely than their peers to be removed from their families (Bywaters et al, 2017). For some young people, the current public health response to youth violence may equate to safety, for some it may disregard their specific needs entirely or, in some cases, it may be a major driver of the harm they are experiencing in their community (Wroe, 2021).

This chapter is concerned with understanding how structural inequalities shape young people's experiences of significant harm beyond their families, and how these inequalities mediate the system response (that is, government policy, the child protection system and its multi-agency partners) to young people who have been harmed. In this chapter, we consider how CS could support us to understand structural inequality and systemic harm when thinking about extra-familial abuse in adolescence. We propose that the framework and its accompanying methods, which have to date considered the contexts of young people's lives when assessing and responding to adolescent abuse, could support us to consider sources of harm beyond parks and peers to, say, poverty and patriarchy. And that, in fact, it is absolutely necessary to do so.

Thinking critically about context

When the CS programme set about 'contextualising' child protection, it started by asking practitioners to understand the contexts where EFH occurs, and to build systems that could target the 'social conditions' of abuse. Quickly, this became associated with assessing places outside of the home. Practitioners assessed and 'mapped' peer groups, discussed abuse taking place in schools or developed assessments of train stations, shopping centres and parks. CS became synonymous with working in places outside of the home, but less so with tackling the *social conditions* – the social, cultural, economic and political structures – that shape these places and may facilitate or mitigate abuse.

Case examples

Callum, 15, was leaving the house and staying away at night. Practitioners were concerned about who he was associating with and his 'risk' of 'being groomed'. Little attention was paid to the fact that he was living in an overcrowded house. Without access to adequate housing, leaving home was often the only way for Callum to find a bed for the night.

In another example, researchers in the CS team were assessing how a school addressed harmful sexual behaviour. During an observation, teachers questioned peer group dynamics and why girls share sexual images of themselves. They did not question that a male teacher was witnessed telling a female student to 'put more makeup on'.

Understanding context means more than just talking about the harm that happens to people in different places but acknowledging the intersection of this harm with broader contextual features, such as poverty or patriarchal gender norms.

CS expands access to child protection beyond the home and families to the contexts where young people experience harm and harm others. However, spaces are not containers for things that happen, they are made of ever-shifting and changing relations between people and places (Massey, 2005). Places are shaped by networks and relations of power, the unequal distributions of which mean that certain places and people are disproportionately impacted by harm (in the broadest sense), while others aren't. In addition to thinking about which places young people are harmed, we might also want to ask ourselves why now, why these young people and whose experiences of place are being prioritised over others?

The street where practitioners have heard that children are at risk of grooming isn't just a space where there might be a lack of CCTV, lighting or appropriate adult supervision. These places mean something to young people. It might be the place you can go to when it rains, the place where she first smiled at you, the spot which falls straight between your two homes or that place where you held him at the end. It might also be that bit of the road the council sold off and now can't put lighting in, the border between two local authorities where no one has claimed responsibility, the place where the youth club used to be. When we're asking practitioners to assess contexts beyond the home, we need to do this with an understanding of the interpersonal, and also the social, cultural and political, relations that influence the harm that might be happening there.

For anyone reading this who has already tried to do a 'peer' or 'location' assessment, you might have run into a few problems or frustrations. Friendships change, people move on, the place that was popular (or risky) last week might not be the same next week. If we try to 'fix' contexts (in both the sense of repairing and in defining) at the level of the individual or place, we run the risk of only scratching the surface of harm, not tackling the root causes of it. When the CS team first started delivery training, the question 'won't this just disperse the problem elsewhere?' was often raised. 'Not necessarily' was often the response, usually followed by an explanation as to why responses would need to be founded on collaborative approaches with welfare at the heart (that is, working *with* young people to make places safer). But the reality of what we have seen is that, too often, approaches focus on disruption and enforcement, and then displacement (and criminalisation of young people) does occur. If we don't understand the structural and systemic nature of contexts, and causes of harm, it is very likely that the harm will just be moved on or embedded further for some young people.

Shifting the child protection lens to spaces outside of the home is not enough to tackle the social conditions of abuse. Inequalities shape young people's experiences of harm in different places, their access to protective structures and the extent to which they are identified as victims or not. When we started developing CS, we first asked practitioners to be able to name the contexts where young people were most at risk ('context weighting') and to consider the language they used to describe young people and the impact this had. We then worked with them to start thinking about addressing this harm. In this chapter, we invite you to think about the possibilities that naming structural and systemic harm can have for changing how we think and respond to young people's safety, and where this leads us. So, in the first instance, we're not asking you to 'fix', say, poverty or the patriarchy – we're asking you to consider it as an essential factor in young people's experiences of harm beyond their families. The next step will be considering how we adapt our systems to mitigate inequalities.

Inequalities and extra-familial harm – rewriting the rules of child protection?

Who writes the rules of child protection?

This section of the chapter considers the evidence that structural inequalities mediate adolescent experiences of abuse and exploitation in contexts beyond their families. It also considers the evidence that the policies, systems and services in place to protect adolescents from EFH are not conceived of or delivered equally and can reproduce or create new harms. This is an important consideration for CS, because 're-writing the rules of child protection' (Firmin, 2020: 251) means we must also be mindful of the social rules operating within child protection that result in the differential treatment of young people and their communities.

The rules of child protection determine which harms are considered a policy priority, a matter for child protection or 'intervention' in families, and what form this intervention will take. Approximately 4.3 million children in the UK live in poverty, with a negative impact on health, social, emotional, cognitive, behavioural and education outcomes (Joseph Rowntree Foundation, 2021). Growing up in poverty is a driver of bullying and experiences of exclusion from peer groups (NHS Scotland, 2018). Child poverty is related to increasing numbers of children in the care system. A recent study (Bennett et al, 2021) concluded that between 2015 and 2020, a 1 per cent increase in child poverty was associated with five additional children in care, approximating that over 10,000 additional children entered care during this period because of rising child poverty. At the same time, tackling terrorism and extremism is a major policy objective for the UK government and is the only harm type with a dedicated paragraph in the 'extra-familial harm' section of *Working Together* (2018). Yet in 2020, only 405 under-20s of the 4,883 referrals to the government's counter-radicalisation Prevent programme met the threshold for discussion at a Channel Panel, equating to a mere 0.003 per cent of young people in the UK (Home Office, 2021). Many have noted the broad and specific impacts of the counter-radicalisation strategy on Muslim young people and their communities, fuelling Islamophobia and marginalising children in their schools and communities (CAGE, 2018). Despite the far-reaching experience of child poverty in the UK and the infrequent occurrence of (and highly impactful response to) radicalisation, the Department for Education's strategy for children's social care (and other key reports) do not mention poverty at all (Bennett et al, under review). A quick search reveals that they do mention radicalisation as a 'rare' threat to young people that, at the same time, is demanding growing resources from local authority budgets (Department for Education, 2016). What is thought of as child harm, the investment afforded to it and the ways in which the child protection system prioritises and targets interventions are dependent on wider political, social and economic agendas. This section, then, is not only concerned with identifying the inequalities that drive adolescent vulnerability to extra-familial abuse, but with identifying the ways the child protection system, its legislative and policy frameworks and multi-agency partners, disproportionately targets, dismisses or distorts young people's experiences of harms in their communities.

Let's take Callum as an example. Policy decisions that prioritise a focus on interpersonal harm, particularly those that are racialised (exploitation, extremism, gangs, trafficking and so on), over structural forms of harm (poverty, racism, patriarchy, homophobia, ableism and so on) determine how services interact with children and families, and the lens through which they view their struggles. It often distorts the ways in which the latter, in Callum's example, poverty resulting in overcrowded housing, can create vulnerability to the former, exploitation in the community.

Inequalities and extra-familial harm

At the time of writing, it is almost 30 years since Stephen Lawrence was murdered by his white peers in the neighbourhood where members of his family lived. The Macpherson report that followed identified significant failures in leadership and professional practice, and institutional racism in the response to Stephen's murder. In 2019, a study of Serious Case Reviews following significant child harm (Bernard and Harris, 2019) concluded that race and racism are significant factors in young people's experiences of harm and of child protection responses (yet often absent from the review).

This is backed by myriad studies suggesting that Black children are over-identified as perpetrators of harm and under-identified as victims. It is perhaps not surprising (although appalling) that almost 50 per cent of the youth justice estate is occupied by Black, Asian and racially minoritised children, who are often noticeably absent in child welfare discourses and services. In 2016, a report revealed that 81 per cent of individuals profiled by the police and its partners as 'gang-affiliated' in Manchester were Black, whereas only 6 per cent of those involved in serious youth violence were Black (the figures were 72 per cent to 27 per cent respectively for London; Williams and Clarke, 2016). The report concluded that the disproportional (and unqualified) application of the 'gang' label to Black (in particular) and other racially minoritised young people informed charging and prosecution decisions with significantly deleterious consequences for young people (see also Amnesty, 2018). A 2021 study by Wroe warned that while Black children were significantly over-represented in 'county lines' cohorts, the hyper-racialised policing of the perceived Black criminal 'gang' could fuel the criminalisation of Black boys and young men who are the victims of exploitation. Yet in 2021, a government report into racial disparities in the UK concluded that racism could no longer explain inequalities in British society, stating that the disproportionate exclusion of Black Caribbean children from UK classrooms (a recognised driver of poor outcomes for children, and of exploitation; Temple, 2020) was a matter of 'aspiration' rather than racial inequality (Commission on Race and Ethnic Disparities, 2021). We clearly have a long way to go.

In the first decade of the 2000s, child sexual exploitation (CSE) became a recognised form of child abuse in British legislation, and by the public and media. Reports of white, working-class girls being sexually abused by organised 'gangs' of working-class South Asian men drew on the racialised idea of the 'gang' or 'criminal other' to spotlight the minoritised ethnicities of (some) perpetrators, while eclipsing the insidious and varied ways in which CSE takes place and the experiences of many of its victims. Research by Cockbain and Tufail (2020) demonstrates that the construction of the 'grooming gang' (not a legally defined term) is inherently tied into an anti-Muslim politics that has been merged with the 'counter-radicalisation' agenda and galvanised by the far right and the right-wing press (despite most perpetrators of child sexual abuse being white men whose trials receive far less media coverage). The research also shows that this obscures the experiences of victims, noting that Black, Asian and racially minoritised victims of CSE were 'almost entirely overlooked' (Cockbain and Tufail, 2020: 6) in the media coverage of CSE in Rotherham. They note that it is not only the media who have failed to acknowledge the diverse experiences of CSE among adolescents, but that mainstream services aimed at providing support to victims are primarily aimed at white girls, despite almost a third of CSE victims being boys and one in five of Black, Asian or minoritised ethnicity (Cockbain and Tufail, 2020). In addition to the racialised political and media coverage of CSE over the past two decades, Davis and Marsh (2020) contend that the obscuring of Black children's experiences of CSE, and other forms of abuse, are the result of 'adultification' where Black children are viewed as more adult-like, sexualised and aggressive than their white peers.

This work by Davis and others demonstrates how some children are excluded from accepted notions of vulnerability. Brown's (2019) work exploring girls' experiences of CSE describes how, initially, the issue had been framed socio-economically, acknowledging that a key component of CSE is the transaction of sex for financial or other resources, and that victims' social class was significant, and a major barrier to their identification by professionals. Policy makers, Brown contends, have since abandoned a socio-economic view of CSE (where unemployment, access to housing or benefits might have been a legitimate local authority response) in place of a narrow 'child protection' view that is concerned only with predatory men and vulnerable girls. Beyond this, Brown argues, the professional idea of 'victimhood' is reserved for 'innocent (white) girls' with a lack of agency, an unrealistic notion that often excludes working-class and racially minoritised young people. Perhaps this is why, two decades later, we continue to hear from professionals that young people are 'putting themselves at risk' or are 'sexually promiscuous' or 'aggressive', and why we see many of the disparities discussed earlier play out across child welfare services.

The research clearly indicates that patriarchal, binary notions of gender (and their intersections with race, class, sexuality, disability and so on) create vulnerabilities to sexual harm in adolescence, and are significant factors in determining if, how and when young people receive help and support. Research from the US indicates that 'Lesbian, gay, bisexual, transgender and queer (LGBTQ) youth are often also identified as being at a heightened risk of victimization' (Hammond et al, 2020: 186). Discussing the experiences of transgender youth, the research notes that this increased risk of victimisation is often a result of young people's structural and systemic marginalisation from their peer networks and legal employment opportunities. The article goes on to note that young people that 'identify as LGBTQ are over-represented in the juvenile justice and child welfare systems and often face significant barriers to obtaining fair and equitable treatment that meet their rehabilitative needs' (Hammond et al, 2020: 186). While the relationship between structural inequalities and experiences of EFH are under-researched, it is likely that many of these observations are applicable to other forms of extra-familial abuse.

'Social models' of disability are informing new approaches in child safeguarding (Featherstone et al, 2018) that are sensitive to how societal structures and norms are disabling and create disadvantages for individuals that are 'viewed by society as having physical, mental or intellectual impairments' (Oliver, 2004: 21, in Featherstone et al, 2016: 10). This is very much true for adolescents' experiences of EFH, with research documenting that young people with learning disabilities

> face additional barriers to their protection, and to receiving support if they are at risk of, or have experienced, CSE. The reasons for this are multi-layered and complex and often appear to be entrenched in the way society perceives and treats young people with learning disabilities. Previous studies on disabled children's abuse point to the part that disablism can play in their lack of protection. (Franklin and Smeaton, 2017: 480)

The authors conclude that a lack of education and training for professionals, social isolation of young people and their families, disempowerment and invisibility and a lack of government guidance all contribute to the conditions that create heightened vulnerability to CSE for young people with learning disabilities.

There has been much to learn from the disability rights movement during the last two years of the COVID-19 pandemic. Disability rights activists have for decades highlighted how social, economic and policy decisions create hostile and inaccessible environments for large sections of society. For adolescents at risk of exploitation, the pandemic revealed 'digital poverty and systemic inequality in access to information and services' in new ways because of (necessary) lockdown restrictions and limits on movement, access and social interaction (Racher and Brodie, 2020: 279). While the authors note that the pandemic led to innovations in the use of digital technology by services to promote access, it is pressing to acknowledge that disabled young people have been structurally and systemically excluded from support services for decades.

The literature discussed here points to the intersecting societal structures of gender, race, class, sexuality and disability and the inequalities they produce in adolescents' experiences of EFH, and how (and where) the child protection system and its partners identify harm and respond. These societal 'rules', while malleable (there is hope!), govern the spaces in which adolescents spend their time (the parks, the schools, the friendship circles) but they also determine organisational and professional spaces – they inform the 'rules of child protection'.

We contend that if we are to fully understand the contextual drivers of EFH in adolescence and, importantly, how to protect young people, there is a need to understand how inequalities are shaping young people's experiences, and professionals' understanding, of vulnerability and risk (Figure 2.1). We also contend that inequalities are shaping and informing harm reduction

Figure 2.1: Intersectional inequalities and young people's experiences of child protection

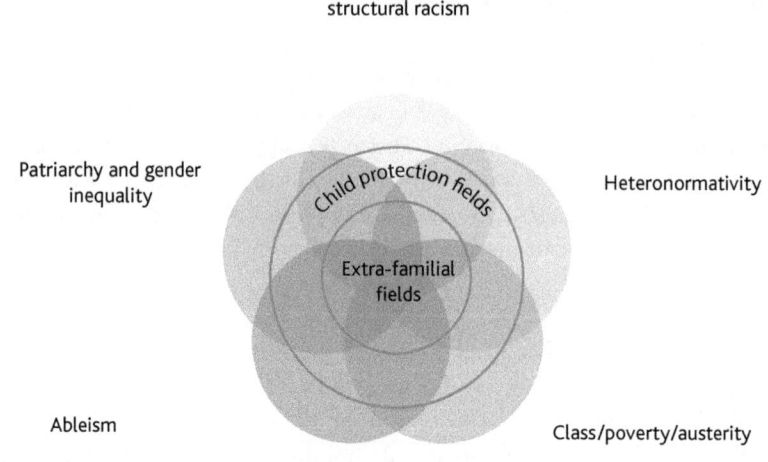

practices, and a differential treatment of young people by children's social care and multi-agency partners.

Broadening the framework: the theory underpinning Contextual Safeguarding

What does this mean for CS? The idea that context matters is grounded in Firmin's (2015) review of nine cases of serious adolescent harm that identified shortcomings in system responses. It is also grounded in the notion that to understand young people's decisions and behaviours, we need to understand the contexts in which decisions and actions are taken – that there is a *reflexive* relationship between environments and individual behaviour. It is specifically rooted in the sociological theory of Pierre Bourdieu, who outlined that an individual's experience in a given context is determined in part by their access to economic, social and cultural resources (capital) (Bourdieu, 1984). For young people leaving their family homes and entering their schools, peer groups and neighbourhoods, their experiences of harm and safety will be determined by the social norms and rules of these spaces, and by the resources they have to navigate these rules. Starting from this point, CS posed the question: what do we know about the rules at play in the spaces that adolescents spend their time that promote safety or harm? And what do we know about how a particular young person, or group of young people, moves in this space, drawing on their access to various forms of financial, cultural and social resource? What system changes need to happen to change the social rules or increase a young person's capital, and how would understanding young people's decisions and actions in this way determine our response to them?

Bourdieu's theory has great utility for thinking about how structural factors – like class or race – interact with an individual's daily experiences of and in the world. Bourdieu's theory bridges (social) 'structure' and (individual) 'agency', explaining the interaction between the two. That class and inequality shape experiences of context is central. Of particular relevance is his idea of 'habitus'. Habitus or a young person's embodiment of 'social rules' is inherently linked with their social class and will influence how that young person engages with and experiences contexts where they may encounter safety or harm, that is, schools, peer groups, neighbourhoods. It will determine their access to capital, their understanding of and propensity to adhere (or not) to the social rules of a given context. Bourdieu's theory tells us that to understand context and a young person's experience in it, we must understand how wider structural and economic conditions influence the capital they can access, their feel for the social rules and, crucially, how *others relate to them* in a given 'social field'.

The child protection system is another 'field' that young people must navigate once they have encountered, or are deemed to be at risk of, significant harm in their communities. As the literature review earlier describes, these inequalities can result in harm, such as system blindness to trans or disabled young people's experiences of harm, or over-intervention and surveillance in working-class or racially minoritised families. Dillon (2019) used Bourdieu to demonstrate how families navigate the 'field' of child protection, the 'rules' of these spaces and the power imbalances that exist between families and local authorities. Dillon argues the 'rules' set by the child protection system are unwritten and made up of professional expectations of how families should present and comply, and that failing to abide by these rules can have very high stakes for families (including removal of children). For young people at risk of EFH in their communities, the unwritten rules of the child protection system (that often target 'behaviour' as a result of individual decision making) can result in young people and their parents being blamed for a range of extra-familial pressures ('lack of parent control', 'risky lifestyle choices') or in adolescent activity such as experimenting with alcohol, drugs or sex being routinely read (for some young people) as indicators of risk, while other pressing factors such as housing or education are ignored. CS has sought to 'rewrite' these 'rules' of child protection (Firmin, 2020: 251), rules that determine how harm in conceptualised, named and addressed and who has the power to do so.

Taking this further, Bourdieu's notion of 'symbolic violence' has been used to understand how 'interventions' in the lives of young people at risk of EFH (and their families and communities) can result in stigmatisation and suffering. The child protection system and its partners, operating within and upholding dominant social rules and power dynamics, can inflict a range of harms in communities as a result of 'interventions' that are ostensibly geared towards creating safety. One example of this might be social care-supported police operations intended to root out child exploitation through the use of undercover policing, licencing and traffic enforcement, increased police presence on the streets and stop and search in working-class areas and/or those populated with racially minoritised or migrant families, reinforcing dominant stereotypes that equate poverty and race with 'crime', criminalising whole communities and damaging trust (Mason, 2019).

Returning to Callum, to understand his 'missing episodes', it is helpful to consider the extent to which his lack of access to financial capital (in the form of housing) led him to draw on his social capital (peers) to find a place to sleep. This *may* increase Callum's risk of harm depending on whether those peers are looking out for his needs (let's not assume they aren't). Callum's 'habitus', informed by his social class, will influence how others relate to him in the various 'fields' he encounters, whether that is his school, friends or indeed professional services. Callum's habitus will inform the resources he has at his disposal to safely navigate these spaces (that is, money, connections) and his feel for the social rules of these spaces. When child protective services encounter Callum, they draw on a set of social rules (including the rules of child protection) to interpret and respond to his predicament, understanding his missing episodes as worrying 'behaviour' indicating 'risky' associations. In the field of child protection, the local authority has significantly more capital (in all forms) than Callum, his family and peers, and begins to set the rules for how his actions will be understood, what he and his parents/carers will need to do to prove he is safe and what types of services or resources will be put in place to support (or disrupt) them (child protection plans, relocations, substance misuse or parenting programmes and so on). Simultaneously, Callum's housing situation, and the inequalities driving that, are unresolved and his family are now contending with the pressures of overcrowding and of statutory involvement in their family or community. This is a form of 'symbolic violence' resulting in a range of harms, including misrecognition, stigmatisation, neglect of basic needs and state interference in private life.

Conclusion

The ideas in this chapter stem from our thinking about the theory and values that underscore a CS approach, and from our research with practitioners in a range of settings who are seeking to make changes to the way they safeguard adolescents. To date, the CS framework has supported local authority child protection teams to target support at contexts beyond the home and has done some initial thinking about what it would mean for the approach to more explicitly name and contend with inequality. This has happened in the development of the CS value base, which, alongside the 'domains', can be used to guide contextual interventions that are rights-based, ecological, strengths-based, collaborative and evidence-based, and through the development of tools, such as the Beyond Referrals toolkit and the Watching Over Working With resource (see the CS website), that facilitate self-assessment and critical reflection on how structural and systems harms are reproduced in schools and social work settings.

It has also happened through collaboration with researchers developing the Social Model for protecting children, a model that foregrounds the 'economic, social and cultural barriers to ensuring children are cared for safely and their relational and identity needs respected' (Featherstone et al, 2020: 2). Initial thinking about the overlaps between the two approaches shows promising opportunities for Social Model ideas to support CS to name and address, say, poverty, and to root practice in co-production with families and communities, and for CS to help transform Social Model ideas into system change in child protection. In Chapter 3, we explore these challenges in more detail, considering how practitioners have grappled with these questions and what they have sought to do about it. We also extend our analysis of what CS can do to support thinking and practice in adolescent safeguarding that is sensitive to inequalities and seeks opportunities to begin to rectify them.

3

Identifying and responding to structural and system drivers of extra-familial harm using a Contextual Safeguarding approach

Molly Manister, Lauren Wroe and Carly Adams Elias

The socio-political power dynamics that shape the world govern the spaces where young people spend their time. Giovanni Rose (2021), a young person living in London, describes this in the poem 'Welcome to Tottenham', highlighted in this extract:

> Welcome to Tottenham.
> The devil's playground.
> We fight over streets we don't own,
> Knife crime's on the rise because the beef can't be left alone.
> Why does no one understand that we just want our youth clubs back,
> Why do they claim they're not racist but label the violence here Black?
> Welcome to Tottenham.

As the extract shows us, young people are aware of how their lives, and subsequently, the risks they face, are moulded by forces that span far beyond their families and communities. Structural inequalities, including poverty, racism and misogyny, are felt by many communities and young people every day (RECLAIM, 2020). Chapter 2 outlined the empirical evidence for the relationship between structural inequalities and experiences of, and responses to, harm in adolescence. If we take anything away from Rose's work, perhaps it should be that young people know more than we do about how inequalities shape the spaces they live in.

Extra-familial forms of harm (EFH), that is, abuse adolescents face outside the home, including criminal and sexual exploitation, peer-on-peer abuse and serious youth violence, and the spaces in which they occur, are shaped and reshaped continually by economic, social and political dynamics (Melrose and Pearce, 2013; Irwin-Rogers, 2019; Wroe and Pearce, 2022). These dynamics can be drivers of harm (that is, economic need as a driver for exploitation) and can shape how governments and professionals respond. When responding to EFH, consideration of how these dynamics play out and how they impact young people's experiences of harm and safety is twofold. First, how do we understand in practice the impact that economic, socio- and political (structural) inequalities have on the prevalence of EFH and young people's experiences of it. Second (and interconnected), what role do policy and professional responses have in reinforcing harm and the inequalities that govern the lives of young people and their communities (system harm). This chapter outlines some of the challenges practitioners face when responding to harm in contexts characterised by structural inequality and how, at times, this is exacerbated by professional responses.

When professionals work with young people to try to reduce the risk they face from abuse outside the home, they are often limited by a system that does not enable consideration of how socio-political forces such as poverty, racism and misogyny impact on how such abuse is experienced by children, families and their communities (Mason et al, 2021). In England and Wales in particular, in comparison to Scotland or Northern Ireland, we see the scaling back of policies that place inequality, prevention and early intervention as central issues in social care (Mason et al, 2021: 2647), which spills out into practice that cannot then integrate a consideration of structural inequality into responses.

As CS develops beyond the confines of the research team and the sites we work with, it is important to pause, take stock of what has been done and think about what the future holds for those seeking to safeguard young people from EFH. This chapter aims to do just that – using data from the CS programme of work to reflect on some of the ways racism, poverty, patriarchy and so on shape the contexts where young people are at risk and how practitioners have, despite sometimes swimming against the tide, tried to integrate these issues into their practice. Chapter 2 laid out the evidence and theory base that points to the necessity, and immediacy, of considering context beyond physical spaces to the inequalities that shape these spaces, and young people's experiences of them. But here we ask, what does this look like in practice?

Practice examples

Over the past three years, the CS research team have worked alongside nine local authorities in England and Wales as they have embedded a CS response to EFH. The local authorities inhabit a multitude of contexts – from small rural villages, beachfront towns, to sprawling inner cities and everything in between. The diverse nature of these places has meant practitioners face a range of challenges when it comes to EFH, and, more generally, the socio-political features of their localities vary. Some deal with, for example, the impact of austerity on services for young people that has meant they have nowhere to spend their time, forcing them into marginal spaces where they are more vulnerable to abuse. Others have witnessed the mistrust between Black young people and the police amid increased stop-and-search powers in built-up cities (Dhumma, 2021). Most are facing the continual challenge of creating safety in school settings where misogyny and homophobia are embedded (Firmin et al, 2019a). All are grappling with safeguarding young people in the spaces outside their homes.

Reflecting on the ways that practitioners are thinking about structural harm when embedding a CS response, we see a range of capacity and inclination within the system. When preparing to write this chapter, we asked our fellow researchers who have been based in CS Scale-Up sites (see the Introduction for more detail) if they had examples of practice that had incorporated consideration of structural inequalities and taken active steps to reduce their impact on young people. We wanted case studies to be brought to us that highlight exemplary practice that had adhered to the four domains of CS (Firmin et al, 2019b) and embodied the values (Firmin, 2020) to address the impact of structural harm when intervening into contexts. Unsurprisingly, the reality was not this straightforward. What we found spoke to a wider challenge identifiable across all social care services (Featherstone et al, 2018; Charmen, 2021), that is, while poverty, racism, homophobia and misogyny shape experiences of harm, services are not designed to integrate this, in some cases, reproducing it.

The ways in which Scale-Up pilots are integrating consideration of structural harm into practice are varied. Four case studies from Scale-Up sites (outlined later) explore how structural inequalities are considered in practice, how structural inequalities are acknowledged as exacerbated or impacting EFH and how professional responses mitigate, reinforce or reproduce inequalities. Each represents a different level of acknowledgement of, and capacity to address, these issues. The case studies represent a small sample. We know, however, that these tensions exist across the sector (Featherstone et al, 2018; Charmen, 2021), and these case studies are indicative of the challenges professionals are facing when tasked with naming and addressing structural harm and its relationship to extra-familial abuse. These reflections help us to understand the challenges and opportunities for incorporating acknowledgement of inequalities in CS work.

"I've made some enemies, but it's fine": the challenge of naming inequalities in service responses

This first case study is a key example of the barriers practitioners face working within a system whereby naming and addressing structural inequality is exceptional, rather than ordinary, practice. It highlights how practitioners we have worked with in Scale-Up sites were able to identify structural inequalities as drivers of harm and how the systems they work within can often contribute to how those inequalities are sustained. Crucially, it shows how engrained inequalities are in the systems set up to address EFH.

In this case, a multi-agency team in a local authority piloted a 'location assessment' – an approach to tackling EFH by assessing risk, harm and safety in a location of concern. This assessment was prompted by serious concerns about the sexual exploitation of a group of girls, and included a range of traditional and non-traditional partners, high levels of buy-in from senior leaders and truly creative interventions that targeted the spaces where young people were experiencing harm. When the assessment was complete, two practitioners reflected on how structural inequalities shaped this location. They noted racism was impacting young people's experience of the space and that responses had reinforced these inequalities:

> '[Location] has been an issue for us with young people and adults since I can remember, even being a child myself, but it was predominantly Black young people or Black adults involved, and there never seemed to be this kind of galvanisation of wanting to do something until the white girls from different parts of the city were involved in sexual exploitation in that area.' (Focus group, CS Scale-Up pilot)

The practitioners highlighted that this was one example of a wider problem – their continual pushing to ensure Black young people were receiving the same level of response as their white peers. They described how their continued reiteration of the issue – beyond the location assessment in question – was met with resistance.

Practitioners described a dynamic not specific to their local authority but common across the UK (Berelowitz et al, 2013; Davis and Marsh, 2020). They described a system that closes support for Black young people but where white young people are offered more, where assumptions are made about Black young people being 'hard to reach', without considering the legacies of institutional racism that have alienated Black communities. Professionals described a culture that assumes that involvement with youth offending teams is sufficient support for Black young people and where white young people might receive support from social care. Ultimately, they described a system that reproduced structural harm, and where practitioners have to fight against the tide to advocate for Black young people to receive a welfare-led response:

> 'a lot of our top-tier young people who are BAME (Black, Asian and Minority Ethnic) did not have any involvement with social care, and we've seen that a lot when they're a statutory requirement or some of

the young people, whereas they've gone to their parents, who happen to be Black parents, and have gone, do you know what, we don't want, get lost, and they do. It's like, really? Is this still happening? You've got young people, young men, young Black men that are really high risk on our list, and they're just really hard to reach, so we close them. Or you say "oh the YOT's involved, so we don't need to get involved all the time" ... I feel like there was more effort put in when we're talking about white young men.' (Focus group, CS Scale-Up pilot)

These observations could be explained by a wider ambiguity about the role of social care in responding to EFH, that is, what threshold must be met, what happens if young people and parents do not consent, or parental capacity to safeguard is not a factor in the harm? What then are the pathways for responding to EFH? However, these professionals clearly noted that case-closure decisions were instigated differentially based on racial disparity and systemic bias in practice.

These reflections are confronting yet important to acknowledge and unpack. Professionals describe being met with resistance and discomfort from colleagues and managers as a result of speaking out about the inequality they were witnessing, suggesting that naming racism in an effort to confront it can rely on exceptionality and risk for practitioners.

Professionals describe the challenge of naming and addressing the ways in which structural inequalities impact young people's lives and confronting how harm is reproduced through service responses. Doing so is essential in order to develop a truly ecological and rights-based approach to extra-familial abuse that is grounded in young people's best interests. However, this should not fall to individual practitioners but be integral to how contextual assessments and interventions are designed and how outcomes are measured.

Naming structural harm and its impact, but now what?

'A social worker who is not from here, all they see is this kid who is involved in some criminal activity or may be being exploited – they don't go where there is a bad area, they don't see what that kid is living in, and the poverty and deprivation.' (Focus group, CS Scale-Up pilot)

Where structural inequality is named, often, it is in relation to young people's backgrounds, or identities and communities, rather than with a focus on the social care system and issues around practice. This next case study highlights a common predicament we have observed in Scale-Up sites: the ability to name structural inequality in contexts where EFH is happening and a feeling of helplessness over what to do next when existing child protection systems are increasingly detached from broader social issues.

In this case, a joint 'location' and 'peer assessment' was conducted by children's social care and Community Safety teams, who were concerned that a group of young people on an estate were being groomed by what they identified as an 'organised criminal group'. One professional participating in the location assessment commented on the legacy of deprivation and poverty on the estate. They reflected on the devastating impact of austerity, including their hope that the assessment would open professionals' eyes to the conditions the community was forced to live with, and how this has contributed to the level of EFH young people were facing.

It was clear to this professional that the real-world impact of political decisions (around investment in communities) and the legacies that are born from them interconnect with how EFH manifests in those places for young people. They noted how new developments were abandoned mid-build after the financial crash, leaving behind derelict building sites in the middle of young people's neighbourhoods. They talked about streets that had been sold off to private investors, leaving no avenue for the local authority to address the lack of lighting and the degeneration of the roads in the area. They stressed how budget cuts had meant the youth club had to reduce the age bracket for attendance, leaving older teenagers with few options for safe places in their community to spend their time. Crucially, they commented that due to the lack of time professionals spend out and about in the community and with many living outside the area, the professionals working with young people 'just don't know these spaces' (Focus group, CS Scale-Up pilot) or the conditions surrounding them that have contributed in part to the rates of violence and abuse in the community. In the end, the focus of the response was not on reducing the impact of structural harm – in this case, poverty – but instead on addressing the 'suspected risk' of young people being exploited into criminality, specifically, organised criminal groups. With the focus established as reducing and disrupting suspected criminality from the outset, social care galvanised around a police-led response to disrupt perpetrators and make arrests. This unfortunately included arresting young people 'where necessary' (Meeting observation, CS Scale-Up pilot). Criminal justice responses to child criminal exploitation (CCE) are a common response in the UK (Lloyd and Firmin, 2020) in the absence of consistent welfare responses that might seek to prevent the criminalisation of young people and safeguard them from harm (Wroe, 2021). Such approaches are not only misaligned from the domains and values of CS – particularly Domain 2 which requires a welfare-led approach to harm outside the home – but they exacerbate inequalities, particularly for already marginalised children.

When naming poverty as part of our work is not the norm, it is unsurprising that actioning against its impact feels nearly impossible. This is not only limited to EFH but is an issue across children's social care, including when intervening into abuse within families (Bywaters et al, 2018). This research details how existing safeguarding systems are often unable to consider the ways in which economic, social and cultural barriers impact children's experiences of harm and protection within families. It highlights how existing systems take a 'top-down' approach to working with families, leaving little capacity to develop community and locality-based approaches that consider the social, economic and environmental contexts in which families and children are living (Featherstone et al, 2018). When it is clear to those working within communities that poverty exacerbates EFH among young people, then it becomes somewhat imperative that responses should consider these issues as paramount. Evidence from Scale-Up sites suggests that professionals are grappling with these issues without having practice frameworks in place to address them.

Naming, responding to and embedding inequality?

> 'I guess we tend to talk about young women as potential victims of CSE and boys as potential perpetrators of criminal exploitation, so we're kind of falling into that a little bit, and it's probably not the case.' (Scale-Up pilot interview)

There have been instances in CS Scale-Up sites where professionals have felt able to name structural forms of harm, and to think about what they might do to reduce their impact. We have observed and been part of some promising conversations, and we have also seen how ingrained these inequalities can be. Where Scale-Up sites have identified and then actioned consideration of inequalities into plans, this has at times gone on to contribute or exacerbate the issue. The case study presented explores how one Scale-Up site sought to rectify gender inequality through changes to service design.

In this Scale-Up site, professionals developed a multi-agency meeting to discuss individuals and contexts linked to cases of EFH, with a broad focus on exploitation and serious youth violence. After these panels had been in action for a few months, it was noted by the multi-agency team that referrals and interventions were mainly for CCE and young men. The CSE social worker pointed out that girls and young women were slipping under the radar and weren't receiving the same level of support. In response, one in every three meetings was replaced with a 'girls' meeting' where girls at risk of CSE were discussed. The intended outcome of the reshuffle was to increase the space for 'girls' issues' related to EFH to be discussed.

Along with professionals in the Scale-Up site, we later considered the extent to which such silos may have further embedded gendered inequality. First, we asked whether categorising CSE and CCE as two separate issues might reaffirm the misconception that these two types of harm happen separately. Research shows significant overlap in the types of exploitation young people experience, risk factors and indicators for such risk (Firmin et al, 2019b), including that sexual coercion, abuse and exploitation can be a feature in cases where young people are exploited into criminality (Berelowitz et al, 2013). In this case, the same professional who raised concerns that girls were slipping through the net for support expressed unease at the separation of these meetings for this very reason – by creating space for 'girls and CSE', how then will we address cases where young people's exploitation cannot be categorised as only CSE or CCE, but where they might experience both?

Second, we reflected on what this meant for how we view the victimisation of boys and girls. Separating these meetings by gender reinforces an assumption that girls are victimised in one way, while boys are victimised in another, allowing for the sexual exploitation of young men to be overlooked (Brayley, 2014) and the vulnerability of young women to experience criminal exploitation to be silenced (Eshalomi, 2020).

Third, some young people's gender identity sits outside cisnormative binaries, meaning that some young people identify as neither male nor female. Trans young people are frequently subject to gender misidentification and hostility (Austin, 2018; McCann et al, 2019) from services. Non-binary or trans young people can experience specific risks in extra-familial contexts due to discriminatory systems, attitudes and laws. Where might a trans young person experiencing extensive criminal exploitation, who had also been sexually assaulted by their exploiters, sit within such a system?

Assumptions about who is considered a victim, who we see as criminal and the ways in which violence and abuse are separated and siloed in ways that often don't reflect the realities of young people's lives all require a challenge to create services that reflect young people's intersectional experiences. In attempts to address the gendered way in which social care systems operate, we acknowledge the need to think deeply together about the root causes of these inequalities and how our service response mitigates or reaffirms societal norms that drive differential treatment in the first place.

Applying Contextual Safeguarding approaches to inequalities and extra-familial risk in adolescence

CS aims to expand child protection systems' access to spaces such as peer groups, schools and neighbourhoods. This has raised questions about the ethical and legal parameters (Firmin and Knowles, 2020) that must be in place to ensure that a CS approach promotes adolescents' rights to protection, participation and privacy, and does not reproduce some of the limitations of traditional child and family-oriented child protection work (Wroe and Lloyd, 2020).

A system that is contextual lends itself to considering how inequalities shape the contexts where young people spend their time. However, this requires rethinking some of the foundations of child protection more broadly, for example, questioning who is supported and who isn't. What does 'support' look like for different people or communities based on race, gender and so on? How are young people's rights balanced, for example, the right to privacy and the right to protection, particularly when child protection systems are expanded into peer groups, schools and neighbourhoods?

The remainder of this chapter will explore how CS could support consideration of such issues. What questions might we ask in order to ensure structural and systemic drivers of harm are accounted for in our assessment of, and response to, EFH in adolescence? This section will explore the domains of CS, with a focus on Domain 1, to outline how the CS framework could enable this approach in practice.

The first domain of CS asks professionals to address the contexts in which abuse occurs, rather than only targeting the individuals within them (Firmin, 2020). This requires assessing the 'social conditions of abuse' – the contexts surrounding the young person that facilitate harm – and inform the behaviour of the young person navigating them. CS Scale-Up sites have sought to do this in various ways, usually be applying traditional child protection methods into spaces beyond the home: this has included expansive assessments of large geographical spaces through to smaller assessments focusing on friendships between two young people. In doing so, Scale-Up sites have adapted their existing policies and procedures to support practitioners to target the social conditions in which exploitation and violence happens.

The question then is, when expanding access to, and also the reach of, child protection, how do we ensure inequalities and system harms are not reproduced and at best mitigated? For example, when targeting a 'neighbourhood' as a social context, social workers and multi-agency partners in Scale-Up sites have conducted surveys, 'mapped' the area to establish 'hotspots' for harm, spent time on the streets speaking with young people and, in some cases, enlisted community members to act as 'guardians' or increased police or Community Safety patrols on the streets. Given what we know about the ways in which inequalities intersect with young people's experiences of EFH (Chapter 2) and the system response to them, what might the implications of these activities be if structural and system drivers of harm are not central to our assessment and planning? Have we considered which young people will be protected by increased guardianship or professional presence, and which will be policed as a result of these system activities? Has the impact on the wider community been assessed, and has community need been addressed, or is the focus on managing and disrupting risk? Can we deepen our assessment of 'contexts' to mitigate some of the risks of expanding child protections' reach into them?

Take a Child and Family Assessment, for example. Scale-Up sites aiming to meet the domain 'target' have adapted traditional Child and Family Assessments, broadening the focus beyond the child in the context of their family (home) to consider the social conditions in which they experience harm (beyond the home), that is, asking questions about peers, or safe and unsafe spaces. Young people's needs are considered in relation to wider community and environmental factors, with guardianship capacity in the community considered in addition to parenting capacity. This has supported sites to incorporate context into Child and Family Assessments.

As we have seen from the literature reviewed in Chapter 2 and the examples from Scale-Up sites described in this chapter, the response to adolescent harm is limited if assessment and support is not sensitive to young people's intersectional needs and the needs of the communities in which they live. Encompassing consideration of the intersectional structures of race, class, ableism and so on, and EFH and community factors such as access to resources (Figure 3.1), we can ask, can children thrive if the community cannot?

Figure 3.1: Assessment to incorporate context

Family context	Extra-familial context
Child's developmental needs	Young person/people's needs
Family and environmental factors	Community and environmental factors
Parenting capacity	Guardianship capacity

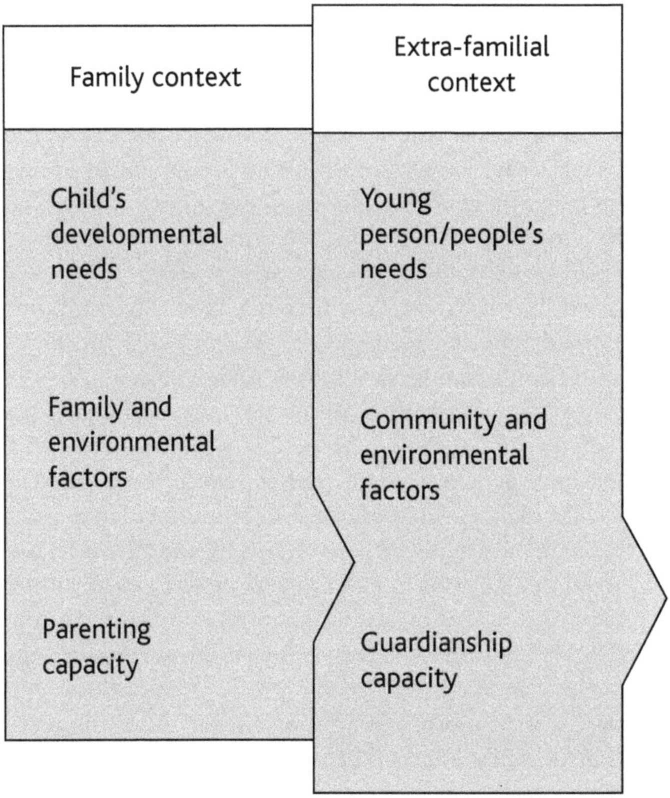

What does it really mean to have access to safety?

One Scale-Up site concerned with the levels of EFH young people were facing in the community conducted an assessment of a park where exploitation was a significant concern. Professionals spoke with members of the community in the surrounding area, including young people, business owners and local residents, to get a sense of the social conditions facilitating EFH. Through the location assessment, they built a picture of the community and how young people live and move through it, getting a grasp on environmental and community factors, including guardianship capacity, that could facilitate safety.

Professionals came to understand how harm was happening in the park, but also that young people and residents were feeling increasingly frustrated at the reality of living in this neighbourhood, particularly around the lack of maintenance of public spaces and the lack of resources and activities for young people and adults.

> 'Young people in [area] overwhelmingly feel fearful and frustrated. They spoke extensively about rising gang violence and they crave more outlets for self-expression, more channels for their energies, more physical spaces in which to congregate safely. Many adult residents and community leaders feel that [area] is forgotten.' (Scale-Up pilot assessment)

Crucially, community members made the link between the safety and wellbeing of young people and the levels of poverty and deprivation in the area. They felt that the lack of spaces in which young people could spend their time was driving them into unsafe spaces where they were potentially vulnerable to abuse and exploitation. Hearing these concerns, the team developed a plan that would incorporate these issues.

One action on the plan was to resource spaces in the community where young people had reported feeling safe; this included the local football facility that had been running in the park for young people. The cost to attend football was £3 per player. While this seemed initially reasonable, the cost excluded many of the young people who lived close to the park, but attracted young people from all over the wider borough who started coming to play football. Feedback from the community led to professionals' realisation that high rates of poverty in the area meant that while the football facility was open to all, it was in fact not accessible to local young people.

> 'In reality, £3 per session is likely to be prohibitively expensive for any young people who live locally seeking to use the facilities with any sort of regularity. An owner of a business near this facility helpfully wondered if the facilities could be made free to young people living in the area.' (Scale-Up location assessment)

Clearly, the assessment sought to target the social conditions of abuse by engaging in a range of activities to better understand the context where young people were reported to be at risk of EFH. Initially, this led to the identification of several areas in the community where young people were unsafe, and spaces, including the football facilities, that had the potential to promote safety and guardianship for them. Deeper assessment of the context, including speaking with community members about local need, established that these safe spaces were not accessible to many of the young people who were experiencing harm in the area. Additionally, practitioners reflected on how crucial it was to conduct this assessment in partnership with services who have different types of knowledge about the community, in this case, where Community Safety professionals had experience and links with the housing teams, meaning they brought a wealth of understanding about how families live and how housing arrangements contributed to the community's social conditions.

Without the knowledge from these community members and the professionals, a dynamic understanding of the context would be impossible, including how structural harm might manifest more broadly and, specifically, around access to safe spaces such as the football facilities. Creative partnership working meant that the local authority was able to hear this need in their assessment and understand how it was linked to young people's experiences of harm.

In doing so, professionals' assessment processes moved from targeting the children and their families (traditional approach), to targeting contexts (contextual approach), to understanding and targeting structural inequalities (structural approach) (Figure 3.2). They moved from a focus on the developmental needs of the child and parenting capacity and guardianship, to the needs of young people and environmental and community factors (including community guardianship), including an intersectional understanding of young people's needs, the resources and needs of the community, and then mobilised local policy and practice opportunities to scaffold safety in and through the community.

The question then becomes, what can professionals *do* about such problems? Upon reflection, the social care professionals leading the assessment reiterated concerns that addressing the issue of funding is out of the realm of social care alone. Instead, they have considered ways in which to utilise and develop partnerships with businesses, services and statutory bodies that have a vested interest in keeping young people safe in the park. Ideas include working with integrated youth services and commissioners to find potential funding sources to subsidise the cost of the sports facilities, and sharing the benefits for the football facility leaders whereby having local young people attend their activities could foster positive relationships in the community.

Figure 3.2: Assessment to incorporate context and structural and systemic considerations

Family context	Extra-familial environment	Structural and systemic considerations
Child's developmental needs	Young person's needs	Young person's intersectional needs
Family and environmental factors	Environmental and community factors	Socio-political, economic factors
Parenting capacity	Guardianship capacity	Local and national governance/policy

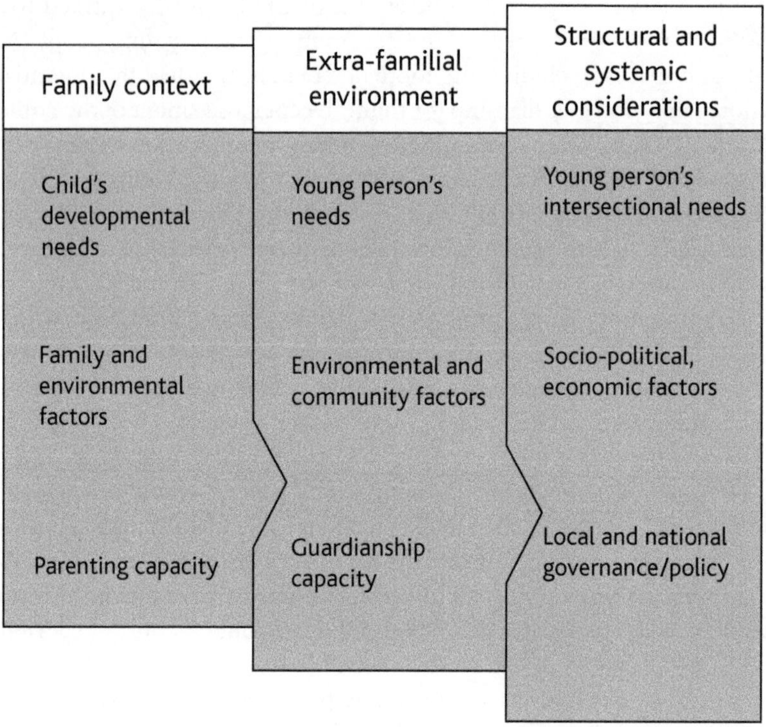

Conclusion

In some ways, it is perhaps easier to incorporate consideration of structural inequality and system harm into child protection assessments, processes and pathways than it is to incorporate such a consideration into extra-familial spaces themselves. As Featherstone and others propose in the 'Social Model' for protecting children, doing so would mean that:

> Assessments and interventions need to actively engage with the economic, social and environmental contexts in which the child and family is living. Some key elements of practice include: valuing children and families' hopes and aspirations and what they say they need to thrive; actively promoting human rights and providing advocacy; fostering positive social connections; recognising the importance of practical help; and crucially taking a situated and dialogic approach to ethics that places dilemmas and decisions in a broader social, political and cultural context. (Featherstone et al, 2020: 1–2)

The Social Model approach requires us to rethink (or return to) the foundations of social work and the role of social workers. Is the role of child protection services to assess, monitor and report, or is it to build relationships, advocate and support young people, their families and communities? Applying this approach to young people's experiences of inequalities and harm in extra-familial contexts could facilitate a truly contextual response that understands extra-familial spaces as shaped by wider socio-political and economic factors.

We are at a pivotal point in our CS journey, one that requires us to reflect back on the work that has been done and think about what we have learnt, and what this might mean moving forward. Implementing CS has not always meant, in practice, the natural development of a system that considers inequality (both encountered and produced by the system) as a core feature of contexts beyond family homes. However, these have been live issues for both practitioners engaged in this work and for young people. CS, with an eye on social conditions, has in part facilitated this awareness, and affords closer examination of how these conditions shape the peer groups, parks, schools and neighbourhoods that young people have to navigate. The next steps for researchers in the CS team and our partners is to more explicitly centre both structural and system harms in our understanding of, and response to, the abuse of adolescents in extra-familial contexts. Critical to this will be being led by the young people who live this as a daily reality, because, as Giovanni Rose's poem reminds us, young people are well aware of how socio-political forces are never far from the places and spaces where they spend their time.

4

Value-informed approaches to peer mapping and assessment: learning from test sites

Carly Adams Elias, Lisa Marie Thornhill and Hannah Millar

Introduction

As local areas have adopted a CS approach, many have increased attention to young people's peer relationships as a source of both harm and protection. This chapter will explore themes which have surfaced while reflecting on the developing practice with peers being piloted in CS Scale-Up sites. We outline some potential benefits and risks, identified in the data, of safeguarding work with peer groups, and use this to reflect on what happens when these practices are employed without the application of the values; how might this impact the young people involved? If CS values are not underpinning the practice with peers, could we do more harm than good?

Within the Scale-Up data, we found multiple approaches employed to help focus on peer relationships and, more specifically, practice which targets the peer group. CS activities can take place at two levels. At level one, professionals embed recognition of extra-familial contexts into their work with individual children and families, using this to inform assessment, decision making and interventions. This might include sitting with the young person and, with curiosity and care, inviting them to reflect on their experiences in their friendships and wider peer relationships, their education settings or the places where they spend their time. Tools including peer mapping or safety mapping (see the CS website) can be used with the young person to facilitate reflections and help understand their experiences of harm in those contexts and, also importantly, their experiences of comfort and support. This can play a valuable role in assessment, decision making and planning for individual young people and their families. At level two, professionals work to actively change extra-familial contexts identified as impacting the safety of young people, meaning the peer group, school or public space could become subject to a safeguarding assessment, meeting or plan. This might include engaging with several members of a peer group, rather than an individual, to better understand the needs, functioning and social conditions which might be contributing to their collective experience of safety. It will also include engaging with the trusted adults who have reach into the group and capacity to provide guardianship to it.

While there is emerging good practice from Scale-Up sites, there is also increasing awareness of potential challenges when establishing practice with peers when this is not underpinned by the values. We discuss the importance of being clear about the purpose and function of peer mapping and assessment and contemplate the notion that *how* we undertake work with peers is as important as *what* we do. We foreground the views of young people to emphasise the importance of engaging and working alongside them in developing this practice. We will draw on what we have learnt from young people and practitioners to better understand the opportunities and limitations of the current system to use and embed this practice in a meaningful way.

Background

Peer relationships and adolescent safety

As children navigate adolescence, they begin to enjoy greater independence from family and develop wider social networks, with their peer relationships playing a valuable and unique role in their lives (Bukowski et al, 2019). At the same time, they become more exposed to harm that happens outside the home, including in their peer relationships (Hackett, 2004; Berelowitz et al, 2013). The harm young people experience in these extra-familial contexts is being increasingly viewed as a child protection issue that requires a social work response (Children's Commissioner, 2019a; Lloyd and Firmin, 2020). As a result, safeguarding practitioners are beginning to consider young people's peer, as well as familial, relationships when responding and are becoming more invested in using practices and tools, such as peer mapping and assessment, to support their safeguarding responses. Peer mapping is the process of drawing maps which show the relationships young people have in their lives. Peer assessment is the process of considering the risks and harms that may be facing a peer group.

As we begin to recognise that peer relationships are relevant to safeguarding (Brandon et al, 2020), this feels instinctively to be a positive move; however, it's important to be mindful that safeguarding practitioners currently work within a policy environment that primarily views abuse prevention through a risk-focused lens (Featherstone, 2016) and a wider research landscape that conceptualises peer influence through a deviance lens (Sutherland, 1947; Hirshi, 1969; Thom et al 2007; Parton, 2010). We must be mindful, then, that this environment could create the conditions in which increased social work attention on young people's peers might only serve to sanction and disrupt, rather than nurture, those peer relationships.

When practice is undertaken through a lens which prioritises criminal justice or focuses primarily on risk, young people and their friendship groups may be criminalised, friendships can be severed by the deployment of non-association orders and young people get relocated far from home (Fine et al, 2003; Wroe and Lloyd, 2020). This approach leans towards the increased surveillance, criminalisation and adultification of young people (Williams, 2018; Wroe, 2021) which is shown to disproportionately impact marginalised young people (Losen et al, 2014; Davis and Marsh, 2020).

Studies have shown that some may assume more punitive approaches to have benefits in disrupting a harmful context (Lloyd, 2019), but they do not always favour the best interests of the children who experience them, particularly the most marginalised (Stein, 2007). While these approaches in theory 'target' a peer group, questions would legitimately be asked of whether they represent a child welfare approach to that target – as required by the CS framework.

Increasing attention on young people's experience of EFH has primarily focused on peer-instigated harm, highlighting the need to understand and address peer groups as a potential context of harm (Hill, 2018; Drew, 2020; Doherty, 2022). A CS approach, however, recognises the presence of a 'peers paradox', where peer relationships can be a source of both harm *and* support (Brodie et al, 2020). While a spotlight on peer-instigated harm has been important, research has also shown that peer relationships can be protective and relevant to safeguarding, with young people affected by EFH often experiencing informal support from one another in a variety of ways (Beckett et al, 2013). This covers a spectrum which includes universal features of friendship, such as having moral support and 'someone to talk to', through to more protective features such as being the first person a young person might disclose their abuse to or meeting each other's basic needs for food and accommodation (Beckett et al, 2013; Latimer et al 2020). The CS approach advocates for safeguarding responses to EFH to be underpinned by strength-based principles, which should encourage safeguarding practitioners to think about building on the strengths of individuals and communities to achieve change, and this equally applies to safeguarding work with peer groups. Understanding the presence of a 'peers paradox' underlines the need to widen our understanding of the nature of peer relationships, and the dynamics of peer groups to include consideration of both the risks and strengths that may be present. This balance is important to inform assessment, planning and interventions with young people and their peer groups, not only to understand the risks but to build safety by identifying and utilising the opportunities for support, comfort and protection that may also be present.

Introducing peers into safeguarding practices

Responding to an increasing evidence base, England's statutory child protection guidance, Working Together to Safeguard Children, was amended in 2018 to recommend that young people connected to shared contexts, or thematic concerns, be considered together during assessments (Department for Education, 2018). Despite this recommendation and the increasing recognition that peer relationships may be relevant to safeguarding assessments and interventions, this does not routinely result in practice which responds to them (Hill, 2018; Drew, 2020; Doherty, 2022). Not yet at least. Research to support the development of CS establishes the potential value of visual peer maps to show peer connections (Firmin, 2019; Sloane et al, 2019). Peer maps can be used to support peer group assessments by providing a basis for practitioners to explore and better understand the relationships between young people as well as the dynamics and social conditions of those groups. It is important to make the distinction that a peer map alone does not constitute the whole assessment and should form part of a wider assessment process. The CS guidance on peer mapping and assessment outlines how these can be valuable tools which can contribute to increased safety for young people, by:

- better understanding the experiences and dynamics in peer relationships and contributing to understanding about safety, harm and support in peer relationships;
- addressing the protection and safety around the young people, rather than changing or severing young people's relationships; and
- contributing to understanding about which context should be the focus for support and/or intervention.

While CS offers a framework for safeguarding practice with peers, it doesn't prescribe a particular method or offer a blueprint for a copy-and-paste approach. This allows freedom and space to be creative and enable different safeguarding systems to design approaches that fit within their individual context. However, it also requires sites to be brave, take risks and challenge their status quo. Scale-Up sites engaged with the Scale-Up Project have been eager to develop and test approaches to identifying, assessing and responding to peers in safeguarding work with young people affected by EFH.

Method

The Scale-Up teams have engaged with children and young people across England and Wales to consider their views and experiences in relation to different elements of CS to inform the research and developing practice. 106 young people took part in consultation activities in person and online. In addition, 78 completed a scenario-based survey and 192 completed general surveys. The respondents were aged between 12 and 21 years old, a mixture of girls, boys and non-binary young people, and representing a wide range of ethnicities. The sample included children and young people with experience of EFH and children's social care involvement, and those without. Data for this chapter have been drawn from practice across four local authority Scale-Up sites (Sites C, F, G and I), where the research team undertook observations, documentation review, focus groups and interviews with practitioners and senior leaders. These four sites piloted new approaches to working with peers, as detailed later. An additional example has been drawn from a site developing CS outside the Scale-Up Project and has demonstrated how the values can be actively applied when undertaking peer assessment while combining this with group work.

Site F piloted a child welfare approach to peer group assessment alongside their usual Child and Family Assessment with individual children and families. Social workers in the assessment and adolescent teams undertook a pilot which encouraged the use of peer-related questions within their assessment. This was to increase understanding of peer relationships and use this knowledge to inform analysis and decision making when considering experiences of EFH.

Site G piloted an approach to peer assessment at level 2 (responses that focused on targeting contexts rather than individual children), by focusing on a peer group of four young people exposed to harm through youth violence. The aim was to understand the motivations, risks and protective factors present for the group and consider how to support them. The assessment was structured around the three themes of the peer assessment triangles: group functioning, guardianship capacity and environmental and family factors, as shown in Figure 4.1.

Site C's approach to mapping and assessment was rooted in an ecological understanding of a peer group's experience following the death of a young person. The young people in the area were deeply impacted by their friend's death. This presented in self-harm, substance use and disturbances in the local community. In this site, efforts were made to understand the social norms of the group and how these were shaped by their collective experience of bereavement and loss. The peers were considered together, which led to a community-wide, child welfare-led response, resulting in timely support for the affected young people.

In response to concerns about a self-harm cluster within a peer group, Site I used peer-group mapping as a foundation for a wider assessment of the peer group's needs. After first establishing the connected young people, the assessment centred around understanding the group's functioning, the interplay with their environment and the guardianship capacity in place to support the group. This was motivated by a child welfare response, with the plan focusing on how to increase safety for the group in relation to self-harm behaviour.

The data were combined and analysed against the CS framework, considering how the practice aligned with the four domains and values, to

Value-informed approaches to peer mapping and assessment

Figure 4.1: Peer assessment framework

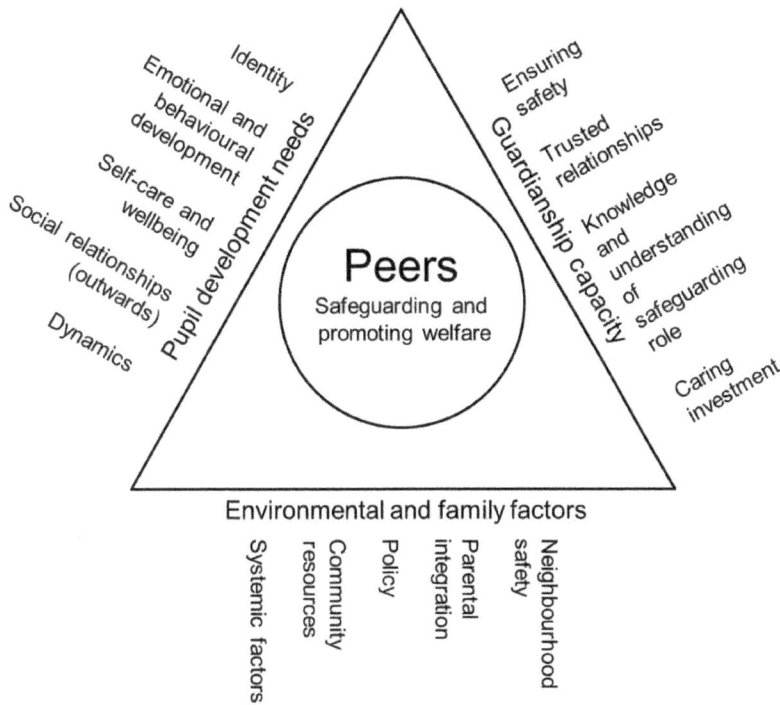

identify themes related to peer assessment and safeguarding. These examples have helped us to develop an understanding about how practice can be aligned with the values and consider the tensions when it does not.

Findings

'I definitely think the idea of peer assessment is a great idea – if it's applied in the right situation, in the right way, it can be really effective.' (Young person, focus group, site F)

When asked during the focus group, many young people who participated were supportive of the idea of peer mapping and assessment, but under specific circumstances. They felt it offered potential benefits "to see the bigger picture" and "to keep tabs on dangerous behaviour to keep people safe" (Young person, survey, Site B). Three interconnected themes emerged that can help consider priorities for developing peer assessments. They include:

- leading with a child welfare rather than crime detection lens;
- building relationships of trust versus relationships of surveillance; and

- moving beyond mapping to understand and respond to the social conditions of abuse.

Each theme is explored here.

Leading with a child welfare rather than crime detection lens

Domain 2 of the CS framework recommends that peer group contexts are incorporated into child protection frameworks and responded to through a child welfare lens when considering EFH. When applying the values, this means recognising and upholding young people's rights, including to protection, privacy and association. Examples from the data highlight the tension when the approach to peer assessment is instead motivated by a criminal justice lens and overlooks those rights.

Young people and their peers are often seen through a lens of risk and deviance. While the intention of peer mapping and assessment to support CS responses is rooted in a welfare-based approach, responses from young people indicated that some were fearful about the potential outcome. Some expressed concern regarding the risk of punitive or negative responses: "It could be important information to help, but could get many in trouble" (Young person, survey, Site C), and "they could have the wrong person getting in trouble ... they might be innocent but got mapped" (Young person, survey, Site E). They were concerned that peer mapping could be used by some to gather and share intelligence about young people without their knowledge and that it would focus on achieving a criminal justice response, rather than safeguarding them. Their scepticism is understandable given the policy and practice environment which is risk-focused and likely to lean towards more crime-based interventions (Featherstone et al, 2016).

Before CS existed, mapping and assessing peer groups had been employed in different settings to inform decisions and responses to young people. School staff informally assess and respond to peer relationships and ecologies every day, especially when considering behaviour management strategies (Hamm and Hoffman, 2016). The police and Community Safety map and assess peer groups for the purpose of detecting and responding to crime or behaviours perceived as 'antisocial' (Chainey and Tompson, 2008). The police 'gang violence matrix' could be described as a method of mapping and assessing peers. The Metropolitan Police describe the gang violence matrix as 'an intelligence tool used to identify and risk-assess gang members across London who are involved in gang violence'. They claim that it also seeks to identify those at risk of victimisation (Metropolitan Police, 2019). However, serious concerns have been raised over the adverse effect being listed on the matrix has for young Black males, who are disproportionately impacted (Amnesty, 2018). While these approaches might target the peer group context, it's crucial to note that they are not driven by child welfare or motivated by seeking safety and protection for young people. Neither are they underpinned by the values of CS, such as being collaborative, rights-based or ecological, and, therefore, they do not align with a CS approach.

It feels important to make this distinction, otherwise we might risk manifesting young people's fears into reality. Site F attempted to avoid this by taking a child welfare approach when a young person was referred to children's social care because they were identified by the police as being present in the park when another young person was wounded with a weapon in that location. The young person was considered by the police as a potential associate of the child who was injured and, if viewed primarily through a criminal justice lens, may have been closed to children's social care at the point of referral. However, through inclusion of questions and curiosity about peer relationships in the Child and Family Assessment, the social worker was able to engage in collaborative conversations with the young person and their parents to better understand their peer group context. They were able to explore the strengths and protective nature of the young person's peer group and understand that although present at the same location at the time of the incident, the young person was not connected to the individual who was harmed and was able to be screened out of social care interventions with the confidence that they were not exposed to harm though their peer relationships. In this example, rather than taking a crime detection approach, the child was seen by children's social care as being potentially in need of safeguarding and support, and an approach of curiosity and care was taken when considering his peer relationships.

Young people's feedback suggests they are seeking reassurance that a child welfare approach is taken, rather than one that might "get them in trouble". We need to be clear that the intention of a peer map and assessment is to take a child welfare approach to help understand and respond to young people's needs, not to criminalise them. Young people shouldn't need to be worried about their peer relationships being criminalised or being seen through a lens of deviance when they should be being safeguarded and supported. Yet such comments by them suggest that this is not always the case.

This perspective was shared by professionals in Site F, who were concerned about limitations within the system and with partners, most notably the police. Some were concerned that the police could potentially "criminalise young people without any real evidence apart from this tool. I'm thinking maybe [for] the young people, there would be concerns about us getting that information and having it on our system" (Social worker, focus group, Site F). Another social worker felt that "we have to be so clear on how that information will be shared so they know. Because they care about us sharing information and they know that we do, but we have to explain exactly under what situation we would share this assessment" (Social worker, focus group,

Site F). To address this, professionals in Site F felt it was necessary to provide clarity about the purpose, including a clear policy framework to inform decisions about when a peer assessment might be necessary. Additionally, taking a welfare-based approach would include seeking active consent and modelling appropriate information sharing which reflects young people's rights to privacy.

Building relationships of trust over relationships of surveillance

Some concerns have been raised about the potential use of CS to increase surveillance over young people rather than build relationships of trust (Wroe and Lloyd, 2020). The importance of trusted relationships to facilitate peer assessment was identified in data from young people and the pilot sites. Domain 3 of the framework recommends that a CS approach would ensure that partnerships are developed with sectors or individuals who are responsible for the nature of those extra-familial contexts. When thinking about engaging with peer groups, this encourages engagement with those who hold existing relationships or reach into them. But it's important to consider if connection alone is enough. What happens when those relationships are not built on trust? Would there be a different impact if the approach to peer assessment were not driven by child welfare and a desire to build trusted relationships with young people, but instead leant towards crime detection and surveillance? To achieve trusted relationships, we should consider how the values can support this and ensure peer assessment is underpinned by a collaborative approach, one where young people, families and communities work alongside professionals to inform decisions about safety.

The example in Site G directly targeted the peer group context and was motivated by a child welfare approach; the assessment presented concern and risk while also identifying strengths and recognising bonds of love and protection in the group. Despite best intentions, the team undertaking the assessment were unable to engage the young people or their parents in the process within the assessment timeframe. To counterbalance this absence, the assessment drew in safeguarding partners to inform understanding and worked with those who held the trusted relationships, primarily a youth worker with a long-standing relationship with the peer group, their families and their local community. This challenges us to consider how we can ensure that young people and parents are supported to participate in the process as active collaborators, rather than passive, or indeed resistant, subjects. How can we ensure peer group practice is something we do *with* young people and families and not *to* them? Are we expecting too much from a system that often views adolescents affected by EFH as 'hard to reach' and holds them responsible if they don't engage?

On occasion, the research team found professionals refer to young people as 'non-engagers' or 'difficult to engage', placing them as being responsible for engagement with a system which they don't feel readily able to trust. There were also examples of authentic commitment to collaboration with young people. During one meeting, a social worker responded to another professional's concerns about a young person's engagement by saying: "It's our job to engage with [*the young person], not the young person's job to engage with us" (Social Worker, observation, Site H). Young people and practitioners highlighted that for them to feel confident, they would need space and time to build trusted relationships. One young person felt that the process should include "trying to gain the trust of a young person or learning about what they're interested in, so that they have a sort of common ground" (Young person, focus group, Site F). Young people could see the potential of drawing on existing trusted relationships. When discussing a case study scenario involving a young person called Luke, one young person suggested it "might just make him slightly more rebellious and slightly more agitated and push him further away from where we're trying to get him to, so if we just keep it to maybe a close teacher, a teacher that Luke is familiar with and has good relations with' (Young person, focus group, Site F).

Developing and embedding collaborative approaches is crucial to ensure practice is underpinned by the CS values. Meaningful collaboration with young people, and families, relies on trusted relationships, because they provide a sense of safety. When young people feel safe, they will feel more comfortable to open up, expose vulnerabilities and engage in help-seeking behaviours. The team observed varying degrees of transparency and collaboration between professionals and young people and families when they developed peer maps. When young people were asked "if social workers are concerned about young people at school – is it important that young people know about this before they map them?", one young person felt that they should be made aware because, if not, "it might anger the people who are being mapped. Social workers are there to help people, not to go behind people's backs" (Young person, survey, Site E). Another young person felt that:

> 'you should definitely include young people because since an adult can be trained in their field of helping young people out as much as they want, but young generations change every single year so you're not going to have enough knowledge written down in a book to teach you how a child is going to act in this day and age – you need young people's opinions.' (Young person, focus group, Site G)

This highlights the need to ensure that mapping and assessment is grounded in evidence and informed by young people's experiences. They are experts on their own lives and peer groups. To earn the privilege of a collaborative relationship, professionals must first gain their trust.

Some young people suggested that negative association with children's social care might impact on their ability to engage with the process:

> 'they'd be less likely to give information because Social Services do have a really bad stigma around them. Even me myself, if I was in the situation and they mentioned that they were from Social Services, I probably wouldn't give as much information because I would worry that my friend would be taken away from their parents, or something drastic like that.' (Young person, focus group, Site F)

This reinforces the need for professionals to consider how they will build trust and transparency to reassure young people and families that, ultimately, they want to avoid something "drastic" like a young person being removed from their parents' care and that peer assessment should be used to explore the strengths in peer groups as well as the risks. If trust and collaboration are important to engaging young people in the process, it's critical to consider how to address the stigma and barriers within safeguarding systems which may prevent social workers from being enabled to work alongside young people to build trusted relationships over time.

In focus groups with social workers, they were mindful of trust and how the absence of it would reduce the ability of peer assessments to be collaborative. They described using their judgement of the relationship to sense the right time to ask questions about peer relationships and building this up over time as trust builds. To work collaboratively with young people and understand their peer groups, professionals will need to invest time developing those relationships, but that means the system will also need to flex (or even transform) to enable them to do this. We also need to consider if we are confident in our understanding of what makes a relationship a trusted one, especially in the context of safeguarding systems where power is not balanced between a social worker and a young person. How can we expect young people to build trust with individual social workers when they have little trust in the system they work within?

An example which focuses on building trusted relationships to facilitate peer assessment comes from beyond the Scale-Up Project, from a local authority who have been developing an approach which combines peer assessment *with* group work. This method involves engaging with the peer group from the start, setting expectations and group agreements, building trust as they progress and having youth workers in the team. The approach is built in reflective space and is an opportunity for critical thinking with the group, while ensuring flexibility, creativity and fun. Collaboration is central to the method; it's not just the process of peer mapping or assessing that is important but *how* it is done.

Moving beyond mapping to the social conditions of abuse

Within the CS framework, when applying Domain 1 to peer groups, we are encouraged to think beyond mapping to understand and respond to the social conditions of harm in that context. A peer map is not a stand-alone activity but should support identifying, understanding and addressing the social norms which enable the EFH to occur within the peer context. To achieve this, the process needs to involve conversations with young people, families and safeguarding partners to gain understanding of the experiences and dynamics in the peer group context. It should provide insight on safety, harm and support in peer relationships. To move beyond mapping towards understanding and responding to the conditions of abuse, we need to take an ecological approach to consider how young people's experiences within different contexts are shaped by inequalities. We will only begin to understand the social norms of a peer group if we take a child welfare approach and build on relationships of trust.

An approach which moves beyond mapping to understand the social conditions of the peer group was applied by Site F, when curiosity and questions about peer relationships were used to guide decision making for a young person who had been placed in secure accommodation on welfare grounds. When the order was granted, the young person's peer relationships played a significant role in the harm they were experiencing. When reviewing the order, the social worker used peer-focused questions to consider the nature of the young person's peer relationships, the changing peer dynamics and circumstances. This informed the decision for them to return to their local area into less restrictive care arrangements. The approach was underpinned by consideration of their rights and was explored collaboratively with them. It looked beyond the connections to explore the social conditions of the peer group. Crucially, the peer map and assessment weren't extractive but resulted in a clear plan and tangible outcome.

Moving beyond mapping by approaching a young person's peer context with curiosity and care can lead to positive outcomes. Young people highlighted the need to consider strengths and protective factors in peer relationships, alongside the concerns. One young person acknowledged that peer assessments could help identify a range of influences and this shouldn't be limited to focusing on risk. They thought a peer assessment "helps you coordinate, 'they're at this place in their lives' and to see who in that friendship group has more negative influences and who has a more positive influence on that person" (Young person, focus group, Site F).

If we are only mapping connections or focusing on risk, we might inadvertently overlook the existing strengths and protective elements within a peer group which could provide a valuable foundation from which to build safety. Practice needs to look beyond mapping alone and consider how friendships are developed, through a myriad of familial links, neighbourhoods, schools and other spaces, through shared values and interests, as well as positive, negative and sometimes traumatic experiences. Peer mapping, when undertaken as part of a wider assessment, could create opportunities to avoid making reductive assumptions and enable professionals to adopt a position of reflection and learning; because if we don't understand the social conditions, how can we offer supportive interventions to the peer group?

Conclusion: creating conditions for ethical peer assessment

Without a clear purpose to safeguard and create plans which address safety, peer mapping and assessment cannot claim to be anything more than intelligence gathering and would therefore not be aligned with a CS approach. For peer mapping and assessment to be aligned with CS, the practice needs to be anchored in a welfare-based approach with a commitment to collaboration with young people. Young people are the experts in their lives and should be involved in decisions being made about them and their safety. To achieve this, practice should prioritise building relationships of trust, rather than surveillance. Peer mapping and assessment must be approached with a sense of hopefulness and curiosity and move beyond focusing on the connections alone to exploring the social norms, dynamics and conditions within the peer group that impact on individuals experience of harm.

The themes presented in this chapter offer foundations to build upon and prompt us to ask whether:

- young people trust the professionals who are leading an assessment of their friendships;
- they can be reassured that peer mapping and assessment will increase safety, rather than surveillance;
- we can reassure young people about the purpose and process of peer assessments;
- we can broaden the focus from risk to consider the strengths and protective nature of peer relationships and include these in the solutions; and
- safeguarding practitioners can collaborate with young people to understand what safety in peer groups looks like for them.

This phase of research has raised some key considerations for development of practice related to peer mapping and assessment. It has surfaced some valuable questions which require further examination, including what makes a safe peer group and what is needed to establish clarity around this? What role do support and protection play in peer relationships and how might exploring this contribute to a strengths-based approach to working with peers? What conditions are needed to build trust, both with individual practitioners and the system they work within? And crucially, is it possible to build such contextual thinking with peers, foregrounding collaborative, rights-respecting, ecological, strength-based approaches, into an individualised social care system that is built on risk?

PART II

Domain 2: The legislative basis of the system

5

Reimagining Community Safety as community safeguarding in response to extra-familial harm

Joanne Walker and Carlene Firmin

Introduction

A central argument to the development of CS has been a need to shift responses to EFH away from criminal justice (particularly youth justice) systems and towards child protection systems (Firmin, 2017; Lloyd and Firmin, 2019). Prior to this, many young people affected by EFH were not viewed as being within the remit of child protection systems, and the contexts in which they came to harm were equally considered out of scope for social work intervention. Efforts to implement CS sought to achieve this shift in two ways. Firstly, by integrating reference to extra-familial contexts (like peer groups and public places) into social work activities (such as when recording referrals or conducting assessments) that had traditionally focused on familial contexts. Secondly, by promoting that child protection, rather than criminal justice, legislative frameworks and associated structures provide the scaffolding for coordinating responses to EFH. The merits and challenges of this have been debated elsewhere in this book (see Chapters 2 and 7, for example) – and some ways forward proposed. However, in the latest testing of CS, the role of a third legislative framework, and associated operational structure, has come into view: Community Safety.

In the UK, CSPs are legislatively responsible for coordinating council responses to crime and disorder. This has often resulted in them leading local responses to contexts associated with higher numbers of crime or antisocial behaviour (ASB) reports, as well as sanctioning (through civil orders) those deemed responsible for those crimes/behaviours.

In local areas adopting CS, social workers have found themselves initiating child welfare assessments of contexts that have also been responded to via Community Safety disruption activity. Individual young people on social work plans due to the exploitation they have experienced have also faced Community Safety sanctions for the ASB they have displayed as a result of that exploitation. In both scenarios, Community Safety responses have risked undermining child welfare approaches to contexts and young people affected by EFH. Yet from a legislative, policy and practice perspective, the principal driver for decision making in the case of such contexts or young people is unclear. If part of one response may undermine the other, which one should take precedence?

In this chapter, we draw upon data from two CS sites who participated in the Scale-Up Project (see Introduction for further details) who sought to overcome this tension, along with examples of how they were compromised by it. We situate these examples within a wider account of England's Community Safety and child protection legislative framework. In doing so we explore:

- whether CSPs are conceptually aligned or divergent from a CS approach;
- what has been required in the testing of CS to create alignment between Community Safety legislation/policy/practices and CS approaches at points of potential divergence; and
- the extent to which CSPs can ever fully align with CS in a consistent, or system-wide, fashion.

Ultimately, the chapter asks whether Community Safety frameworks can ever play a core role in the delivery of CS, an approach where a child's welfare, rather than crime prevention, should be paramount.

Background
Community Safety and children's safeguarding – an overview

Community Safety Partnerships (CSPs[1]), originally named Crime and Disorder Reduction Partnerships, were given a statutory footing (that is, became a legislative requirement) through the 1998 Crime and Disorder Act. They were introduced into every local authority/council area in the UK with the remit to 'tackle crime, antisocial behaviour, substance misuse, environmental crime and issues around re-offending' (Darlington, 2019). Thirteen years later, in 2011, the Police Reform and Social Responsibility Act formalised a relationship between Police and Crime Commissioners (elected officials who oversee police and fire services across a local force area) and CSPs – with the latter being reportable to the former.

CSPs were introduced nine years after the Children Act 1989 – the legislation that underpins England's child protection, and wider safeguarding, systems. They were also functioning for five years prior to the introduction of Local Safeguarding Children's Boards, changed to Safeguarding Children's Partnerships in 2017, whose function is to 'coordinate local work to safeguard and promote the welfare of children' in every local authority/council area in England (Plymouth, nd) (Figure 5.1).

Figure 5.1: Legislative and governance arrangements for safeguarding and Community Safety Partnerships

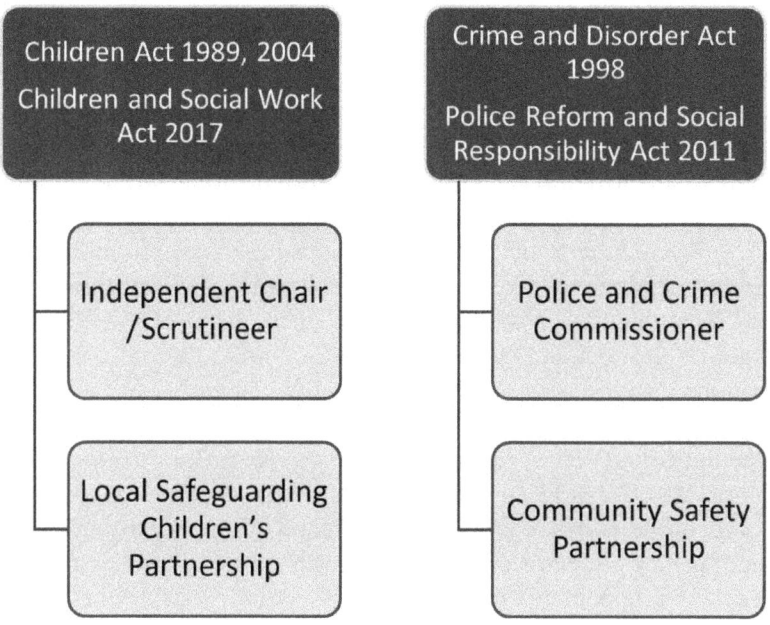

Community Safety Partnerships and extra-familial harm

Community Safety responses to EFH, and the role of CSPs within this, can be seen in England's policy, commissioning and practice frameworks.

Firstly, government policies, to varying extents, have presented EFH within a Community Safety agenda. The Home Office (the UK government's policing directorate) have developed various policies related to forms of EFH. These include guidance on responding to 'gangs' and 'serious youth violence' (HM Government, 2018a), 'child criminal exploitation' including via county lines drugs distribution (Home Office, 2018), domestic abuse in young people's relationships (Home Office, 2011) and CSE (Home Office, 2020). These policy documents note roles for CSPs in identifying, and reducing, the rate at which this harm occurs and associated indicative behaviours – such as that which is deemed 'antisocial'.

In 2020–21, the UK government came under increasing pressure to respond to the impacts of serious violence on young people and to reduce the rate at which young people were groomed and exploited into drugs distribution. Part of the response to these calls was to propose a 'serious violence duty', through which CSPs would:

> prevent and reduce serious violence, including identifying the kinds of serious violence that occur in the area, the causes of that violence (so

far as it is possible to do so), and to prepare and implement a strategy for preventing and reducing serious violence in the area. The Duty also requires the specified authorities to consult educational, prison and youth custody authorities for the area in the preparation of their strategy. (Home Office, 2021)

Policy frameworks, therefore, clearly outline roles for CSPs in reducing incidents of EFH. These frameworks have been reinforced through national and regional commissioning activities. In 2018, the Home Office funded 29 CSPs £17.7 million to develop interventions in response to serious youth violence (Children and Young People Now, 2018). Funded interventions included youth outreach workers offering targeted support to young people thought to be at risk of experiencing or committing violence, and trained practitioners within police custody to identify children at risk of violence. In 2019, the Home Office provided £35 million to establish 18 Violence Reduction Units (VRUs) across England to: 'tackle the root causes of serious violence. VRUs will bring together police, local government, health and education professionals, community leaders and other key partners to ensure a multi-agency response to the identification of local drivers of serious violence and agreement to take necessary action to tackle these (Home Office, 2020: 4). VRUs have, in turn, funded CSPs to deliver a range of local interventions in response to EFH. They also utilise data sets developed by CSPs to track trends in EFH and monitor performance.

From a practical perspective, the response of CSPs to EFH can be seen at both 'levels' of the CS approach. At Level 1 (responses to individual young people and their families), Serious Case Reviews have found a range of Community Safety sanctions used to influence the behaviour of young people affected by EFH. For example, both Jaden Moodie (Drew, 2020) and Corey Junior Davies (Hill, 2018) received Community Safety or ASB sanctions in the months and years prior to their murders in the context of criminal exploitation. These civil orders were served in response to the challenging behaviours these young people displayed in public places as a consequence of their own victimisation/exploitation. On some occasions, such interventions occurred prior to any wider safeguarding response; on other occasions, they were served in tandem with child welfare activity (but not necessarily in a coordinated fashion). The author of the Serious Case Review for Corey Junior Davies described how a sanction-based response to Corey occurred in the context of:

> the borough's strategic approach to youth violence which centres assessment, intervention and review of case work with gang affected and at-risk young people *within the community safety partnership*, and where the Youth Offending Service and the Police Gangs Unit are

the most actively engaged partners and lead on the two multiagency forums to explore risk and vulnerability. (Hill, 2018: 15; italics added)

At Level 2, CSPs regularly coordinate responses to locations and groups associated with 'antisocial behaviour' or crime and disorder. There will likely be many occasions when such activities mean that CSPs intervene with locations or groups associated with EFH, when the harm in question is viewed through the lens of crime, disorder or ASB. Indeed, a range of publications have documented the work of CSPs in disrupting incidents of EFH in this respect (Harrow Council, 2018; Home Office, 2020; LGA, 2019). In 2018, Harrow Council published their *Community Safety, Violence, Vulnerability and Exploitation Strategy*, in which they made various commitments to commissioning street-based interventions with young people (via youth work intervention) to reduce their involvement in 'antisocial behaviours', as well as noting the role of policing disruption activities to address weapon carrying in public places. Reports by the Local Government Association in 2019 and the Home Office in the same year highlighted the role of licencing enforcement in intervening with business establishments associated with the exploitation of children and young people. Such responses to locations and groups are common to Community Safety practices, and often a primary source of contextual responses to EFH in local areas. Whereas children's social care, under the wider remit of safeguarding children's partnerships, have been historically focused on intervening with children and families effected by EFH in those contexts (Lloyd and Firmin, 2020; Firmin and Lloyd, 2022).

Community Safety responses to extra-familial harm through the Contextual Safeguarding framework

CS promotes responses to EFH that target the contexts where such harm occurs. Given the extra-familial focus of CSPs, and their engagement with EFH at policy, commissioning and practice levels (outlined earlier), it is important to examine whether their existing remit supports the delivery of CS. After all, if social care can draw upon CSPs, and integrate with their work locally in ways that national policy is yet to achieve, then this could open a critical route to intervening in peer group, school and community contexts where EFH occurs – contexts which have often felt to be beyond the reach of traditional social work responses.

Table 5.1 illustrates how the activities of CSPs map against the four domains of the CS framework. As Table 5.1 illustrates, the work of CSPs aligns with the CS framework to a limited extent. Synergies are evident in what CSPs target (locations and groups), who they work with (partners who can influence what happens in those locations and groups) and the impact they measure (change at a contextual as well as an individual level).

Table 5.1: Remit of Community Safety against the Contextual Safeguarding domains

	Contextual Safeguarding	Community Safety
Target	Social conditions (and associated contexts) of abuse.	Physical locations and groups where EFH (if conceptualised as crime, disorder, ASB) occurs.
Legislative framework	Child protection and child welfare.	Crime and disorder.
Partnerships	Young people, families and others who can build protection and safety in extra-familial contexts.	With statutory and community agencies who can disrupt crime and ASB in extra-familial groups and locations.
Outcomes	Increase in safety at a contextual and individual level.	Reduction in, and prevention of, crime and disorder at a contextual and individual level.

However, the discord between the legislative framework of CSPs and those centred by the CS framework (Domain 2) is significant. CSPs have a statutory responsibility in respect of reducing/preventing crime and disorder – whereas children's social care, and safeguarding children's partnerships, have a statutory responsibility in respect of safeguarding, and promoting, the welfare of children and young people. While these are not necessarily mutually exclusive goals, they are not the same. As has been noted elsewhere in this book (see Chapters 2 and 12, for example), criminal justice and sanction-based interventions can undermine children's welfare rather than promote it. For example, CSPs may use dispersal orders to address complaints about ASB by groups of young people congregating on a high street. This type of intervention will move young people away from the location – and complaints of ASB will reduce as a result. However, dispersing young people from public places where they are visible may push them into locations where they are out of sight. This is turn can increase, rather than decrease, young people's exposure to risk and harm. Moreover, young people who are racialised and marginalised in other respects are more likely to be the subjects of such complaints than their peers – increasing the risk that they will be pushed into precarious contexts where there is little guardianship or support should they require it. A child welfare response to a group of young people in a similar situation (as illustrated in Chapters 4 and 13) would involve working alongside those young people to understand their needs in that context, and better meet them, to promote wellbeing.

The potential lack of focus of children's welfare in the activities of CSPs, and therefore lack of alignment with Domain 2 of the CS framework, also limits the conceptual synergy between the work of CSPs and the other three domains of the CS framework. In terms of Domain 3, CSPs tend to work in partnership with criminal justice agencies – and wider council services such as housing, licencing and so on – to utilise sanction and disruption tactics that reduce/prevent crime. These interventions do not foreground partnerships with young people and families. They may even frame young people as the target of partnership interventions. This framing leaves CSPs misaligned with Domain 1 of the CS Framework. A CS approach calls for systems to target the social conditions of contexts in which EFH occurs (Chapters 2, 3 and 12). Research suggests that one such social condition can be the perception of young people as deviant, and therefore excluded, as opposed to valuable, and therefore included (Measor and Squires, 2017). Surveillance-based interventions such as increased CCTV and police presence in public places are common to a Community Safety agenda but may not create conditions in which young people feel valued and included. Rather, such interventions may simply displace young people into areas where they are even more vulnerable (and out of sight). As noted previously, a reduction in complaints about a location (a contextual outcome used by CSPs) could indicate young people are more vulnerable (as they are no longer in a location) rather than any safer.

Conceptually, therefore, a lack of consideration of children's welfare fundamentally compromises the alignment of CSPs with a CS agenda. And yet, their statutory remit, and their reach into extra-familial contexts, mean they will feature in efforts to embed the approach in any local area. In this chapter, we explore the practice implications of this conceptual tension through data from local areas that have implemented a CS framework – and included CSPs in that endeavour. In the process, we identify whether synergies can be forged, and what might be required to achieve this, in the face of conceptual discord outlined thus far.

Learning from the Scale-Up Project

The CS programme has been working with nine local authority areas in England and Wales to develop CS system responses to EFH (Scale-Up Sites A–I). The system change process occurred across three stages: create, test and embed, each stage lasting a year. Within the 'test' year, Scale-Up sites carried out formal pilots to test aspects of the 'on paper' CS system proposed during the 'create' year. Learning from the pilots was used to revise and adapt local systems prior to embedding. Researchers from the CS team collected data from pilots using a range of qualitative methods (see Chapter 1).

Data collected from pilots undertaken in two Scale-Up sites provide an insight into any alignment or tensions between CSPs and CS, and the possible role that CSPs can play to implement the CS framework.

Pilot 1

Pilot 1 was carried out in Scale-Up Site B between October 2020 and May 2021. The pilot involved a new structure to coordinate multi-agency responses to CSE. It featured 'complex strategy meetings' chaired by children's social care and an associated location assessment to identify and assess concerns about CSE related to a particular road within the area. Researchers carried out nine meeting observations, document reviews of all key material related to the pilot, three interviews and three multi-agency focus groups of pilot participants.

Pilot 2

Pilot 2 was carried out in Scale-Up Site C from July to October 2021. The pilot introduced a structure to coordinate Community Safety and children's social care responses to locations associated with EFH. During the pilot, the site conducted a multi-agency location assessment of a local housing estate where there were concerns of child exploitation and young people at risk from organised criminal group (OCG) activity. Researchers carried out eight meeting observations, reviews of paper resources used for the pilot and the final assessment document, and two multi-agency focus groups of pilot participants.

Analysis

For the purpose or the chapter, research data from both pilots were analysed to explore:

- roles of a CSP within a CS system;
- the implications and challenges of the pilots for Community Safety and child protection processes; and
- what the four CS domains might look like for a CSP system as a result.

Findings: Community Safety roles in a Contextual Safeguarding system

The pilots: an overview

The CSP was involved as a key partner in Site B's pilot, alongside other multi-agency partners including children's social care, the police and Voluntary and Community Organisations. They were a partner agency in the complex strategy meetings and the related locality meetings and sub-working group. As part of the response, the CSP contributed information they held pertaining to the local area of concern and explored licencing options available to target local shops that were selling alcohol to young women experiencing CSE.

A location assessment was undertaken during the pilot to develop a place-based plan that addressed CSE within the area. One feature of the location assessment was surveys with young people, residents and businesses. These aimed to understand the issues from the perspective of people using the space and to identify any potential community guardians. The CSP conducted the resident surveys that formed part of the location assessment.

In the Site C pilot, a location assessment was led by the CSP. This was the first time the CSP had carried out a CS-informed approach to a location assessment. For the assessment, the CSP carried out neighbourhood consultation activities with community members. They also undertook a visual audit to map locations of concern. This involved taking photographs and visiting locations of concern identified by data on crime and ASB. These activities were intended to identify anything in the location under assessment that might act to make a young person vulnerable. As part of the assessment, children's social care professionals consulted with young people they knew to ascertain areas where young people felt safe and unsafe. Finally, the CSP distributed leaflets in the local area to increase community members' understanding of exploitation and signs to look out for to support the identification of young people at risk.

The assessment was overseen by a multi-agency CS panel, created as part of the pilot. The panel was led by children's social care and involved multi-agency members. Following completion, the location assessment was used to inform a peer assessment carried out by children's social care and overseen by the CS panel.

Across these two pilots, we identified three themes that characterised a shift in the roles played by CSP when they participated in a CS response to EFH.

Partnership working

Under a CS response, the nature of the partnerships that CSPs engaged with changed. In both pilots, the CSP worked with children's social care and voluntary organisations, whose priority was safeguarding the welfare of young people. These agencies had not been typical partners of the CSPs in previous responses to EFH:

> 'I've not really worked with any of those who sat down at the table before, because we have a whole different sort of workload and the way we work with young people and families and others out there as part of the safer community remit and I felt a little bit out of my depth at the beginning, because all of those professions worked directly with children.' (Member of the CSP, multi-agency focus group, Pilot 2)

The nature, as well as the type, of partnerships that CSPs used also changed. For example, engagement with community representatives, such as local residents, had a different focus – the welfare of young people. In Pilot 2 in particular, the CSP reached out to a range of partners to inform an assessment of young people's needs in the location. They engaged with shop owners, businesses, local community and church groups and young people to learn about their needs and concerns in the community:

> I think one of the positives from the neighbourhood assessment which I picked up was looking at that wider contextualised involvement from local community organisation and shop keepers and so on because when we discussed it, we went out and talked to them about it if they would want to be involved in any future developments of this from having posters in the window to being a safe space for young people ... they see the kids hanging out outside of shops, drugs and whatever they're doing out there and they were all keen to play a role in it so I think that is why a conceptualised network is really positive and we make a point of involving our residents. We're not successful unless we involve local people.' (Member of the CSP, multi-agency focus group, Pilot 2)

Through community engagement, the CSPs were able to identify potential community guardians (individuals or groups who play a role in safeguarding young people in the community) for the local area and possible locations that required a safeguarding response.

Furthermore, in both pilots, working with new partners and asking different questions of existing partnerships enabled CSP professionals to identify new information about locations of concern and safety. For example, in Pilot 2, CSP engagement with young people identified that young people felt safe in local youth activities and spaces that had community guardianship. Similarly, in Pilot 1, the engagement work with residents identified previously unknown concerns pertaining to a bus shelter.

Influencing data sets and information

In respect of partnership working, adopting a CS approach altered the activities of CSPs. However, on other occasions, the involvement of CSPs in CS pilots changed how children's social care responded to EFH; the influence occurred in the opposite direction. One example of this was the data that was used to identify, and understand, extra-familial contexts impacted by EFH. In both pilots, CSPs offered information that influenced the data sets used by multi-agency partnerships to design responses to EFH.

The multi-agency partnerships involved in the pilots felt that data shared by CSPs provided important information which shaped their response to the locations of concern: "We worked together on the [location name] complex strategy meeting and the plans and in fact ... Community Safety were quite instrumental in getting the geography, the architecture around the [location name] so that it was safer" (Multi-agency professional, multi-agency focus group, Pilot 1). Data held by CSPs included recent statistics related to reported crime within the area and how this related to the geography of the location, as well as knowledge related the location's legacy and history based on their data sets, such as the 'reputation' of places among services. This historical knowledge was deemed to be invaluable by the multi-agency partnership. It enabled them to understand stigma related to certain areas and the reasons these spaces had legacies that might influence residents and other communities'/agencies' views and relationships with the space. Pilot participants viewed that without this data, children's social care had gaps in knowledge while planning responses to locations:

> '[it] would have been absolutely amazing, to know that information prior to working with that cohort of children that are in that area and even though I've worked in [area name], I still don't have that knowledge that [CSP lead] has and I would never know that ... [the CPS's] team is great because we know you work in the community and you have that sense of community and I think it would be great to understand and to help understand the child and what they're facing in the community.' (Professional from children's social care, multi-agency focus group, Pilot 2)

In Site C, the location assessment was used to inform the development of a peer assessment carried out by children's social care and overseen by a multi-agency panel. Despite the focus of the location assessment on maintaining safety for young people in the area, the data it generated were largely used within the peer assessment to support police activity. For example, locations of crime and ASB identified in the location assessment were mapped against the addresses of young people who were included in the peer assessment. The CSP used the data to pursue crime and disorder responses to these young people rather than a welfare response. Such an example demonstrates how CSP data, and CSP use of welfare assessment data, can influence the tone and focus of a multi-agency response back towards crime and disorder, even if that response involves children's social care.

The purpose of a Community Safety Partnership response

Working towards a CS framework appeared to shift, in parts, the purpose of a CSP. The purpose of both pilots was to provide a welfare response to EFH rather than a response driven by a crime and disorder framework. Therefore, when the CSP provided data pertaining to crime and disorder, as part of Pilot 1, the principal purpose of this was to assist a safeguarding response to a group of young people and location where they were at risk of harm. They were also called upon to use licencing legislation and provide interventions into locations of concern, such as a bus shelter, to reduce the risks young people faced in the area. In Pilot 2, the purpose of the CSP shifted as the pilot required them to view young people through the lens of safeguarding (and therefore see them as at risk of harm in their community) instead of through the lens of ASB, crime and disorder (when they were viewed as the source of risk to 'the community'):

> 'I work very much seeing these young people, we don't see the background for these young people, and so on, so what we see is a name on the daily reports and I think the young lad, he is 11 or 12, we knew he was causing issues in his local community, antisocial behaviour, some racial taunting of local residents, but it was only when he was caught trying to throw drugs over the prison wall at [area name] that we thought, hang on, this is a little bit more ... it makes us a little bit broader ... it is just thinking that although they are a nuisance and causing a nuisance, young people also need that extra support and I think it gives us a little bit more understanding as to how to think about the young people in our communities.' (Member of the CSP, multi-agency focus group, Pilot 2)

This changed perspective impacted the response provided by the CSP. They moved from a position of sanctioning young people they identified, to one where they often referred these young people to children's social care and engaged in local activities to support their needs, such as youth activities and clubs. Such a response was focused on safeguarding welfare.

Maintaining this shift of purpose to a welfare response that worked alongside young people and their wider communities was sometimes challenging for participating CSPs and their partners. In Pilot 1, for example, the CSP queried the value of resident engagement when the data such activities sourced mirrored information they had already collected through other means: "I always felt like we didn't necessarily learn that much from that specific exercise because, or that we didn't already know essentially" (Member of the CSP, multi-agency focus group, Pilot 1). On other occasions, the needs identified by the local residents appeared in conflict with what the CSP were able to offer. Despite pilot activities seeking to shift towards a focus on local needs and welfare, participants did not always feel this was feasible within a CSP legislative framework:

> 'Yeah and I think coming from a fairly traditional community safety background slash world where essentially we're kind of about telling people what they can and can't do, and when they do the stuff they're not meant to be doing, going and getting court orders to try and oblige

them to do it, a lot of it is about saying to people "don't do this" or "do that", and then mandating it, putting consequences in place when they don't ... that sort of traditional community safety approach is, if it even is that, is not particularly good or doesn't feel particularly comfortable in talking to the community, because if the community says "actually, we want it all to be footloose and fancy free round here, and not have very many rules", and we can't really work that. It's a bit like, well, that can't happen actually ... because we sort of exercise powers on behalf of the authority ... So talking to communities, it feels a bit odd.' (Member of the CSP, multi-agency focus group, Pilot 1)

These tensions are understandable given the legislation underpinning the CSP role. As outlined at the outset of this chapter, the traditional purpose for CSPs pertains to crime and disorder. The response toolkit that CSPs draw upon is focused on changing behaviour through ASB, crime and disorder sanctions, a response that does not lend itself to welfare-oriented outcomes.

Can Community Safety and Contextual Safeguarding ever align?

Across both pilots, professionals reflected that the approaches taken by CSPs were novel. Feelings of 'unfamiliarity' and being 'out of their depth' with welfare responses highlight the little integration of CSPs within safeguarding responses to date, and that the adoption of CS is a diversion from their current position. This was evidenced most prevalently by the minimal partnership working between CSPs and children's social care prior to the pilots, as well as a lack of understanding by Community Safety professionals as to the role of children's social care and the vulnerabilities of, and risks faced, by young people they would typically identify through crime and disorder processes. A particular barrier to this integration previously, identified by both pilots, was the misalignment of traditional CSP responses which focused on crime and disorder in locations affected by EFH as opposed to the welfare of children in those same contexts.

Both pilots applied a welfare framework to locations affected by EFH and the CSP was asked to contribute to this process. A welfare approach was promoted when CSPs worked in partnership with agencies that have statutory responsibilities for safeguarding; both pilots were overseen by children's social care. Within this structure, the CSP was able to provide data related to locations of concern, such as geographical mapping and crime statistics. Although multi-agency partners saw this data as important, if its inclusion in an assessment were to be prioritised over young people's views (or used instead of them), it would pull children's social care activity away from CS rather than support an alignment with it.

The positioning of the CSP within the community and their knowledge (from a particular perspective) of the location also enabled the CSPs to consult with members of the community as part of a CS location assessment, identify potential community guardians and raise awareness of risks within the community. Pilot 2 also demonstrated the role that CSPs can play in conducting observations of locations through a safeguarding lens to identify risks and protective interventions, such as introducing low lighting. CSPs' role in consulting with community members and young people, however, is only aligned with CS if they are able to engage with the views expressed by these groups and ensure that they are foregrounded in the assessment. Where these views are dismissed or minimised, again, CSP activities risk moving children's social care efforts to assess locations away from a welfare and CS response.

CSP professionals reported that working alongside agencies with a statutory safeguarding responsibility provided them with a greater insight into the vulnerability of young people experiencing EFH. This increased knowledge enabled CSP professionals in Pilot 2, for example, to have a greater consideration for the welfare of young people they encountered in relation to EFH. Partnership working and data sharing in relation to EFH, however, does not necessarily always lead to the prioritisation of young people's welfare. If contextualised data are used to pursue a crime and disorder response, as was done in the peer assessment in Pilot 2, then questions are raised as to the value of multi-agency working and information sharing and to whose purpose it serves.

To ensure a safeguarding response is prioritised in relation to EFH, a welfare lens needs to be applied to the following questions: what information is being gathered, from which sources and for what purpose (and that this is made clear to young people and members of the community sharing information)? What data should be shared with different agencies and why? If agencies are working together, do they have a shared purpose where a child's welfare, rather than crime prevention, is paramount? In order to do this, questions may also need to be explored related to the nature of the relationship between multi-agency partners, the power within these relationships and the extent CSC is able to provide a safeguarding response to EFH.

If we organise the activities of CSPs against the four domains of the CS framework, we see where the activities observed during pilots were aligned or divergent from CS (Table 5.2).

Within Scale-Up test sites, doing Community Safety was not the same as doing CS. There are significant divergences between the two approaches, predominately predicated on a misalignment of the legislation underpinning them – and their associated purpose. In the pilots discussed in this chapter, CSPs were able to achieve some shift in the response they provided, moving from a position solely focused on disrupting crime and disorder to one that

Table 5.2: Community Safety Partnership pilot and future activity against Contextual Safeguarding domains

	Community Safety	CSPs in CS pilots	For CSPs to maintain CS
Target	Physical locations and groups where EFH (if conceptualised as crime, disorder, ASB) occurs.	Physical locations and groups where EFH (if conceptualised as crime, disorder, ASB) occurs. Tensions arise regarding the extent the CSP approach can work with other measures of EFH, that is, the perceptions of residents of harm. CSP in Pilot 2 was to a greater extent able to view EFH using a wider remit in their assessment (including the perceptions of young people the community).	The definition of EFH would need to be reconceptualised. EFH and the social conditions related to it would need to be perceived through a welfare lens informed by children's rights where an understanding of the lives of young people and communities is foregrounded.
Legislative framework	Crime and disorder.	Purpose of the response was more than crime and disorder and worked within a structure that was largely underpinned by welfare legislation. This was led by CSC. Partnership working between CSP, CSC and the police can also lead to the pursual of a crime and disorder response.	The legislation underpinning the CSP would need to change to ensure a better strategic alignment between welfare legislation and crime and disorder legislation with child protection and child welfare being prioritised.
Partnerships	With statutory and community agencies who can disrupt crime and ASB in extra-familial groups and locations.	With statutory and community agencies who can provide a safeguarding response to EFH and locations.	Formalise partnership working between CSP and statutory and community agencies who can provide a safeguarding response to EFH and locations. Flow of information sharing to inform welfare responses only.
Outcomes	Reduction in crime and disorder at a contextual and individual level.	Worked towards both welfare and criminal justice outcomes without always considering whether the two were aligned. Moreover, contextual outcomes tended to be measured in respect of crime, whereas welfare outcomes were measured for individuals.	Welfare of young people and communities prioritised: increased safety and welfare at a contextual and individual level is prioritised over reduction in crime and disorder at a contextual and individual level. Safety reconceptualised to ensure that young people are viewed as members of the community.

was also minded to safeguarding and child welfare. Analysis of pilots against a CS framework, however, identified tensions in relation to the hierarchy of data that continued to inform CSP responses to EFH, and, within this, the centralisation of the voice of young people and the community.

Partnership working between agencies that are underpinned by differing legislation was shown to support some movement towards developing a response with a shared purpose of safeguarding young people, and, in the process, prioritising child welfare legislative frameworks. However, business as usual is not a pilot. The challenges emerging from the pilots also raised questions as to the feasibility of CSPs working to a CS approach as a sector more generally. If the two approaches ultimately work in accordance with different legislative frameworks, these tensions could eventually undermine a sustained focus on child welfare in partnership responses to EFH. As things stand, CSPs could never lead CS work. This would need to be overseen or led by children's social care to ensure it remained underpinned by child protection legislation and characterised by child welfare activities. The relationship between children's social care and CSPs also requires further definition so that information sharing between the two structures is for the purpose of child welfare first, and on all occasions, rather than risk some activity slipping towards enabling crime and disorder responses to individuals and groups of young people.

To maintain CSP sector involvement in CS, a better strategic alignment between the two legislative frameworks is required, one that ensures policies guiding CSPs enable them to realise their duties while also aligning with child protection legislation, rather than at times undermining it. Welfare does not currently form part of the framework underpinning the CSP role. Thinking about the title of 'Community Safety', however, does provide scope to think about the role of CSPs in safeguarding and promoting the welfare of young people. Community Safety could be reconceptualised so that young people were viewed as community members requiring responses to promote their safety, rather than current interpretations that often see 'communities' as in need of protection from young people.

Note

[1] Referred to as CSPs from 2010 onwards in England.

6

Contextual Safeguarding beyond the UK

Delphine Peace

Introduction

CS has been shaped and primarily implemented in England and Wales, yet the issues it confronts are not unique to the UK. The CS team have begun exploring the applicability of the CS framework in European and Australian contexts as part of the 'Contextual Safeguarding Across Borders' (CSAB) project. This project specifically explores the feasibility of CS as an approach to support safeguarding responses to refugee and asylum-seeking young people in Europe, and Indigenous young people affected by EFH in Australia. Beyond exploring the international transferability of a CS approach, the project also explores the ways in which CS can support child protection responses to acknowledge and address the impact of structural inequalities in young people's lives – such as poverty, racism, sexism and so on – on their experiences of harm. Safeguarding refugee and asylum-seeking young people has become a salient child protection issue across Europe, particularly over recent years in the wake of the so-called European 'refugee crisis'. Refugee and asylum-seeking young people, in addition to facing significant risks of EFH on their migration journeys and within their host countries, face an additional set of structural barriers within European child protection systems that are ill-equipped to protect them (Degani et al, 2015; Dimitrova, Ivanova and Alexandrova, 2015; D'Addato, 2017; Giovannetti, 2017; Barn, Di Rosa and Kallinikaki, 2021). In Australia, research has highlighted that young people from Indigenous communities can also be particularly vulnerable to forms of harm and discrimination situated within social welfare interventions (Ivec, Braithwaite and Harris, 2012).

This chapter is based on the European strand of the CSAB project. Particularly, it draws from a literature-scoping review that was conducted as part of this project to better understand how EFH is responded to in Europe. The chapter focuses broadly on European challenges to responding to EFH and does not go into depth about responses specific to refugee and asylum-seeking young people – this aspect of the study has been published elsewhere (Peace and Wroe, 2022). This chapter aims to explore the applicability of CS in other contexts. It begins by presenting key trends and challenges across European child protection systems related to responding to EFH, before offering some initial thoughts on how CS speaks to these challenges.

European responses to extra-familial harm: key trends and challenges

'Extra-familial harm' in a European context

In the UK, the term 'extra-familial harm' refers to a range of different forms of abuse that adolescents can experience outside their families – such as harm from their peers or sexual or criminal exploitation by adults. The term 'extra-familial harm' does not feature in the European (anglophone) literature and policy documents that we have encountered as part of our scoping review for the CSAB project – perhaps unsurprisingly, as this term was coined within a specific UK policy context. Like in the UK, systems to address child abuse in Europe seem to primarily address abuse within familial settings, with state interventions based either on supporting parents to better safeguard their children, providing families with socio-economic support or protecting children from risks situated within their home environment/families via targeted one-to-one support or by placing them into care (Gilbert, 1997; Spratt et al, 2015; Merkel-Holguin, Fluke and Krugman, 2019). Increased awareness of child sexual abuse in Europe has primarily focused on abuse within the family or institutional settings (Bruning and Doek, 2021). Nonetheless, European regional policy frameworks over the last 20 years have drawn attention to forms of harm that young people can experience in extra-familial contexts – with a particular focus on sexual abuse (including CSE) and the trafficking of children (see CoE, 2005; CoE, 2007). As such, our scoping review for the CSAB project mainly focused on these forms of harm. European regional policy frameworks prompt European member states to address CSE and child trafficking through a rights-based approach and child-sensitive protection systems. However, when it comes to social policy, health or education matters, the European Union can propose a broad approach but cannot impose new laws; nor can it prescribe how member states, and which agencies, implement recommended policies. This can lead to inconsistent applications of child protection measures across different countries and poses a number of challenges in terms of addressing these forms of harm, as we will explore later.

Although CSE and trafficking feature more prominently as forms EFH in European frameworks, research about these forms of harm in European settings appears limited. The papers that we identified mostly focused on the sexual exploitation of children perpetrated by adults, and on the trafficking of children for the purpose of CSE. In Europe, the form of trafficking and CSE that appears to have received the most attention is the 'Loverboy' method – whereby traffickers (often adult men) groom young women or young men to enter into a 'relationship' with them and use their influence to exploit them, for instance, via the sex industry. This has been mainly reported in Eastern European countries and in Germany (Child10, nd). There seems to be less research about other forms of trafficking (such as labour trafficking) (Barner et al, 2018) and abuse and exploitation between peers. Another trend that struck us is that the overarching focus on violence against children in Europe is primarily focused on forms of violence that children experience or witness – but specific considerations about protecting children and adolescents who may be both victims and perpetrators of violence, including when forced into exploitative situations, remain largely absent (Brunin and Doek, 2021).

Although European literature looking at CSE and trafficking is emerging, the papers we came across suggest that child protection systems in Europe generally struggle to respond to these forms of harm. These flag some key systematic challenges that will look familiar to UK readers.

Shared trends and challenges around responding to child sexual exploitation and trafficking in Europe

The scoping review surfaced three key trends and challenges that resonate particularly well with the UK context.

Falling through child protection nets

Regional European policy frameworks have called for the improved identification and protection of victims of CSE and trafficking and provide mechanisms to allow for this. However, there continues to remain a lack of both identification and suitable child protection responses, which means that many adolescents who have experienced these forms of harm fall through child protection nets. While many European countries have 'National Referral Mechanisms' (NRMs), which are special referral processes to improve the identification, referral and support of victims of human trafficking, these are inconsistently applied with varying thresholds for identification and service provision (Palmer, 2019; Gregulska et al, 2020).

One underlying challenge is that in most European countries, the identification and protection of child victims of trafficking are not addressed as a separate *child* protection and child-rights issue. As such, there is an absence of distinct measures in place to identify and protect children, including a lack of risks and needs assessments, a lack of specialist accommodation and support, as well as a lack of special funding allocations for child protection responses (Gregulska et al, 2020). For example, while the trafficking of women and girls for sexual exploitation remains the main form of trafficking identified, in the large majority of European states, there are no public institutions and/ or national action plans to address this specific form of trafficking (Gregulska et al, 2020). Specific documents considering the enhanced vulnerabilities of women and girls to trafficking for sexual exploitation were identified in only three European states – Germany, Spain and Sweden (Gregulska et al, 2020). Identification rates are even lower for child victims of trafficking for the purpose of labour exploitation (CoE, 2019).

Rather than being framed as a child protection issue, child exploitation through human trafficking is predominantly defined, and addressed, within a narrow criminal context – and particularly within the frame of illegal immigration concerns, as opposed to being addressed within a human rights focus (Barner, Okech and Camp, 2018). This trend can be observed in Europe and beyond, with efforts to combat trafficking primarily focused on prosecuting perpetrators and a generic lack of holistic support for the protection and rehabilitation of victims (Barner, Okech and Camp, 2018). In many European countries, children are not protected by law from criminal prosecution for offences they commit in the context of trafficking (UNICEF, 2008), and the identification and assistance to victims in some countries, particularly in countries of destination, are largely driven by victims' willingness to cooperate with the criminal justice system (OSCE, 2019). For example, in Belgium, adult and minors' entry into the NRM system is voluntary and dependent on collaboration with the police. This can pose an additional barrier to accessing services for adolescents who might be reluctant, or afraid, to engage with the police (Gregulska et al, 2020). Similarly, in Ireland, the police service is the only body responsible for formally and legally identifying victims of trafficking – this has shown to undermine the early identification of victims and possibly exclude a large number of women and girls trafficked for sexual exploitation (Gregulska et al, 2020). In some countries, such as Hungary or Poland, without formal identification, victims – including children – cannot access state-funded services and support offered through the NRM, while other countries, such as Austria or Finland, have low thresholds for entry into their NRMs, and services are not conditional on formal identification (Gregulska et al, 2020). In some countries, victims of exploitation receive no child welfare support but are criminalised and placed in detention facilities – this is the case, for example, in Italy, Greece and Hungary (Degani et al, 2015; Dimitrova, Ivanova and Alexandrova, 2015; OSCE, 2019; Palmer, 2019). Asylum-seeking adolescents who have been trafficked across borders are particularly vulnerable to this trend, as considerations of their migration status often obscure their child protection needs (Forin and Healy, 2018). Adolescents who have been trafficked into criminal activities, such as labour exploitation, forced begging or theft, are also largely criminalised (Degani et al, 2015; Dimitrova, Ivanova and Alexandrova, 2015).

Our scoping review for the CSAB project identified limited examples of countries that had specialised child protection provisions in place for victims of CSE and/or trafficking. In the Netherlands, there are targeted programmes for young people affected by CSE – including both 'open' and 'secure' facilities. In some cases, admittance to care facilities (often enforced through judicial authorisation) is preventive when it is strongly suspected that a minor is at immediate risk of sexual exploitation or when there are strong suspicions but no substantial evidence that the exploitation is taking place (Aussems et al, 2020). In Sweden, moreover, children who are presumed victims of trafficking are placed in specialised housing with reinforced support (OSCE, 2019). Meanwhile, in Bulgaria, children who have been identified as victims of cross-border trafficking abroad and are repatriated are placed in residential centres (known as 'crisis centres'). The centres offer a range of social services, including social and psychological support, crisis intervention and legal counselling (OSCE, 2019).

A lack of partnership working

There appears to be, furthermore, an absence of clarity about which state agency is responsible for identifying and protecting victims of CSE and trafficking (Degani et al, 2015; Dimitrova, Ivanova and Alexandrova, 2015; Muraya and Fry, 2016). In some countries, like Greece and Cyprus, this responsibility sits with social welfare agencies – but in practice, due to their lack of capacity, civil society organisations provide the majority of services (Palmer, 2019). In some countries, like Belgium, there is a specialised centre for victims of trafficking coordinating responses at national level; in other countries, civil society organisations act as this coordinating body – like in the Netherlands or Poland (Gregulska et al, 2020). While in other countries, like France or Italy, there is no central national coordinating agency, and assessments of needs and support provision tend to sit with civil society organisations, depending on their capacity to do so (Gregulska et al, 2020). Noteworthily, only half of European member states have inter-governmental committees ensuring the collaboration of various governmental actors – and not all of these interagency bodies include specialised civil society organisations (Gregulska et al, 2020). Civil society organisations are notably influential in Finland and Germany, where they play an important role in shaping policies (Gregulska et al, 2020). The absence of data, lack of information sharing and lack of cooperation across agencies and organisations, moreover, further reduce opportunities for identification and complicate referral processes in many countries (Degani et al, 2015; Forin and Healy, 2018; Gregulska et al, 2020)

Victims often receive (unsuitable) care provisions that can increase their vulnerability to extra-familial harm

One form of response evidenced in our scoping is the use of residential placements to protect adolescents from CSE or trafficking. Sometimes, these placements can include secure facilities and detention centres. In Norway, for example, some adolescents are placed in detention to prevent them from leaving care and returning to the control or influence of a trafficker (OSCE, 2019). Moreover, a review of 20 multi-national projects to support child victims of human trafficking in Europe flags a number of structural shortcomings in child protection services for children residing in temporary accommodations, such as unsuitable and unsafe accommodation, a lack of wider support from child welfare services and a lack of coordinated response, including around ensuring the safe return of minors to their home country (Palmer, 2019). These gaps apply to adolescents from European countries as well as those who have been trafficked from abroad into Europe. Another study comparing child protection responses to child trafficking across European countries highlights the lack of training available to staff in shelters run by child welfare services or by the judicial youth protection services in regards to supporting child victims of exploitation (Degani et al, 2015).

In some cases, the unsuitability of placements can increase young people's exposure to harm, whereby they go missing from their accommodations due to poor living conditions in shelters and/or continued links with their exploiters (Degani et al, 2015; Dimitrova, Ivanova and Alexandrova, 2015; Muraya and Fry, 2016). In some countries, like Hungary, there are no protected houses or shelter facilities for 'third-country' national minors – despite the country being a popular transit stop for smuggler nets transporting migrants to Europe and beyond. Instead, trafficked third-country nationals identified as victims of trafficking – including children – are accommodated in reception centres for the duration of the procedure, without any access to psychosocial assistance or support (Degani et al, 2015). As we have seen previously, across Europe, asylum-seeking adolescents with irregular migratory status, and/or unaccompanied adolescents trafficked from abroad, are often placed in temporary accommodations – such as shelters or hotels, or detention facilities, despite United Nations guidelines condemning this practice (UNGA, 2010). Detention facilities, shelters and informal encampments have been flagged as settings where adolescents – including those affected by exploitation or trafficking – can experience multiple forms of violence and abuse, including CSE and trafficking (Freccero et al, 2017; FRA, 2020).

Opportunities for Contextual Safeguarding

In light of these common challenges, there seems to be a number of opportunities for a CS approach in Europe.

Emphasising extra-familial harm in adolescence as a child protection issue

As we have seen, many child protection systems in Europe are ill-equipped to respond to CSE and trafficking and, in practice, many adolescents affected by these types of harm fall through child protection nets, or end up being criminalised. CS could provide a theoretical and practice framework for framing CSE and trafficking as child protection issues, and emphasise the need for comprehensive, welfare-led responses, as opposed to responses that are primarily focused on punishing crime or addressing behavioural issues.

Although our scoping review for the CSAB project focused on CSE and trafficking, as these are forms of EFH most recognised at a European level, we found some discussions about other types of EFH – including peer-on-peer abuse, sexting, 'youth violence' and 'gang involvement' (Fraser, Ralphs and Smithson, 2018; Stanley et al, 2018; Tomaszewska and Schuster, 2021). These are forms of harm which, as we see in the UK, traditional child protection systems find difficult to address as they often involve adolescents who straddle victim/perpetrator identities. For example, some authors have raised concerns about recent developments in European policies against 'gangs' – notably, the use of civil gang injunctions, police gang units, intelligence databases and multi-agency working practices, and their potential to focus disproportionately on young people from Black, Asian and minority ethnic backgrounds (Fraser, Ralphs and Smithson, 2018). This echoes concerns raised in the UK (see, for instance, Williams, 2018).

Although we only found a small amount of literature about youth work in Europe, the material we identified suggests that discussions around EFH are also largely absent from the European youth work policy agenda, and limited to combating radicalisation (Ord et al, 2018). European youth work appears mainly focused on preventing drug abuse or 'risky behaviour', promoting sexual health and, more broadly, on fostering the participation of young people in society through a range of means (Ord et al, 2018).

Could CS offer a theoretical framework to prompt more discussion about these forms of harm, and help to frame them as child protection issues warranting welfare responses? Could it help us explore whether challenges encountered in the UK, in relation to addressing these types of harm, are also present elsewhere? Different social work, youth work or youth justice contexts could also offer valuable learning to a UK context.

Working with adolescents, including those who are victims of, and involved in, criminal or harmful activity

CS could further shed light on the need for child protection responses to understand, and work with, the dynamics of adolescence. There seems to be an absence of discussion about the protection needs of adolescents in Europe, and a lack of evidence of responses to protect and support adolescents who may be both victims of and engage in harmful or criminal activity – including as a result of being forced into exploitative situations.

Yet looking at how different countries in Europe respond to youth offending and work with older adolescents and young adults, some contexts might be more favourable to welfare-led responses to EFH. Social services are involved to various degrees in youth justice systems in Europe, with some countries that have adopted a 'welfare' approach and others that have adopted a 'justice' approach (Rap, 2015). In a 'welfare' model, social workers are closely involved in the youth justice process and advise the judge on the need for protection or care (such as in Belgium, France and Italy). Whereas in countries that follow a 'justice' approach (such as the UK and Ireland), social work services work independently from the youth court, and social workers play a less active role. Other countries in Europe adopt a mixed model (such as Germany, the Netherlands, Greece and Spain) whereby social services are independent from the youth court, but there is a possibility to implement early interventions soon after the arrest of the young person, as part of a wider welfare approach that characterises these countries. Germany, the Netherlands and Croatia offer interesting examples of specific juvenile court protections for young adults based on educational or rehabilitative approaches for young people involved in 'delinquent' or criminal behaviour, and less reliance on incarceration (Matthews, Schiraldi and Chester, 2018). The Netherlands is a particularly interesting example in this respect. Over the last decade, it has implemented a special 'adolescent criminal law' for young offenders aged 12 to 23. This policy change was influenced by wide research on young adult offenders, including neuroscientific studies showing that brain functions are not fully developed at 18. This makes it the country with the highest age limit for juvenile justice provisions (Pruin and Dünkel, 2015). In Scandinavian countries, furthermore, child welfare agencies do most of the work that is normally attributed to juvenile justice agencies in many other European countries, and sentences are mitigated for young offenders under the age of 21 (Pruin and Dünkel, 2015).

Perhaps CS could lend itself well in countries where criminality is seen as a welfare issue? Countries where youth justice systems are characterised by an approach of minimum intervention, giving priority to non-punitive and rehabilitative responses, and in which youth justice and welfare approaches are more closely intertwined, are more likely to align with Domain 2 of the CS framework (responding to adolescent harm using child welfare legislation). These settings could offer some valuable learning to other countries like the UK, where there is a marked divide between child welfare and youth justice services. The UK has been described as having a much more punitive youth justice system compared with other European countries, with England and Wales having the lowest criminal age of responsibility in Europe (along with Cyprus and Switzerland) (Pruin and Dünkel, 2015).

Intervening in contexts

While contexts are acknowledged in international guidance, it seems that child protection responses are rarely used to intervening within them. In Europe, child protection interventions continue to centre largely on parenting and the behaviour of young people, rather than addressing broader social inequalities that might influence exploitation (Radford, Allnock and Hynes, 2015; Sethi et al, 2018). Importantly, child protection systems themselves can be contexts of harm when they do not adequately protect and support adolescents.

Could a CS approach offer a pathway for intervening within contexts – such as supporting protective peer relationships or making places in the community safer – that might be useful in European contexts? In some places, this approach is already well established. Indeed, there are many overlaps with CS and social pedagogical or ecological models of child welfare interventions – particularly in Germany, where social work and social care are shaped by the concept of 'lifeworld orientation'. This approach shares many similarities with Bourdieu's theory, which underpins CS, highlighting the importance of understanding social environments in order to understand young people's individual behaviours and experiences and drawing on these environments to provide holistic support (Grunwald and Thiersch, 2009). Germany has a stronger focus on community interventions and group work through its tradition of 'mobile' or 'spatial' youth work rooted within local boroughs, churches and civil society organisations. According to this approach, social workers and youth workers work with young people in the locations in which they spend time. In Germany, social work and youth work are closely intertwined. It would not be unreasonable, therefore, to think that CS would align well with the German system and similar systems where social and youth work in community spaces is more prominent. In a similar vein, one study exploring youth work across England, Estonia, Finland, France and Italy highlighted a tension between the degree to which youth work focused on individuals or collectives (such as peer groups and the wider community) (Ord et al, 2018). English youth work appeared more focused on individuals than youth work approaches in France or Italy which were more geared towards the collective, with a stronger focus on 'creating bonds' between young people and adults in the community and improving young people's sense of belonging in their peer groups and in the community – an approach that looks very similar to the ambitions of CS. It would be interesting to explore whether such youth work and community-based social work have been specifically applied to protecting adolescents from EFH in other countries.

Youth work, moreover, could be an avenue for engaging with the social conditions of harm, such as poverty and discrimination, that can enhance adolescents' vulnerability to engage in EFH. Finland offers an interesting example of such an approach, with an increase of youth work targeted at adolescents with fewer opportunities. 97 per cent of Finnish municipalities (as of 2015) had at least one or more detached youth workers dedicated to reach out to adolescents who were not in education, employment or training, to offer guidance and access to public services (Ord et al, 2018). This approach forms part of a wider shift in European youth policies from traditional universal provisions towards measures focusing on 'youth at risk' (Ord et al, 2018) – similarly to the UK, where this shift has underpinned New Labour's reforms of youth work (Ord et al, 2018). Yet this development can have many negative consequences for young people across Europe given the importance of universal service provisions to preventing harm and ensuring young people's wellbeing – such as providing them with spaces to hang out and positive activities – and could contribute to separate services for 'at-risk' adolescents. Could CS help draw attention to the importance of universal youth provisions to engaging with contexts? CS could further raise concerns about how language is used in policy and practice to describe 'high-risk' or 'problematic' behaviour, that would imply that adolescents are in some ways responsible for the harm they encounter? It seems that in the youth work arena, too, CS could offer relevant caution against a focus on individual behaviour change and criminal reduction.

Opportunities for developing contextual interventions with adolescents might be further challenged in a context of declining youth work funding that can be observed throughout Europe, and even in countries where it is traditionally more embedded than in the UK, such as Germany, Austria and Finland (Seal and Harris, 2016). Youth work generally struggles to secure sustained funding and gain recognition within political advocacy and youth development and faces continuous pressure to 'prove' its value through outcome and impact measurements (Williamson, 2020). As discussed elsewhere in this book (Chapters 11 and 12), measuring outcomes for contexts is a new approach that professionals and researchers are currently grappling with, and there are probably many opportunities to learn from other settings.

Partnerships

Similarly to the UK, the absence of national strategies for safeguarding adolescents who are victims of exploitation means that responses tend to fall between European youth justice, child protection agencies and civil society (Lloyd and Firmin, 2020; Wroe, 2021). On the one hand, there is an evident need for better partnerships to address EFH in adolescence. Would CS work better in settings where civil society organisations and youth work are more prominent and work more closely with statutory agencies?

On the other hand, the 'statutory framing' of CS, which has been conceptualised and tested primarily within statutory child protection settings, might also have its limitations in countries where civil society organisations play much more prominent roles as welfare providers. Perhaps even more so in countries where, in the absence of statutory responses, civil society organisations and large non-governmental organisations (NGOs) provide most of the service delivery. This is notably the case in Eastern and Southern Europe and particularly for victims of exploitation. A CS approach would probably look quite different in those settings.

In some places, multi-agency integrated working might surface tensions for youth work or civic organisations linked to fears of losing their independence and their distinctive capacities to engage with and build trusting relationships with young people. In the UK, these tensions are certainly present in the voluntary and community sector (VCS), whereby the emphasis placed on information sharing between professionals in response to EFH can be seen by some practitioners as undermining principles of confidentiality, trust and consent with young people (Ord et al, 2018). These tensions might be more present in European child protection systems informed by socio-pedagogical approaches that emphasise trust, confidentiality and voluntary participation over more individual, statutory approaches (Seal and Harris, 2016). In the UK, we are seeing how some applications of CS, if misinterpreted, can lead towards relationships of monitoring and surveillance with adolescents, in the name of child welfare (see Chapters 4 and 5). It is probable that the nature of the UK child protection system, with its higher focus on risk, 'antisocial behaviour' and crime reduction, is to some extent more conducive to this trend. Yet, as we have seen, the European-wide shifting emphasis on targeted interventions with 'high-risk' young people warrants caution in this respect.

Concluding thoughts

This chapter has surfaced a number of challenges reported for European child protection system responses to EFH that resonate particularly well with the UK context. There is overall an absence of discussion about EFH in Europe and an absence of evidence of responses that intervene within contexts. The focus is mostly on CSE and trafficking. Young people affected by CSE or trafficking tend to fall through child protection nets. In the absence of child protection responses, responses to victims of child exploitation – particularly associated with trafficking – are still largely situated within the criminal justice system. There is a lack of clarity about which agency is responsible for safeguarding victims of CSE and trafficking, and an absence of partnership working. The absence, and in some cases unsuitability, of child protection responses can enhance adolescents' vulnerability to EFH.

In light of these similarities, the chapter has considered opportunities for using CS to reinforce framings of EFH as a child protection issue; highlight the specific safeguarding needs of adolescents, including those who straddle victim/perpetrator divides; offer pathways for intervening in contexts; and encourage creative partnerships. It has also noted certain aspects of various child protection systems that might be more conducive to CS, and others that may surface similar, and even new, challenges to those we see in the UK. If CS might be useful as a lens to understand other child protection systems and contexts of harm, these settings in turn have much learning to offer to further enrich the CS framework.

Although this chapter focuses on Europe, many of the trends and challenges discussed are present across the world, and there are many research avenues for exploring the applicability of the approach in a range of other settings. Colleagues in the CS research programme are, for instance, looking at the connections between CS and the decolonisation of child protection systems in relation to British colonial legacies in Australia, New Zealand and Canada (see Chapter 7), and exploring broader issues around structural inequalities (see Chapter 3) that are without doubt relevant to many countries.

7

Decolonising practice: 'doing' Contextual Safeguarding with an ethics of care

Vanessa Bradbury-Leather and Sue Rayment-McHugh

The authors of this chapter are non-Indigenous academics and practitioners. We wrote the chapter because we believe good intentions are not enough. Many professionals involved in safeguarding practice are white and located in privileged positions within an ongoing colonial society. We believe that non-Indigenous social welfare practitioners, policy makers and leaders need to do more to reimagine practice, to challenge the mistakes of the past that have filtered into the present and to advance ethical ways of thinking and doing. We acknowledge the need for this work to be undertaken in partnership with First Nations colleagues and leaders. They hold critical knowledge to inform and transform systems and practice and are already leading this journey. It's time for the rest of us to catch up. This chapter urges critical thinking about past and contemporary practice. It is not intended to replace essential and valued First Nations and minoritised ethnic perspectives and leadership, but to stand in solidarity with, and advocate the importance of, dismantling colonial legacies for the mutual liberation of all. As we move forward with this chapter, hold in mind this *whakaaro* (thought) from kaumātua (Māori elder) Koro Hata Temo: "Sometimes what I'd like to say is, the problem with you guys is you never lived in our world ... but you forced us to live in yours" (Koro Hata Temo, 2016). Koro Hata's whakaaro challenges us to disrupt colonialism as norm, keeping us alive to the many ways of knowing and being that can enrich our practice. This chapter is an attempt to disrupt the all-encompassing nature of settler colonialism, and to reimagine the world (through the lens of child protection) with First Nations' values in mind.

A call to reflect and rethink

CS is now well established and scaling up throughout England, Wales and Scotland, bringing context to the forefront of current safeguarding practice. Following this growth and success, it is timely to reflect on this practice and experience and explore more deeply its application with communities who have been disproportionately impacted by child protection systems. Not only is this relevant to the UK context but it seems particularly important now, given current plans to test the applicability and feasibility of CS in international settings, including in British settler postcolonial nations. Indeed, this raises the ongoing impact of colonial legacies as a key contextual consideration, and a need for accountability in practice for the UK's colonial past.

Taking time to reflect on the implications of embedding CS in these contexts is about ensuring CS operates with an ethics of care, avoiding repetition of destructive colonial practices, challenging and speaking to the structural conditions of harm, and is informed and led by those who have been most impacted by excessive child protection intervention. To advance CS in these contexts, this chapter considers past oppressive practices and their lasting impact into the present, how CS challenges these harmful legacies through its values, where tensions remain and why it is important that practice is shaped by these principles and values when we 'do' CS.

Looking back to move forward

We begin by looking back to former British colonies, Aotearoa New Zealand, Australia and Canada. Over a century since 'post'-colonialism, First Nations youth, among Black and other minoritised ethnic young people, are disproportionately over-represented in each of these state's child welfare systems (Family Matters Report, 2017; Ontario's Human Rights Commission, 2018; Mā ori Inquiry into Oranga Tamariki, 2020; Australian Institute of Health and Welfare, 2021; Cenat et al, 2021). There is growing evidence in these contexts to suggest that structural harm in child protection systems is an inherent result of the ongoing legacy of Britain's colonial past – where social work has its roots in colonial policies of assimilation as a result of the importation of British child protection service design into these settler contexts (TRC, 2015; Wai, 2021). Under the directive of 'residential schooling' and later the 'sixties scoop' (McKenzie et al, 2016), and 'stolen generations' (Human Rights and Equal Opportunities Commission, 1997), social workers became 'instruments of social control' and 'participants in the process of dispossession and oppression' (Bennett, 2013: 19–20), enacting government policies and processes of the era, supporting children to be removed from their homes and displacing First Nations children from their lands, families and communities. Such state policies were tied up with prejudiced and harmful assumptions around the ability of First Nations mothers and families to take care of their children and a so-called need to assimilate First Nations' children into white settler society (Bennett, 2013; McKenzie et al, 2016).

What does this tell us about our system? What social practices and processes result in the ongoing over-intervention of racialised families? While these 'post'-colonial nations have diverse experiences, they share the similar constraining force of systems built on Eurocentric values and service delivery. This includes a heady mix of individualism, one-size-fits-all interventions, the perpetuation of deficit narratives and a seemingly punitive system that intervenes in the lives of individuals rather than the social-structural conditions of harm. These policies have a legacy of intergenerational trauma, disadvantage and loss of protective family, kin and social structures (Dudgeon et al, 2010). There remain critical questions about how current foster care statistics are an extension to these colonial dynamics, connecting past and current child protection practice (Cuneen and Libesman, 2000). Eurocentric, expert-led, individualised practice continues to override community-led, local ways of knowing and being (Mabuvira, 2020); and the colonial nature of the system is maintained as invisible – continuing to impose capitalist systems on stolen land as if apolitical and natural (Cook, 2020; Hyslop, 2022). This has resulted in deep and entrenched mistrust of social welfare professionals and mainstream child protection systems by Indigenous and minoritised communities (Malthouse and Oates, 2021).

Similarly, in the UK – the home of the empire and the root of colonial policy – there is likewise an over-representation of Black, disabled and minoritised ethnic young people in the system (Bernard, 2020). Black children move from home to home more often, receive fewer support services, remain in care for longer, are less likely to be reunited with parents and are less likely to be adopted (Epstein and Gonzalez, 2017; Davis and Marsh, 2020; Duffy Rice et al, 2020). Immigrant families are subject to child protection interventions for raising their children in ways that sit beyond 'British' parenting values (Okpokiri, 2017). More broadly, the system is set up to victim blame, often responsibilising women and girls for the abuse they encounter, or framing mothers as having a rational 'choice' to leave abusive relationships, symbolic of a shaming and punitive system that views needs primarily through a risk lens (Featherstone et al, 2016). Moreover, the paradox between the victimisation of white girls and the adultification of Black girls is telling of the deep-rooted norms and values that inform which young people are deemed most in need of support (Davis, 2019).

This puts the dominant British white, Western and neoliberal child protection system and its moral underpinnings into tension, that the role of the system assumes it is inherently good (Featherstone et al, 2014). But what is the role of child protection and who does it serve? Who decides and who benefits? At what point did we decide that it was better to remove children from their families, and fund foster families and state care, rather than resourcing the families and communities themselves (Clarke and Yellow Bird, 2021)? 'Self-care' and 'keeping yourself safe' from harm remains the dominant narrative over collective care (Wever and Zell, 2018). Trauma-informed responses continue to centre individuals, rather than holistic notions grounded in community (Linklater, 2014; Clarke and Yellow Bird, 2021). On a systemic level, addressing harm seems to focus more on punishment, rather than healing and restitution. Though our system is built to protect, are tones of assimilation (towards white British/Eurocentric norms and values) reflected in regulations, policies, practice? Is the information we collect about young people and families proportionate or about watching over, or even maintaining control of, them (Wroe and Lloyd, 2020)?

It is necessary that we locate current policy and practice within its historical and political context so that we can understand how these colonial legacies are not just in the past. They are ongoing. Imprinted into the fabric of our society, they have become the norm, shaping the way we know the world and subsequently practice within it.

Decolonising social welfare

There are international calls for the decolonisation and indigenisation of social welfare (for example, Rankopo and Osei-Hwedie, 2011; Gray et al, 2013; Schmid, 2021). Such calls include replacing imposed Eurocentric, bureaucratic and non-relational dynamics of the system with collective helping strategies built on reciprocity, mutual obligation and community-led decision making (Mabuvira, 2020); foregrounding Indigenous knowledges and approaches (Osei-Hwedie and Boateng, 2018; and for social work practitioners and scholars to 're-interrogate the assumptions they hold, trouble the child protection mindset and fundamentally re-theorise and reposition child welfare' (Schmid, 2021: 12). Leaning into the concept of 'decolonisation' and not simply 'anti-racism' allows us to recognise the intersecting nature of colonialism that has its roots in oppression – heteronormativity, racism, classism, ableism, homophobia, sexism – that shapes dominant norms and values in social welfare.

To put this into context, current strategies introduced to counter the impacts of systemic harm are often implemented in silos, abstracted from the structural conditions that sustain them. For example, culturally sensitive and competent social work practice and family group conferencing (FGC) that shifts decision making through restorative practice are both measures being implemented to recognise systemic racism in social welfare (Connolly, 2004; Baltra-Ulloa, 2013; Vinsky, 2018). However, while important and well intentioned, there are warnings that such interventions are becoming 'mainstreamed' within child welfare structures and distanced from their original aims (Cunneen and Libesman, 2000; Desmeules, 2007). For example, FGCs that emerged as an acknowledgement of the need for Māori-centred practice to counter systemic racism in child welfare have, in some instances, become co-opted and used to justify heavier intervention by police or child protection systems (Desmueles, 2007), or continue to be framed as an 'alternative' solution, despite proven effectiveness. At the same time, cultural competency training for social workers often focuses on individual practitioner behaviour and aptitude, rather than engaging with, and challenging, the structural underpinnings (Eurocentrism) that sustain system harm (Baltra-Ulloa, 2013). Moreover, these interventions frequently rely on individuals and groups, rather than being mandated or formalised within structures.

With little challenge from the state to address the institutional nature of harm, decolonial social work scholars (see Gray et al, 2013) have criticised how merely recognising oppressive social care practice and including culturally competent and alternative interventions into the system do little to challenge the power dynamics that lead to harm. As anti-colonial scholars Fanon (1986) and Coulthard (2014) suggest, the politics of recognition function to leave the dominant system unfettered, where colonial legacies go undisrupted and continue to marginalise racialised (as non-white) people.

Calls for a transformative agenda of decolonisation are being led by First Nations Peoples, who have the language to name the devastating impacts and dynamics of colonial legacies, having fought (and they continue to fight) for nearly four centuries for the right to self-determination – to *know* and *be* beyond coloniality (Talaga, 2018). Such calls have advocated for the repatriation of Indigenous land and life (Tuck and Yang, 2012), creating knowledge systems that centre the often untold history of minoritised communities (Simpson, 2004), and celebrating a plurality of knowing and being (De Sousa Santos et al, 2007). Indigenous knowings have advanced movements for liberation, grounding social justice practice through an ethics of care, and fuelling momentum around restorative and transformative justice.

This chapter is titled '"Doing" Contextual Safeguarding with an ethics of care', as a nod to the idea that intrinsic to a decolonial approach is the need for us to be critical about the role social work as a profession has played, and plays, in 'caring'. It invites a critical understanding of social work's complicity in practices of colonialism, dispossession and family rupture, and the ways in which voicing and interrogating these power relations can provide a blueprint for antidotes moving forward. How we can instead be held by a collective ethic premised on relationality, trust, mutuality and connectedness (Okun, 1999; Walker et al, 2006; Pease et al, 2018; Wever and Zell, 2018), conscious to the colonial context in which our discussions and practice take place, and inviting the many ways 'care' in the profession can be understood and practised beyond Western, white, neoliberal and individualist frameworks.

It is therefore crucial that in this route towards 'decolonising social work', this process must include 'those excluded and exploited by the system, who possess exactly the perspective and wisdom needed to fix it' (Villanueva, 2018: 9). It is necessarily a journey of unlearning and relearning the structures we occupy (Fanon, 1986; Nandy, 1988). This is important and necessary, not to replace one knowledge for the other but to ensure that in the process of decolonising child protection, we do not unintentionally reproduce systemic harm by defining systemic change within Eurocentric terms/structures. What, then, does this mean for CS?

Contextual Safeguarding as a route towards decolonisation?

CS gives us hope that transformation is possible. In the UK, enthusiasm for CS seems to have livened practitioners – providing the language and momentum to practice differently, to rewrite the rules of child protection, to create new systems and processes that are concerned with targeting contexts rather than individual behaviour. Through practical and tangible processes of system change at a holistic level, it seems to have provided relief from a limiting system that is highly bureaucratised, risk-averse and blaming. It has given voice to the people working within the system to effect change, while providing those impacted by the system a language to describe the challenges they face (Firmin, 2022).

In that respect, we can see how CS as an approach leans into challenging some of the harmful legacies intrinsic to Eurocentric practice, by locating the harm young people encounter within the social conditions of abuse – challenging the norms and social rules that enable harm – rather than as individual failings of parents and carers of young people. It pushes us to think not just about the interconnections and interactions of individuals, families and communities, but the 'voice' of more-than-human space and place too – how a stairwell, a park, a hallway embodies its own agency (Simon and Salter, 2019) – and how we can support the creation of safety in these spaces, not merely disrupt and displace those who spend their time there.

When we are given the freedom to think and practise beyond the individual, we are afforded the reflective space to step back from practice as normal and ask some uncomfortable questions: what are the consequences of a system set up to seek out 'troubled families' rather than contextual circumstances that lead to harm? The development of the values that underpin CS speak to the tensions that these reflective questions raise, to ensure that, while the approach remains flexible, the intention and underpinning ethos remains intrinsic: that practice be collaborative, evidence-informed, rights-based, ecological and strengths-based.

One example we have seen from CS as a route towards decolonisation is through the piloting of a CS approach to FGCs (see Owens et al, 2021). Opportunities to use FGCs to respond to a context rather than an individual were explored – where a peer group, school or community location was the subject of the conference, as opposed to an individual child and family. This process shifted the traditional child protection focus away from parental capacity towards understanding community capacity. In a park associated as a historical 'hotspot' for harm, for example, the focus shifted away from asking individual young people not to frequent the area to identifying steps to make the space safer. This included creating a 'community guardianship' network of people with a reach in the area, including local shopkeepers, bus drivers, the school and so on. This was not about surveillance but working *with* young people, rather than against them – bringing in some key decolonial principles that allowed collective helping and community-led decision making. Moreover, the joining up of restorative principles with a CS approach seemed to facilitate wider reflective discussions of systemic harm that were shaping young people's experiences of safety in the area, where the community actively leaned into solutions to challenge racism, sexism and stigma towards adolescents. In that respect, the intertwining of these two approaches created an effective space for communities (from voluntary community partners, young people and residents to multi-agency professionals in the area) to link up and be creative about the way they worked with the social conditions of contexts and created safety.

Tensions within a statutory system

While the conditions are certainly there for CS to drive a decolonial agenda, and we have witnessed enthusiasm from practitioners in leading this change, this is not without its limits. Challenges remain when system change is dependent on individual practitioners, rather than supported by collaborative partnership input, buy-in and engagement; where there is systemic change but not cultural change; or when practice is distanced from the values – doing to, rather than with, young people; and when continuing to centre primarily behavioural and/or criminal responses to welfare-based issues. Although from the outset, this could be deemed as teething problems for system change, against the backdrop of colonial legacies, there are consequences to treating CS as business as normal with a new label. As Schmid (2021: 14) says, 'it is no longer sufficient to put "new wine into old wineskins" and progressive aspects must be supported and integrated into a new comprehensive model that is not punitive, individualistic, adversarial or primarily statutory-led'.

The recent Waitangi Tribunal report (Wai, 2021) from Aotearoa New Zealand regarding the disproportionate rates of tamariki Māori in state care provides some stark questions for implementing reform into a system that has, by its design, been set up to disenfranchise First Nations peoples:

> growing inequalities and disparities in child protection are not inevitable outcomes of individual choice, they are substantially the

choice of legislative outcomes of which society has choices (Wai, 2021; cited in Hyslop, 2021) ... piecemeal reform – no matter how well-intentioned – will ultimately fail another generation of children if the same factors placing inhumane stress on families continue unabated. (Wai 2021: 179)

The statutory system sits within a wider relation of power, and as Jordan (2012: 12) has highlighted regarding past reform, 'whatever its ethical principles and philosophical commitments, social work is prone to take on the features of the political culture in which it is practiced'. How, then, can we harness and utilise the enthusiasm gained thus far with CS to speak to and challenge the confining nature of statutory frameworks?

This raises some difficult questions for CS. What does this mean for an approach where there has been a deliberate move to implement ('include') this into a statutory system that has been central to oppressive practices and caused profound harm for First Nations and racialised young people? There remain tensions and challenges, therefore, for embracing a truly decolonised CS approach, while underpinned by a child protection legislative framework, and where day-to-day CS practice is embedded within statutory child protection services. With 'context' central to CS, it seems fundamental for the context of colonisation and past oppression, and subsequent mistrust of some statutory authorities, to also inform CS responses, particularly for First Nations or marginalised communities (Firmin and Rayment-McHugh, 2020). So if the aim is to repair damage associated with past or current colonial practice, or at least to cause no new harm, some tough questions need to be asked about how, or if, this can be realised within a statutory system. Could the interrelationship between CS in the UK and the statutory child protection system, and the application of this elsewhere, be seen as contradictory for First Nations or minoritised ethnic communities? Does it further feed into colonial dynamics that an approach 'over there' knows best? How do these communities make sense of this?

The design of a pilot CS project in Australia (2013–19) provides a useful example of how an ethics of care was operationalised in a project aimed at reducing the extent of sexual violence and abuse by young people in a small, remote Aboriginal community (see Firmin and Rayment-McHugh, 2020). Importantly, an understanding of local cultural and community history (looking back to move forward) was fundamental to developing a framework for practice on this project, built on an ethics of care, including respect, relationality, empowerment, strengths focus and partnership. The project was based at an Australian university but was community – not statutory – led in its design and implementation. In a departure from mainstream safeguarding practice, community engagement was prioritised first, above collaborations with child protection, police and justice authorities. This decision reflected a historic and ongoing community history including forced relocations to a mission settlement, and related and ongoing issues of fear and mistrust of statutory government authorities.

As part of this approach, engagement and partnership with local community members became central to understanding the problem, designing and implementing prevention activities with a community focus and ensuring a community voice informed all aspects of the project. This was considered critical to its success. Thus, a local advisory board of community members was established to work in close partnership with university practitioners and academics. A 'Neighbourhood Survey' was also undertaken as a forum for whole-of-community input into the safety of local children and young people and to discuss ideas for addressing abuse risks (Neighbourhoods Project, 2017). Moreover, to build genuine connections with community members and an enhanced understanding of the local context, non-Indigenous project team members resided for short periods in the community and engaged in community events and activities, including efforts to learn the local Indigenous language and enhance cultural knowledge and understanding.

This is just one example, and not the only way forward. The challenge for CS is how to acknowledge the varied impacts of historic and ongoing colonisation and embed a decolonising approach, considering the central role of child protection services in existing UK practice. At a minimum, checks and balances seem necessary to protect against unintentionally increasing state intervention in the lives of vulnerable youth, inadvertently paralleling past destructive child protection practice. Even if no further harm is done, strategies should be developed to address the risks and barriers that may prevent or prohibit effective engagement with a statutory child protection-led CS approach for communities who have experienced disproportionate intervention. Perhaps most importantly, alternative, innovative ways to operationalise CS practice outside of formal government/state systems should be explored and encouraged to prevent potential harm and enhance outcomes for all youth and all communities. These questions will become increasingly important as CS internationalises.

The path forward

So where does that leave us as practitioners and academics navigating this space, and as communities and young people impacted by them? Voicing the sentiments of social work practitioners documenting and reflecting the process of change, we acknowledge the difficulty of 'consistently practicing well in this demanding context', and how statutory child protection work is often experienced as a 'consuming world of its own' (Hyslop, 2022: 3). But we need critical reflexive action to move beyond the paralysis that advocating and implementing change often creates, understanding how feelings of discomfort, limitation and paralysis are often more reflective of wider power dynamics at play (Idahosa and Bradbury, 2020). To move forward, we must shift to creating organisational cultures of *collective* accountability and care – so that we create spaces to hold on to the discomfort and say when/where we have got it wrong, while being guided by the wishes and wisdom of those impacted by the system.

There are no linear or quick-fix ways of addressing the complex nature of colonial legacies. However, there are steps we can follow so that we don't get completely lost within, or sucked back into, the colonial structures and practices that have been reproduced over the years, becoming naturalised and rendered invisible (Pease et al, 2018). Alongside the CS values that foreground and underpin everyday practice, we must take a step back and hold close the reasons why systemic change is necessary in the first place, before we rush to implement this approach devoid from its institutional context. As Wroe (2020) suggested, CS is not simply a technical solution to a systems problem but a conceptual and ethical one. We must therefore care for system change in an ethical way, guided by wider principles of critical reflexivity, relationality, relevance, reciprocity, collectiveness and a plurality of knowing and being in our pursuit towards implementing/embedding CS. In Figure 7.1, we have represented these principles in a circle – urging you to consider how these intersect with current CS values. We have made an attempt to outline what some of these principles might mean in practice and follow the figure with reflective questions to guide thought around the implications of integrating an ethics of care with CS values.

What we have described is not to be prescriptive but to provide some parameters to support the journey – practical steps to name and challenge these issues and counter them through ethics and values. It is reflection, conversation and discussion on these issues that may lead to the greatest change and improvement in policy and practice, and a genuine integration of an ethics of care with CS values. Our aim in this chapter is to provide you with prompts, rather than answers, in recognition of our shared learning journey as we embed CS in our practice. When thinking about how we can integrate an ethics of care with CS values, we encourage you to journal, discuss or reflect on the following questions.

CS already requires us to ask:

- When targeting the social conditions of abuse, how do we ensure we do not fall into the same deficit narrative but instead celebrate the strengths of communities?

Decolonising practice

Figure 7.1: Practising with an ethics of care

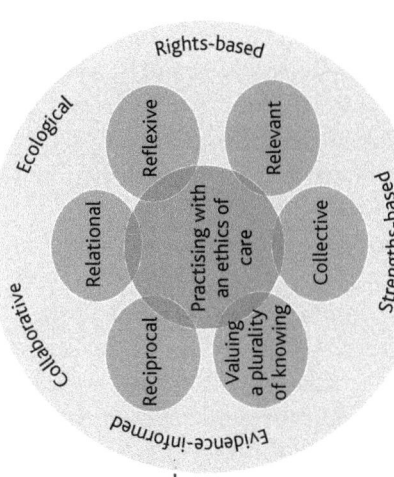

Relationality, not just of understanding how young people, their families and communities are located in context; but how we, as practitioners, academics and students, are positioned in these spaces. Leaning into compassion and care that neo-liberal practice/systems have tried to fervently distance us from: What is our positionality and responsibility in these spaces? Who has the authority to answer to systems changes, how is power configured and who decides? (Hyslop 2022)

Critical reflexivity so that we make visible these invisible power dynamics, and ensure we name systemic and intersectional harm when we see it: racism, sexism, homophobia, classism, ableism – shifting the locus of harm to the structural conditions, rather than young people, families, or individual practitioners.

Relevance, so that we respond to the calls from First Nations and Global Majority activists who advocate that the pursuit toward transformation must be shaped by a 'nothing about us without us' ethos. Grounded, not in the ideas of 'experts' abstracted from the realities of those who the CP system are there to support, but in the needs of those on the ground.

Collective, so that systems change is holistic and systematic - including various stakeholders, young people and families; rather than dependent on individual practitioners and groups where the result is often piecemeal, distanced from or siloed from challenging the institutional context. Leading change from the ground, while advocating for our legislative frameworks to catch up.

Engage with a plurality of knowing and being, so that we challenge the universal nature of traditional child and family social work service delivery: being critical that there is no such thing as a universal child, family or community. That we must continue to be flexible with our approach, so that we understand communities in context; how concepts of family, care, more-than-human space and place are understood. How communities can thrive through their own definitions of wellbeing when supported with resources and tools, and are not seen as problems. Challenging Western, white, heterosexual and able-bodied privilege intrinsic to traditional policy and practice.

Reciprocity, not just for the young people, families and communities that CP systems are there to support; but for practitioners, recognising the limiting nature of neo-liberal statutory frameworks that have narrowed connection through bureaucratic processes – to consider how we all suffer from this way of living, and the distress we feel from working in these systems that have traditionally not produced the healing that people need.

99

- How can we ensure we are reflective of the wider structural/political/intergenerational context in which practitioners, young people and their families are embedded?
- What's the importance of creating solutions collaboratively, with young people, families and communities at the centre?

Mindful of what has been raised in this chapter, a decolonial approach requires us to ask something new of CS. Questions to guide this journey may include:

- Why are 'colonisation' and 'decolonisation' important concepts when we think about CS in practice? Why is it important to weave these considerations into what we do?
- To what extent do colonial contexts remain at the forefront of current CS practice decisions?
- Why must we name systemic harm and be accountable to challenging it?
- Is CS oversight always helpful for children and families at risk of EFH? What are the unintended consequences of this?
- Are there other innovative ways to operationalise CS in an international context?
- How can we 'practise' with an ethics of care?

These conversations continue to be exploratory as we consider the conditions necessary to embed CS in ways that can challenge social and structural conditions of harm – challenge, rather than replicate, harmful practices in traditional forms of child protection. These are beginning conversations, to which we don't hold the answers – but we urge you to address them as you go. Don't agonise – organise.

Conclusion

We set out in this chapter to contribute to the advancement of CS by challenging current thinking and practice. We discussed decolonisation as intersectional, and more than just anti-racist practice. We have promoted a need to look back in order to move forward and highlighted ongoing practice tensions. We have encouraged implementation to be embedded through an ethics of care, centring plural ways of knowing and being, challenging the ways we know and practice in the world and reframing how we understand safety and the role of state intervention.

Moving forward requires social welfare organisations, CS leaders and practitioners alike to critically reflect on current practice, acknowledge opportunities for improvement and be willing to imagine (or reimagine) scope for improved practice that moves beyond the colonial context to a place of equity and justice for all. It is our responsibility to do so. We must accept that this may be uncomfortable, and we are unapologetic about this. Change is often uncomfortable. But it is time; it is long overdue. Our past 'best' has not been good enough for First Nations and minoritised communities, who continue to face over-excessive intervention. We hope this chapter contributes to the conversation.

PART III

Domain 3: The partnerships that characterise the system

8

"If you want to help us, you need to hear us"

Hannah Millar, Joanne Walker and Elsie Whittington

Introduction

The title of this chapter, "If you want to help us, you need to hear us" (Scale-Up focus group, Site 7), are the words of a young person who participated in our research. While this sounds simple, the current child protection system is not set up in a way that prioritises youth voice and participation (Tidsall, 2017; Warrington and Larkins, 2019; Whittington, 2019).

Since 2019, researchers in the CS teams based at the University of Bedfordshire and Durham University have had the opportunity, within the limitations of COVID restrictions, to work with young people in nine council-level areas as part of the Scale-Up Project (see Chapter 1 for a project summary). This element of the project presented an opportunity to begin thinking about how services can work with young people *as partners* to inform and develop CS approaches. This work has taken place in the context of wider calls for children and young people to be included in co-designing, evaluating and being more proactively involved in service development and safeguarding (Tidsall, 2017; Warrington and Larkins, 2019; Whittington, 2019).

In this chapter, we present emergent findings from work undertaken with young people as part of the Scale-Up Project, including the Young Researcher's Advisory Panel (YRAP) at the University of Bedfordshire and their longer-standing work on participation as protection (Hamilton et al, 2019). In doing so, we highlight how young people's views align with the need for CS values, in particular collaboration, and how participatory practices can support this. We also offer insight into some of the methods we used as part of the Scale-Up Project to engage young people in critical conversations about safeguarding responses to EFH.

What do we mean by participation?

In this chapter, and in our practice as researchers, our understanding of 'participation' is grounded in children's rights. Article 12 of the United Nations Convention on the Rights of the Child (UNCRC) advocates children's right to have their views taken into account in matters that affect them. In relation to this, the UNCRC make clear that 'effective inclusion of children in protective measures requires that children be informed about their right to be heard and to grow up free from all forms of physical and psychological violence (UNCRC, 2009). Within the field of safeguarding, there is arguably a 'false juxtaposition of participation and protection' (Warrington and Larkins, 2019: 133). Child protection concerns can be used to undermine, block or limit children's rights to participation in decisions that will affect them (Tidsall, 2017; Warrington and Larkins, 2019; Whittington 2019). Protection rights are often prioritised above participation rights, limiting investment in setting up and maintaining structures for young people to be heard across practice, policy and research.

Landsdown and O'Kane (2015) offer a continuum of modes of participation with young people spanning 'Consultative', 'Collaborative' and 'Child Led'; each mode presents varying of degrees of involvement and ownership. 'Child Led' enables the maximum opportunity for young people to be involved in decisions about issues that affect them; whereas 'Consultative' seeks to gather young people's views but may go no further than this. There is a place for engaging with young people across all levels in order to increase their participation within child protection and wider safeguarding systems.

In this chapter, we seek to promote a practice of participation that goes beyond consultation but recognises that being fully child- or youth-led may be logistically challenging and daunting in some policy, practice and safeguarding contexts.

Young people, the child protection system and participation: feeling unheard and unimportant

It has been well documented that the current child protection system was not developed to intervene in EFH (Hanson and Holmes, 2014; Chard, 2015; Firmin, 2017; Violence and Vulnerability Unit, 2018). Similarly, child protection systems in the UK do not prioritise participation, resulting in young people reporting that they do not feel valued, heard or respected when in contact with professionals intended to support them (Beckett and Warrington, 2015; Hallett, 2016; Factor and Ackerley, 2019; Lefevre et al, 2019; Hampson et al, 2021). These system failures have resulted in young people failing to be supported and protected when facing EFH, experiencing processes of exclusion, criminalisation and unwanted and inappropriate intervention, as well as individual negative encounters with professionals (Beckett and Warrington, 2015; Hamilton et al, 2019; Billingham and Irwin-Rogers, 2021). In the absence of child protection responses to young people who are experiencing forms of harm outside of home, young people can find themselves facing responses from organisations that are responsible for addressing crime and disorder in community spaces (see Chapter 5 of this book for further details). This can result in young people being subjected to disruptive methods, such as surveillance and dispersal practices, and punitive and criminal measures, rather than a safeguarding and welfare-led response (Wroe and Lloyd, 2020).

These responses and encounters can erode a young person's sense of worth and value in the world (Beckett and Warrington, 2015; Hamilton et al, 2019; Billingham and Irwin-Rogers, 2021). This is something that Billingham and Irwin-Rogers (2021) consider by applying a lens of 'mattering' to consider the minority of young people who commit violent crimes. The concept of 'mattering', defined here as 'The perception that, to some degree and in any of a variety of ways, we are a significant part of the world around us' (Elliott et al, 2004: 339), reminds us there is great risk to young people if what constitutes that young person's world fails to make them feel like they are truly part of society. Processes of exclusion (Just for Kids Law, 2021) and over-policing (Elliot-Cooper, 2021), for example, can produce greater risks for some groups of young people in their school and neighbourhood contexts. If young people experience harm from institutions that have a responsibility to safeguard, it is unsurprising that they may not trust those in protective roles (Elliott et al, 2004; Billingham and Irwin-Rogers, 2021).

The impact of these system failures can be felt by certain groups of young people in particular. EFH of all kinds can affect any young person. However, failings within institutions such as education, and structural factors, including racism and poverty, can result in some groups of young people being significantly, and disproportionately, affected by EFH (see Gov.uk 2019/20; Youth Justice Board and Ministry of Justice, 2020/21; Perera, 2020; and explored in further detail in Chapters 2 and 3 of this book).

In 2019, data surfaced that confirmed increasing numbers of 16- and 17-year-olds are entering the care system (Children's Commissioner, 2019b). This has been linked to experiencing harm outside of the home and complex dynamics that are exacerbated at home due to harms beyond the front door. Children's social care involvement, in some of these cases, can lead to young people being relocated away from their familial contexts and the breaking of significant protective relationship networks (Firmin and Owens, 2022). Parents, carers and young people are often not included in the planning and decision making around relocations due to EFH (Firmin et al, 2020), and, at worst, the intervention can leave young people and parents/carers feeling responsible for the harm that has occurred and unsupported to increase protection (Pike et al, 2019). SPACE, an organisation in the UK with a specialist focus on keeping children who have been criminally exploited safe, have written about the blame that parents face when seeking support from children's social care and how they find themselves being offered 'a host of professional suggestions, advice and courses that will have no bearing on their child's exploitation, nor halt their imminent harm, criminalisation or death' (SPACE, 2021). This evidences what CS seeks to change, and that is to create a way of working that can intervene in the contexts where harm occurs and remove a culture of blame on individuals, whether the young person and/or their parents/carers.

It is, therefore, important that child protection systems are rooted in, and respond to, the reality of the lives of young people. This involves listening to young people and what their trusted networks are saying. Some may argue that the Children Act 1989 ensures that young people are heard as their 'wishes and feelings' should be taken into consideration. However, as Dillon's (2021) work highlights, this process can be misrepresented as participatory working but effectively functions more as a 'tick-box' exercise: 'Wishes and feelings has seemingly become a task to do, rather than part of a "revolutionized" participatory process to meaningfully embed children's opinions into their own social work intervention' (Dillon, 2021: 9). One way to shift from the tokenism of 'tick-box' practices, as identified by Dillon, is to create a culture grounded in relationships developed with trust. There is a growing body of literature on the importance of relationship-based practice (Ruch et al, 2010; Hennessey, 2011; Megele, 2015; Bryan et al, 2016, Lewing et al, 2018; Hamilton et al, 2019; Lefevre and Hickle, 2022), which is valuable when thinking about developing meaningful safeguarding processes. Research has found that children desire a good relationship with their social worker (Cossar et al, 2016; Dillon et al, 2016; Muench et al, 2017). However, relationships take work and time, and there is no model, formula or flow chart that prescribes *how* to build a relationship of trust with a young person. What is critical to consider is the role of power dynamics between young people and professionals like social workers (McLeod, 2007; Hickle et al, 2017; Hamilton et al, 2019; Corney et al, 2021; Smithson and Jones, 2021). For instance, Corney et al (2021) draw attention to the need to challenge 'adultism', which positions adults as all-knowing and the sole experts in young people's lives, often making decisions for them about their safety, for example. This highlights the need for professionals to be reflective and to promote participation as a means to overcome 'adultism' and to partner with young people 'to optimise young people's participation' (2021: 5). In short, children do have a voice, but they will only be heard if it is facilitated by adults who genuinely listen and can act upon their views.

This brief review has aimed to highlight the importance of services and systems working with young people to understand their experiences, and making them matter, but also their potential role in increasing young people's risk of EFH when approaches involve surveillance, exclusion and even criminalisation. By not listening to or creating ways for young people and their trusted adults to be heard, safeguarding processes may fail in doing what they are meant to.

Methodology

As noted in the introduction to this chapter (and detailed in Chapter 1 of this book), since 2019, the CS research programme has tracked the work of nine local authorities in England and Wales who implemented a CS response to EFH through the Scale-Up Project. To ensure that CS approaches designed in participating sites drew on and spoke to the lived experiences of children and young people, a strand of *consultative* participation work was piloted as part of the Scale-Up Project. This strand had two key aims: to find out young people's views about CS responses to EFH, and secondly, for these views to support changes being made within their local area to respond to EFH.

Scale-Up site consultation methods

To consult with young people, a mixed-methods approach was used, consisting of surveys, focus groups and interviews. This chapter draws on data from focus groups and interviews across the nine sites.

We developed a series of different scenario-based activities to use during interviews and focus groups which gave young people an insight in how CS would work when responding to harm in different contexts. The scenarios were based upon a range of real-life cases of young people experiencing harm outside of home and exemplar responses from Scale-Up sites. Responses included peer, school and location assessments, and safety mapping, in addition to scenario-based activities. The type of harm and proposed CS response used in the interview or focus group was dependent upon the aspect of the CS approach being trialled in the site. For example, if a site was looking to implement a location assessment, the focus group or interview in that site would explore a scenario involving harm in a community space and the possibility of using a location assessment to respond to this.

In addition to scenario-based activities, some young people were asked to carry out document reviews as part of the interviews or focus groups. These involved participants reviewing paper-based materials that were being revised as part of a Scale-Up site's efforts to adopt CS. For example, young people were asked to review a 'thresholds of risk' document for EFH and policies related to context conferences. Where appropriate, the documents and guide questions were shared in advance of the activity and referred to throughout the interview and focus group.

Interviews and focus groups gathered young people's views on CS responses being piloted in their area. The method of interview or focus group was often chosen in consultation with organisations who were supporting participants and the young people themselves. In the national sites, the gatekeepers were all VCS organisations and in the London sites, gatekeepers were either VCS organisations, social care or youth offending

Table 8.1: Breakdown of the focus group and interview activity and themes per site

Site	Activity	Contextual Safeguarding approach considered	Number of young people
1	1 x scenario-based focus group	Conducting a location assessment	3
2	1 x scenario-based focus group	Conducting a school assessment	5
3	2 x scenario-based interviews	Conducting a peer assessment	2
4	1 x scenario-based focus group	Conducting a location assessment	5
5	1 x scenario-based focus group	Safety planning meetings	5
6	3 x focus groups	Conducting a peer assessment (x 2) Safety planning meetings	1 x 18 1 x 10 1 x 7
7	3 x interviews 1 x focus group	Developing a thresholds document for accessing support Conducting multi-agency meetings on EFH	10
8	2 x interviews	Safety planning meetings	2
9	1 x focus group	Conducting a school assessment	4
		Total	66

team practitioners with an existing relationship with the young person. Table 8.1 presents a breakdown of the focus group and interview activities, and responses explored in each.

Working with the Young Researchers Advisory Panel

In addition to work with young people who were living in Scale-Up sites, the CS research programme engaged a group of young people who had formed a Young Researchers Advisory Panel (YRAP – we pronounce it Why-rap) at the Safer Young Lives Research Centre in the University of Bedfordshire. The YRAP were established in 2016. They aim to challenge the marginalisation of young people's voices in safeguarding sectors and the maintenance of damaging power imbalances within both organisational and public responses to this form of abuse (Hamilton et al, 2019; see also YRAP, University of Bedfordshire). Members of YRAP are aged 17–24. They come from a variety of backgrounds, and all share a passion for raising

Table 8.2: Consultation activities with the Young Researcher's Advisory Panel

Participatory practice with YRAP members	Number of activities
Online workshop to pilot scenario and focus group methods	3
Workshop to unpack meaning of 'being heard'	1
Workshop at residential weekend to develop a youth-friendly definition of CS	1
Online meetings to co-produce a CS resource for young people and work with a designer	5
Developing a conference workshop for CS conference	4
Delivery of 'Don't judge us, help us' workshop at CS conference	1

awareness against sexual exploitation and violence (Young Researchers' Advisory Panel, 2017).

Seven YRAP members were involved in supporting and consulting on the Scale-Up Project in two ways. Firstly, they reviewed and piloted consultation resources referenced earlier, providing feedback and advice on scenarios and questions. They also led on the creation of a resource which explained CS and could be shared with young people and professionals alike. These activities were conducted via a series of online and in-person workshops with YRAP members, as detailed in Table 8.2, and visualised in images in Figure 8.1.

Ethics and limitations

This work was given specific ethical approvals by both the University of Bedfordshire and Durham University, in addition to the broader ethical approval granted to the Scale-Up Project. Ethical approval considered informed consent, voluntary engagement, anonymity, participant welfare and a right to withdraw. The project was committed to a trauma-informed approach (SAMHSA, 2014) and the use of the third-person lens through scenario-based activities sought to minimise the possible impact of discussing relatable and (re)traumatising experiences. The scenarios enabled young people to reflect on the professional response and the system without having to share their own experiences, but, naturally, some young people felt comfortable to draw on these, as the data shows.

The work reported in this chapter commenced as the COVID-19 pandemic, and associated restrictions, impacted the UK. This added an additional layer of challenge to activities which were already complex and required a level of care and attention. The restrictions meant that any scope to develop longer-term relationships with young people which could lead to more collaborative or even co-produced research was not possible.

Figure 8.1: Young Researcher's Advisory Panel group developing work and thinking through safeguarding

A consultative approach enabled us to work within the restrictions, running activities online or in one-off in-person sessions at voluntary sector or statutory organisations who were offering in-person support. All participants were engaged through a gatekeeper who could support the young person throughout the research process.

The approach to understanding young people's views and their implications was qualitative, and sample sizes are small, and, as such, the data presented in this chapter are not necessarily representative of all young people in all Scale-Up sites. We mitigate this limitation by presenting our findings in this context, and what these views invite us to consider when developing CS work in the future.

Analysis

For the purpose of this chapter, focus group and interview data were analysed thematically across two stages using NVivo 12. Firstly, the data were analysed against three thematic areas: 1) Young people's thoughts on different CS approaches, such as peer mapping or location assessments; 2) What young people thought would be required to make these approaches effective; 3) Any barriers identified by young people that might prevent an effective CS approach.

At a second stage, further manual analysis was then undertaken to identify 'conditions' or factors that young people identified as important in a CS response across these three areas of analysis. This process identified three broad themes that cut across the three thematic areas analysed in stage one. In order to understand these themes against specific elements of a CS approach, such as location assessments, a tagging system was created using Microsoft Excel. Focus group and interview data were tagged against the key element of a CS approach explored in the research activity, as outlined in Table 8.1. For example, the focus group carried out in Site 2 was tagged against *school assessment*.

Conditions for Contextual Safeguarding: "If you want to help us, you need to hear us"

In the main, young people who participated in this project supported the idea of CS; however, they were yet to experience a system where CS was fully embedded (engagement happened during the testing phase). They were not able to comment on what it would be like to be part of a peer assessment or to feel the impact of services adopting safety mapping activities with young people. However, they were able to share what they believed to be the necessary components of, or conditions in, a service for them to be comfortable with, and supportive of, the implementation of CS.

Our analysis identified three overarching and interdependent themes – rights, relationships and collaboration – in young people's accounts of the service conditions for effectively adopting CS. These conditions align with the four domains of the CS framework and foreground the values that underpin the approach.

Rights

Young people identified approaches that upheld and promoted their rights as a crucial component of any response to EFH, and that this condition was essential to the implementation of CS. Young people discussed their rights in relation to two particular elements of a CS approach: the right to have and be in safe spaces, whether this is in public space or a space that they can call their own; and their rights in respect of how their information is shared, used and for what purpose.

Space

The right to be in public space and to be a young person in this space was identified in data from across the engagement work with all young people, and was particularly discussed in two focus groups exploring the use of location assessments. Young people discussed having a lack of spaces to spend their time and the impact of this on their feelings/experience of safety in public spaces and exposure to EFH: "I think it would be a nice, better kid ... yeah, kid environment. [Laughs] And so they don't have to be afraid" (Focus group, Site 4); "[Because there are no spaces for young people,] they've got to walk around in the street listening to music" (Focus group, Site 1). When discussing the lack of spaces in the community for young people, participants not only shared how current community spaces are unsafe but also that some are unpleasant to be in: "if you go there, first of all there's rats and you hear them running about but you can't see them, and if you're sitting down just trying to chill out and you're hearing like – scuttering" (Focus group, Site 1). When talking about a CS assessment of a location, young people identified that the condition of spaces, and what they offered young people, were key points to consider. They described places where you could have "fun" and how "stupid little things ... like a drink stall, or ... water fountains or vending machines or things like that" (Focus group, Site 1) can make a space safer and inviting for young people.

In addition, young people referred to the importance of somewhere they can be themselves without being surveilled as a key element of a safe space and something young people should have a right to. One person, for example, described what they considered to be a safe youth club:

> 'because going to a youth club, this is the one place you're supposed to feel secure, you're supposed to act the way you act truly, your true form. You do not want to feel confined, it's not after school club, it's a space where you can relax and offload. If you feel like this person is going to go and tell my mum if I'm doing this or that, you're not really going to want to be around in an area where you feel like you're being watched 24/7.' (Young person 1, interview, Site 7)

Another young person talked about the need for a space that is less punitive and more understanding: "but I think if it was police roaming around, people would feel a bit like, you know, even if they are just smoking like one spliff or whatever and they're just like chilling out, they're not killing anyone by doing" (Focus group, Site 1). The significance of young people having access to inclusive, safe spaces was described as countering other exclusionary processes young people may experience in other spaces.

Information sharing

Further to a right to space, young people raised questions about the impact of CS on young people's rights in respect of information that was produced, or shared, about them. Young people identified potential challenges with how information-sharing activities interacted with young people's rights to privacy and how this in turn related to whether they felt respected by, and could trust, professionals. This consideration emerged most predominantly when young people engaged in the scenario-based activity involving peer mapping and peer assessment practices.

Young people understood that in relation to safeguarding duties, professionals may need to share certain information about them. Although they often expressed frustration with the practice and described it as a potential barrier to help seeking from professionals, they also generally understood and recognised its place in safeguarding practices. It was in this context that young people outlined three expectations that they had in respect of information sharing as part of a CS approach:

1. a young person's right to know how their information is shared and used;
2. for this information to be accurate; and
3. for information to be shared on a need-to-know basis only.

Young people described that they "have a right to know what things are being talked about them" (Focus group 1, Site 4). To facilitate this, young people noted a need for transparency and trust between a young person and professionals who help them, so that they can confidently make informed decisions about what to share: "youth workers, someone around there, not much authority but they understand safeguarding and they understand confidentiality and how much you can tell them before you go forward" (Young person 3, interview, Site 7). They also highlighted how information should be shared on a restricted basis: "I understand that maybe information needs to be shared but I do think it should be quite contained because maybe the individual may not feel safe or feels unhappy to be in a situation" (Focus group, Site 6). As this quote highlights, restricted, considered and accurate information sharing was not only highlighted as important in the aspect of rights but also because of the potential consequences of information being shared inappropriately or inaccurately. This concern appeared particularly relevant to the practice of peer mapping, where young people highlighted the potential risks of inappropriate information sharing. Young people noted the potential for rumours to spread around their schools or for them facing acts of retaliation from peers should others find out that they had provided a young person's name to a professional or put them on a map of a peer group. In a similar vein, young people also felt that assumptions about their connections and activities could be made by professionals when completing the assessment. In doing so, they noted the negative stereotypes or judgements that could be made about them as a consequence of misinformation.

Relationships

Young people often centred relationships with professionals as key to both mitigating concerns about information sharing and addressing their requests for their rights to be respected: "I think you have to establish a relationship, definitely" (Young person 1, interview, Site 7); "if you want it to be effective, you've got to build that relationship with the young person" (Young person 2, interview, Site 7). Partnerships, as the third domain of a CS framework, promote a vision for safeguarding that features a broad professional and community network working together, but also with, and alongside, young people and families to increase safety. We heard from young people that to feel included and part of such an approach, relationships of trust must underpin this work. We asked young people what trust means when working with professionals and received various responses – many suggested you needed to feel comfortable to "just talk". But that is not always easy, and there is a responsibility on professionals to create environments that achieve this.

Relationships with social workers

The second domain of the CS framework requires that responses to EFH are welfare-led, and therefore coordinated by children's social care. However, young people who participated in this study identified a number of potential challenges in establishing trust with professionals within children's services, challenges which could in turn trouble the second domain of the CS framework. Some of the young people engaged in this study held negative views and preconceptions about social care, and this in turn impacted their ability to trust social workers: "There is quite a stigma surrounding Social Services and it's a really negative one" (Focus group 1, Site 6); "Social workers give me stress" (Focus group 1, Site 7). Others viewed intervention by children's social care as significant, and were concerned that this in turn would increase feelings of anxiety and worry among young people impacted by EFH:

> 'I think maybe first it shouldn't be social workers because that is what actually will worry a younger child, like once you're doing something bad, like, "Oh yeah, you'll just get social services involved", as a young child you're thinking, "Oh my gosh". Like social services is a big thing, it's not something small, it's a big thing.' (Young person 3, interview, Site 7)

Other young people reflected on how negative experiences of social workers impacted trust: "I feel blamed and I am always being told 'you've done this, don't lie to me, I know you did this" (Focus group 1, Site 7).

> 'I'm telling you when one professional breaks your heart and your trust, for you to trust another one is pretty damned hard, because you just band them in the same group ... trust isn't always just about letting you know what's going on, it's also about you pitching in and them feeling like, "Okay, this is a responsibility I have, this is going to be something that impacts my life, I need to have some say in it, I need to say something ... You're still going to be vulnerable if you have somebody making all decisions.' (Young person 1, interview, Site 7)

Young people who participated in this study suggested that trust needed to be mutual and not transactional. The statutory position of social work, preconceived notions of social work intervention and experiences that undermined confidence in social workers were all identified as examples that would undermine the extent to which young people could trust social workers. Creating conditions in which social workers can collaborate with young people – to shift perceptions and manage inherent power imbalances – therefore seems crucial for the second domain of the CS framework to be feasible.

Relatability and relationships

Considering more about which factors support partnership working between professionals and young people, rooted in relationships, one of the points that young people shared was that relatability with their worker was significant. Talking to adults or professionals is not easy, as one young person identified: "I think, for a lot of young people, it's harder to talk to adults" (Focus group 1, Site 1). This is perhaps even more challenging if you are experiencing, or at risk of, harm, for fear of being blamed, moved away or even put at further risk.

Being able to relate to a professional is something that young people highlighted as a way to overcome the initial suspicion that may come when services attempt to engage them. Relatability could be characterised in a number of ways, including through age, ethnicity or lived experience. During a consultation on location assessments, a group of young people reflected on their personal experiences of being able to connect with workers: "It's like even like the younger workers here, like even if they're not my worker, I find that even being around them, it's more of like an up vibe, because they're just like younger and they know what's going on" (Focus group, Site 1). Another young person in that same group added that: "if you're not already like comfortable speaking to adults you know, it's like you're not going to be comfortable speaking to a random adult, where I think if it was like younger people, it would be more kind of, oh yeah, actually like you're just talking" (Focus group, Site 1). The young people we spoke with often cited youth workers as professionals who they had found to be relatable. When asked during an interview who they thought could facilitate a young person to share their experiences of harm outside of home with social care, one young person responded:

> 'I think having a youth worker, I think sometimes teachers, I know in my high school we used to have mentors in school that you could build a relationship with and speak to, they would have so many different

children, but they'd still have like a buddy connection with you when it was like you one on one.' (Young person 3, interview, Site 7)

Relatability, therefore, was not only described as key to developing relationships of trust between professionals and young people but also as potentially supporting engagement with voluntary agencies first as a gateway to statutory support.

Collaboration

The relational approaches young people outlined previously create the conditions for collaboration. In their accounts, young people who participated in this project routinely described the importance of being involved in plans to keep themselves and their peers safe. For them, collaboration emerged from trusting their worker, and through collaboration, trust could also be built: "getting to that point of the relationship between social worker and young person where you can actually implement change, not only as a young person taking an initiative, but to help the social worker help them, it's actually working, it's coming into effect" (Young person 1, interview, Site 7). In this sense, the value of collaboration, one of six underpinning CS, appeared central to young people's accounts of how the approach should be adopted.

Collaboration was discussed as particularly important when undertaking peer assessments, as well as the absence of collaboration. Young people discussed how, in the absence of collaboration, professionals and adults might assume quite a lot about young people without really understanding the drivers for their behaviour. In the context of peer assessments, young people questioned the ability of professionals to accurately do this without talking to young people involved:

'This seems really idealistic to me ... this idea that maybe Luke was peer-assessed successfully because it can be very difficult to understand what's going on in a child's life from an adult's perspective, or maybe from another person's perspective, and you never really know what Luke himself is going through ... Although the detached youth workers and the youth centre would have definitely helped, I feel like the peer assessment might have been a little bit more tricky than suggested.' (Focus group, Site 6)

In the same focus group, young people believed that a collaborative approach to peer assessment would involve the following:

'engaging with young people will give them a deeper insight into what's actually going on because if they just decide to just look at something with a bird's eye view and see this and this is happening, they won't know what's happening at ground level, what's actually going on with the young person.' (Focus group, Site 6)

Relationships of collaboration likely develop over time. As the young person cited earlier in this section reflected, they were able to build a collaborative relationship with their social worker through "consistency, trustworthy relationships, open space, reliability, stuff like that is majorly important" (Young person 1, interview, Site 7). In the interim, direct conversation with young people about their lives, rather than relying on professional or data-driven accounts of risk, seems a sensible starting point when attempting CS activities.

Foregrounding the values of Contextual Safeguarding: conditions for implementation

In this chapter, we shared the service conditions that young people described as central to the safe and effective implementation of CS. For the young people who participated in this project, CS is best implemented in services that adopt a relational approach, underpinned by trust and relatability, and which strive for collaboration and power sharing between young people and adults, rather than surveillance and monitoring of young people's behaviour. Confidential, accurate and ethical peer mapping, peer assessment and wider information-recording processes within a CS approach were also of particular importance to the young people we spoke to. Young people discussed the need for CS to be used in ways that value young people. For them, the approach should work to not only create safer spaces for young people but also to create enjoyable environments in which young people can be themselves in the community, thrive and have fun.

These findings indicate that, for our participants, the values of CS are an essential component of the response. Implementing the four domains in the absence of the underpinning values – particularly those of collaboration, rights respecting and being rooted in an understanding of young people's lives – will likely result in implementation activities that would concern young people. Practitioners and service leaders, therefore, need to consider whether they have created the conditions in which CS can be implemented in a value-driven manner.

Speaking to young people as part of the Scale-Up Project has demonstrated the importance of both proactively listening to young people to inform safeguarding processes and the need to produce ethical responses to EFH. Our learning through this project, and the findings it generated, lead us to conclude that participation work must not be seen as an add-on – something to do once CS approaches are up and running. Instead, we advocate that it is essential to understand and value the relationship between children and young people's participation and protection as a key part of safeguarding (Hamilton et al, 2019; Warrington and Larkins, 2019). It is essential to view and treat young people as 'both/and' not 'either/or' (Lefevre et al, 2018) by recognising them as rights-baring citizens who can and should have a say in things that affect them even when they are in contexts and situations where they require protection or intervention.

Participation is not easy, as this chapter has set out, and does not hold all the answers. However, starting with young people and seeking to include them holds, and opens, real potential to do things differently. CS can create a space to step back, undo, review and rebuild with young people, so systems can better protect them from harm outside of home. Prioritising the values of CS in its implementation could lead to not just 'rewriting the rule of child protection' but towards co-producing the rules.

9

Parents as partners: destigmatising the role of parents of children affected by extra-familial harm

Lisa Marie Thornhill

Introduction

> 'I mean I kept my ⋆ Jack in after I found – I found out he'd been selling drugs, him and me other daughter, and I rang the police on him and I rang the social services, and then I got put on a child protection plan, but under "neglect". Now, that's you who's trying to save them, not trying to neglect them. He [social worker] said it wasn't neglect of the parents just that's what it's classed under … I mean, I was heartbroken. Do you know what I mean? I was heartbroken.' (Jayne, parent, Scale-Up Project)

What are the options for parents if they are concerned about their child being at risk of harm outside of the home? What might go through your mind if you were tidying your child's room and you found a large quantity of drugs or a knife? Would you try and address the situation yourself? Call the police? Call children's social care? Jayne shared her experience after being asked how responses to this type of harm could improve. When she started to tell her story, she talked about how initially she felt that she was doing the right thing – being a good parent – by contacting children's services and the police, although this clearly wasn't easy. And then the pain and frustration when it was her parenting that became the focus of workers' attention and not the harm Jack was experiencing.

In this chapter, I explore some initial findings on the role of parents when their child is at risk of EFH. Using the data captured through testing CS, I will outline some of the ways parents and parenting were discussed in cases and some initial findings about what happens when safeguarding systems attempt to shift the focus from parents to contexts where their child experiences harm outside the family. Parents play a pivotal role in protecting children from harm. I argue that social care has the opportunity to change systems and practices to prevent the stigmatisation of parents and bring parents in as partners. I begin by drawing upon the literature base which supports collaborative working with parents before moving on to consider the challenges presented by the current policy and practice framework when children experience EFH, drawing on research from the Scale-Up Project.

The role of parents in protecting from extra-familial harm

Prior to joining the CS team, I was a frontline practitioner working with families affected by intra-familial and extra-familial child sexual abuse for 14 years. During practice, and in my doctoral research (Thornhill, 2019), I reflected on the stigmatisation that can happen with what are often referred to as 'non-offending parents' (NOPs). NOPs (most often mothers) are at risk of being blamed for harm they did not inflict on their children and for failing to protect them from abuse they couldn't have known about, either because it happened outside of the home or because of the grooming process. Recent literature calls for NOPs to be recognised as secondary victims (Duncan et al, 2020; Serin, 2021). By responding to parents as secondary victims of the harm caused by EFH, we have a firmer foundation for working compassionately and collaboratively with parents and to establish relationships for working with young people.

Parents are vulnerable to being blamed or responsibilised for harm outside of the home in a variety of ways, for example, for failing to control, failure to supervise, failure to report or challenge behaviour or failure to meet their child's needs. Parents report feeling isolated, guilty, stigmatised and ashamed about the harm their child has experienced (Duncan et al, 2020; Firmin, 2020). In their study on the parents of 'gang-involved' young people, Aldridge et al (2011) found that parents of young people affected by EFH were aware of parent-blaming narratives and rejected them. Parents did not see themselves as responsible for the harm experienced by their children. However, recommendations by professionals for interventions focused on their parenting, for example, by providing a parenting course, made them feel angry, mistrustful and resentful towards the professionals as a result of the inferred judgement. Experiences such as this are not isolated to experiences of EFH. In their work on domestic abuse, Featherstone and Morris (2021) highlighted how social work practice routinely focuses on the role of mothers where fathers and men are broadly absent. In their work, King et al (2021) discuss the growing emphasis within neoliberal narratives on individual responsibility and resilience, ignoring the systemic and structural barriers which inhibit people to provide the roles expected of them. Providing the example of parents, they note the very real structural and systemic barriers – such as poverty – which can inhibit parents to give children what they need. Yet within a discourse of responsibility and resilience, these systemic barriers are viewed as individuals neglecting their duties.

Chapters 2 and 3 in this book highlighted the social justice and ethical imperative to recognise systemic and structural barriers in cases of EFH. In relation to parents, it is clear that failure to do so can instead responsibilise parents for the harm of their children. It is worth noting that even in cases where there may be harm within the home, this rarely exists in isolation from systemic and structural causes such as poverty (Featherstone and Gupta, 2018). Responses which focus on parents decrease the likelihood of collaboration. Often, engaging with young people requires professionals to first establish the trust of adults who the young person themself trusts. If young people bear witness to professionals blaming and shaming the adult they love and trust, then it's unlikely that they will be willing to engage. Furthermore, racialised reporting of harm outside the home and the structural inequality that exists within child protection systems create a significant risk of Black and ethnic minority parents being more likely to be blamed for harm their child experiences (Carden, 2017).

Focusing on parents as a response to EFH misdirects resources from the understanding of the complex interplay between the social conditions of harm and the ecological experience of the individual young person (Aldridge et al, 2011). The wider description of Jack's situation indicated that he was being criminally exploited. Jayne's account indicated that she was a conscientious parent who wanted to do everything in her power to make sure her child was safe. However, when she reached out for help, her son was placed on a child protection plan, under the category of 'neglect'. While some efforts were made to reassure her that the category of neglect did not reflect her parenting, the outcome remained; Jayne was heartbroken. Her experience, and many others like hers, shows that the system response needs to change. Professional capacity to acknowledge the social conditions and work in a compassionate, collaborative way are hindered, to some degree, by the policy and practice frameworks.

Policy, practice and parents

System responses and decision making in relation to children that experience harm are underpinned in English law by the level of harm a child may experience. If a child is experiencing harm, English law outlines (to some degree) how bad that harm would need to be for a child to receive support from social care services. In theory, the worse the harm is, the more likely a child is to get support. However, how the law is interpreted in policy is slightly different. In safeguarding English policy *Working Together* (HM Government, 2018b), the primary focus of social work assessment and intervention is on parenting. While this focus might be appropriate for cases where families may be more closely associated with the harm that is happening and require support and help, in cases of EFH, this may feel misaligned. At the beginning of this chapter I introduced a quote from a mother, Jayne. Jayne's son Jack was placed on a child protection plan under the category of 'neglect' despite it appearing there were no concerns about parenting. In 2019, Lloyd and Firmin explored children's social care decision making for children victimised in extra-familial settings. Jayne's experience aligns with Lloyd and Firmin's (2019) findings in relation to parental engagement as a contributing factor related to inconsistent decision making among professionals. Parental engagement with social services was identified as a factor in deciding to progress or close a referral. Paradoxically, parental refusal to engage was used as a reason to escalate or close a referral, as was the level of parental concern. There are problems with both incidences: parents are either left to manage the risk of significant harm on their own or may have their own parenting become the focus of an assessment and plan.

Since 2018, England's statutory guidelines, *Working Together to Safeguard Children*, has been updated to include harm outside the home. In some ways, the argument to include EFH in statutory guidelines and focus on context is a battle easily won. Professionals, parents and policy makers will agree that it is 'common sense' to focus on a context where abuse is occurring rather than the individual young person who has been affected and their family. However, rewriting these rules in practice presents new challenges for practitioners to work through. These challenges can be seen in the detail of the social work responses to EFH and the decision-making processes that inform these responses. In the following sections, I look at the role of parents in cases of EFH and when testing CS.

Research with parents

The CS team have been tracking decision making and responses to parents in relation to EFH since 2017 (Lloyd, 2019; Firmin et al, 2020). The Scale-Up Project was a three-year, multi-site project working with nine local authorities to adapt their system approaches to harm outside of families (see introductory chapter for further details). As part of the Scale-Up Project, we wanted to further work with parents to understand their experiences of social work when their children were experiencing EFH. The role of parents has been a feature of the Scale-Up Project in multiple ways. Across the nine Scale-Up sites, the CS team considered how parents were engaged in cases of EFH and developed approaches that looked beyond responsibilising parents, and also addressed contexts where young people experienced harm. For example, in one site, 'safety planning meetings' were undertaken within existing child protection arrangements, where meetings focused on the level of harm and context of that harm, and plans aimed to tackle these contexts rather than solely focusing on parenting. We also sought to engage parents in discussions about the child safeguarding system and CS to seek their views on proposed changes under the framework. As part of this, we captured data through focus groups, interviews, case reviews and observations on responses to parents within social care systems. In addition to this data, I held two focus groups with parents themselves via the support of organisations that work with parents of children that have experienced EFH.

This data confirmed what most researchers and practitioners working in this area already know: EFH is extremely distressing for parents. But even more so, the child protection system is not only inadequately designed to respond to this form of harm but can actually be harmful to the families and parents who are involved within it. The parents we spoke to helped us to understand what happened when their child was at risk of harm outside of the home and the child protection responses that followed. Parents also provided us with insights into how things could be done differently. Their experiences have helped us to further our understanding of the challenges facing both parents and professionals when young people are experiencing EFH. We have seen, heard and read about practitioners doing their best to keep young people safe, practitioners who clearly care deeply for the families they are trying to help. We have also seen practice which places unreasonable demands and overwhelming pressure on parents. It is important to foreground that it is not our intention to scrutinise individual practice. Practitioners are operating in a system which is not designed to respond to harm outside of the home. Systemic constraints of the system can lead to emotional harm being inflicted on parents who reach out for help. I draw now on some of these findings by focusing on two aspects of social work practice: language and the structure of child protection processes.

Language: whose fault is it anyway?

Evidence from Scale-Up sites evidenced that language, and how the parents were discussed by professionals, played a central role in how they were, or were not, responsibilised for the harm their children experienced. I begin with two stories: the first is a composite case study – a story formed from evidence drawn from our findings from multiple cases and sites we have worked with – the second from one site developing a new approach to child protection conferences.

Paulina and Bart

Paulina is the mother of four children. They all live together in a two-bedroom flat. Over the last year, her eldest son Bart has been spending more time away from home and has been skipping school. Paulina is worried about her son because she has seen him with money and he has a new phone. Paulina and Bart have started to argue a lot and it upsets his younger brother. Sometimes, when Bart doesn't return home, Paulina gets worried about him but she's also a little relieved – one less argument. Bart's school made a referral to children's social care and the social worker told Paulina that she is worried that Bart might be being 'criminally exploited' and has told Paulina to stop him going out. Paulina doesn't know what this is, but she is worried they think Bart is in a 'gang'. The social worker has tried contacting Paulina lots but sometimes her phone runs out of battery or she's at work and she can't answer. Paulina is scared that social services might take her children away. A few years ago, Bart's dad Piotr was violent to Paulina and her children had to live with her sister for a while. In a child protection meeting, the social worker told her that "the reason they can't live with you is because you refuse to leave him". When she was told this, she was devastated; she thought she was a victim but was told she was to blame. Now she just wants to block it all out. After trying to contact Paulina, the social worker writes this on Bart's case file:

> [the parent] has developed excellent skills in deflecting and rejecting support and assistance from professionals and family members. CSC have been involved many times and have not been able to complete any work with this family due to [the parent's] denial and disguised compliance while the situation deteriorates. (Case file, Scale-Up)

Sadly, these words are not isolated. During the Scale-Up Project, we saw many instances of parents being referred to as 'compliant' with the exploitation of their children or as 'neglectful' or 'collaborating' with abusers. It can be easy or tempting in these instances to criticise the practitioners themselves. But much like the need to understand the harm children experience in context, so too must we understand the harm that can be inflicted by systems themselves. Often, the pull of individualised practice persists, and some parents continue to be blamed and held accountable for risk outside of the family home (as well as any harm inside it).

As a team, we reflected upon the commitment and dedication of the professionals we worked with which ran at odds with the evidence we often saw. We witnessed the struggle of experimenting with new ways of working in combination with the gravity of the responsibility when a child might be shot, stabbed or killed, and how this can draw professionals to cling to established patterns of practice that blame parents for all the risks young people face. For example, the idea that it might be easier to 'just' leave an abusive father rather than tackle the violence itself, to think that parents are 'compliant' with abuse rather than the reality that parents may be responding to trauma in ways they can, to recommend stopping a child going out rather than respond to the housing needs or tackle those that are exploiting him. Given the blame, shame and stigma parents of young people who experience EFH report, denial and disengagement would be an entirely expected response. I share now a second story.

Finlay and Sharon

Finlay (aged 12) was previously known to children's social care and placed on a child protection plan under the category of 'emotional abuse', but social care has had contact with his family for some time. The most recent initial child protection conference for Finlay stated:

> Since September 2020 the social care records indicate Finlay had been associating with members of the *** gang. He had been trying to cut contact with them as they have been asking him to hold weapons and he's been present when they have attacked people – things Finlay doesn't want to be part of … it is believed there were threats of stabbing Finlay. (Case file record)

The young person's mother, Sharon, feared for her son's safety on his journey to, and while at, school. Sharon was reluctant to send her son to school as a result. The chair of the conference noted on more than one occasion that 'this wasn't the first time an initial child protection meeting had been convened' (observation from child protection conference) and, in fact, Finlay had been on a child protection plan before. I winced slightly at the repeated reference, wondering how it would have felt for Sharon to have this point laboured.

During the meeting, there was a palpable tension between Sharon and professionals and a danger of reaching an impasse while discussing Finlay's educational needs and Sharon's commitment to being full-time employed to provide for her family. I reflected on her participation in the child protection conference – during her lunch break via an online platform – and what it meant for her to participate. Despite initial consensus among professionals that there were no parenting concerns, it seemed as though there was a retreat to focus on parenting through the repeated reference to the previous child protection plan. A question was asked as to how many hours Sharon was working and if Finlay was being adequately cared for. Meanwhile, Sharon, who was clearly exhausted, took the opportunity to steal a bite from her sandwich. At this point, I couldn't help but wonder if the meeting was about to descend into combat.

However, this meeting was about trying something new. The CS lead suggested a plan, one which focused on creating safety for Finlay in his school, and on his journey there by providing a support worker from the team to take Finlay out for breakfast and then accompany him at school. Sharon offered a mild protestation that she was unsure Finlay would agree, but what was most notable was that her whole mood and demeanour changed to one of relief. I observed the shift in dynamics between the professionals and Sharon when the focus was on context. It appeared Sharon felt relieved and supported by these suggestions and part of a collaborative effort to protect her son. Sharon was not alone: the professionals also seemed to exhale a sigh of relief. Child protection systems can – and often – focus on considering the question of 'what can a parent do differently to protect their child?' In this meeting, practitioners worked together around the idea of 'what can we do differently to protect this child?' While the shift to consider this wider context is subtle, the impact it can have – as with Finlay – can be large. But practitioners need to be supported to do this work.

The structure of child protection

The earlier examples, and the extract from Jayne at the start of this chapter, highlight how crucial the structure of child protection is. Whether that's the need to label the harm – with categories that appear to signal parental responsibility – the structure of meetings or the legacy of how things have always operated, the design of systems plays a central role in how, or if, parents are engaged as partners. Alongside our work to document the role of parents in cases of EFH, we are in the early stages of understanding how parents experience safeguarding responses. I share now initial engagement with parents (only mothers were involved) as part of two focus groups we conducted with parents who had experienced the child safeguarding system when their children had experienced EFH. Mothers were engaged through two organisations that worked with parents and children impacted by EFH. When the mothers shared their experiences of children's social care, it was evident that they did not experience services as compassionate or collaborative. The responses indicated that the mothers found the experience of intervention extremely stressful, as can be seen in the following quotes from parents discussing their experiences of social care involvement: "I echo what all the other parents have said about the daunting prospect of social services or any safety agencies questioning the parent" (Focus group, Scale-Up); "It makes you feel like you're treading on eggshells" (Focus group, Scale-Up);

> 'Your whole life's been put on hold. Not nice. It's not … it's like living on pins. That's what – that's what she was saying, and then I said it's like your life is on eggshells until it's over, and it feels like a lifetime, even if it's six months, a year, two years, it's the longest time of your life. And it's depressing, it gets … it – it affects the whole family.' (Focus group, Scale-Up)

Despite the fact that their children were experiencing harm from outside their families, the women here discussed feeling like they – and their parenting – were under scrutiny. For these women, it seems their lives were put on hold, while they and their families were the subject of questioning. As the women spoke, I wondered how the additional stress might impact on a parent's ability to be emotionally present and available for their child(ren). Another parent commented on the daily impact and intrusive thoughts about how their lifestyle may be negatively judged by social workers:

> 'all I'm doing is panicking … constantly got that in the back of your mind, you can't do this, you can't go out, you can't … you know, I've cancelled going out on, er, a works night out, just because they'll turn around and go, "well, she … you was drinking, where were your kids?".' (Focus group, Scale-Up)

Such reflections demonstrate the additional strain experienced by parents when children's social care was involved in their lives. Instead of receiving help to minimise the harm happening to their children, they felt scrutinised.

The focus groups also highlighted a gap in responses to address harm in context. Parent descriptions indicated that system responses focused on restricting young people's behaviour and relied on them to enforce those restrictions:

> 'Cos you know when – when you're trying to do, you know, you've got to say no to this or I can't do this because – because of a child protection you – you know. You can't do, you know, you can't stay out or, you know, and they can – and they can blame – can blame us and it's not us. Do you know what I mean? It, you know, we're just trying to help. But when there's extra restrictions on top rather than support, we – we're not neglecting them, we're just try … we're ju … we're trying our best, but it ain't working. Do you know what I mean? And we're, you know, it's not just one person getting punished, it's everybody. That's how I – that's how I feel, pun … like we're being punished for it.' (Focus group, Scale-Up)

While practitioners do not generally set out with the intention of 'punishing' or 'blaming' parents, extracts like the one here reflect a common narrative that many parents discuss when coming into contact with the child protection system (Gibson, 2020). As colleagues in the CS team have highlighted elsewhere (Lloyd and Firmin, 2020), the focus on parenting in policy seeps into the very fabric of how social workers are trained to consider who causes harm and who has responsibility to prevent it.

In response, we have been developing system changes that bring parents in as partners to this work. I shared examples of these new approaches with parents in the focus group. Using animations, I presented examples of what a 'safety meeting' (where the focus is contexts and not individuals) could be like. Perhaps unsurprisingly, the parents were enthusiastic about the prospect of a different approach, one where they did not feel punished or blamed. It was evident that language professionals used was important to parents. When I shared details about the structure of safety planning meetings, parents seemed to be reassured by the language used to describe them, for example, the name 'safety plans' as opposed to 'child protection plans'. Language focused on safety appeared to communicate to parents that the process was rooted in collaboration:

> 'there's a whole world of difference between the phrase "child protection conference" and "safety conference". Like, the child protection, for me, I would be saying, "well, why – why are you questioning about my child's protection? Like, I'm trying to do everything I can to keep my child safe". But, the safety conference, it just seems as though, okay, it's just about their safety.' (Focus group, Scale-Up)

> 'There's a difference between, I think, this – like many have said – this stigma behind protection services.' (Focus group, Scale-Up)

During the focus groups, it was interesting to witness how freely mothers shared their experiences with me and the other women in the group. It was evident that hearing and sharing their experiences had a beneficial effect, perhaps reducing feelings of isolation and stigma. Both groups commented the experience had been positive for them. In one of the groups, there was discussion about setting up a regular meeting for parents. There seemed to be something special about sharing experiences, connecting with people who had been through similar experiences, knowing that they were not alone, perhaps affirming that they were not to blame.

It is not only parents that felt the social care system was stigmatising and blaming parents. Young people themselves discussed this in focus groups. A young person offered their view about parents being sent on a parenting course when their child was harmed outside of the home: "they've [social care] definitely handled it the wrong way when they blame the parenting for something that weren't their fault. They can't control what happens outside the house" (Young person, Scale-Up focus group). When safety planning was introduced to the group, young people continued to express concern about the possibility of parents being judged:

'Because the way they lay it out is them getting inside the parents' head and make them think that they're a bad parent, no matter what anyone says after they hear "you could've then prevented your child from getting hurt", they're always going to think they're a bad child, they're bad parents from that point forward. So, they'll attend all class they're able to, to prevent people from calling them a bad parent.' (Young person, Scale-Up focus group)

When I talked to young people about the idea of safety planning, I was slightly surprised at the level of commitment and concern about their parents. Young people expressed concern that their parents might feel judged by children's social care and obliged to attend parenting courses. The previous quote caused me to reflect upon parental rights and their ability to decline intervention and the consequences for them. If young people at risk of significant harm outside of the home are managed under child protection arrangements, and there are no concerns about parenting, what happens if the parents decide to withdraw consent? Who is accountable if the context doesn't change?

Conclusion

The emerging findings raise questions about how child protection system design, and the culture and language of social work within this system, responsibilises parents in cases of EFH. Parents report experiences of shame, stigma and isolation when their child(ren) have been harmed or are at risk of harm. While new shifts in policy call for 'contexts' to be the focus of assessments, even in sites that are actively trying to do so, the pull towards discussing parenting is strong. While there have been some encouraging developments during the Scale-Up Project, it is clear that more work is needed to understand ways to bring parents into this process. Even if the intention is to focus on context, without clear and available interventions that can tackle harm in context, it is likely that workers will default to what is available to them: parenting courses and parental support. It is also notable that data captured was limited to mothers. We cannot offer any findings in relation to the role of fathers in keeping young people safe outside the home.

Initial discussions do, however, suggest that there is cause to be hopeful: when systems are designed to focus on context, this can shift the focus on where the harm is. Can this structural change create an opportunity to unite professionals and parents to develop plans designed to increase safety outside of the home? While work with parents in CS is in initial testing, we hope the approach can provide practitioners with a framework and language to support collaboration with parents and reduce stigma and blame.

10

What can we learn from multi-agency meetings to address extra-familial harm to young people?

Lisa Bostock

Every day, practitioners work together to safeguard children and young people. Assessment of risk to children is a uniquely challenging task and the onus is on social workers and other safeguarding professionals to 'get this right' for children and young people (O'Neill, 2007). Yet risk assessment is beset by the navigating tensions between knowing how best to act based on agreed 'facts' and 'not knowing', curiosity and uncertainty (Mason, 1993). Identifying risk of EFH adds an additional layer of complexity for practitioners who must manage many unknowns regarding the social conditions of abuse. To navigate such tensions, multi-agency meetings have been developed to support practitioners to explore different perspectives on risk, and plan context-specific safeguarding responses for young people at risk or experiencing EFH. In recent times, there has been a proliferation of such meetings with the aim of creating safety for young people. However, in what ways do these meetings support partners – including young people and families – to embed a CS approach to EFH?

What we do we know about multi-agency safeguarding meetings?

Partnership working is enshrined within child welfare legislation and positioned as central to protecting children and young people (Department for Education, 2018). A series of high-profile reports into child deaths and analysis of Serious Case Reviews have repeatedly identified problems with multi-agency working, particularly difficulties with information sharing across organisational boundaries (Ward et al, 2012). To address these difficulties, multi-agency meetings represent an opportunity to build relationships between agencies, share information and, critically, make sense of information that often can be quite patchy in making decisions about how best to intervene to protect children (Salmon and Rapport, 2005). For multi-agency working to be effective, a series of inter-related factors is required, including existing good relationships, a shared value base and clear aims and objectives, as well as access to a range of interventions (Cameron et al, 2012).

Addressing EFH via a CS approach is dependent on developing new relationships with non-traditional safeguarding partners with knowledge and reach into contexts beyond the home where young people might be at risk (Firmin, 2020). It also creates opportunities for the professional network to draw on multiple perspectives about what might be happening for young people with a view to developing new and creative solutions to address harm across a range of contexts. In using CS to respond to EFH, practitioners may be faced with multiple perspectives and competing narratives, for example, narratives of multiple families and peers within a peer group affected by serious violence and conflict, businesses who are affected by the increased violence in the area and the school environment in which some of the harm occurs (Lewis et al, 2022: 4).

Across many areas, multi-agency meetings have been introduced to support identification and planning in response to young people at risk of or experiencing EFH. Some meetings have a specific focus, for example, CSE; others have a wider remit to respond to all forms of EFH, including intervening in locations of concern. These meetings bring together information from multiple sources, including police intelligence, social care and local practitioner knowledge, to support identification of risks to young people from different contexts with a view to making timely, and developing effective, safety plans (Lewis et al, 2022).

They provide an important opportunity for practitioners to have the space to consider multiple perspectives, test assumptions and ensure plans are evidence-based and informed by holistic analysis. While there is a literature on the importance of multi-agency working to address CSE (see Coy et al, 2017), little is known about what happens within multi-agency meetings to address EFH. This chapter draws on new data collected from across ten sites working to develop a CS response to EFH. It is based on 16 observations of multi-agency meetings across three of those sites, providing evidence of how practitioners discuss EFH within the CS framework.

Addressing extra-familial harm through multi-agency meetings

The CS programme has been working with ten local areas to implement CS across nine involved in the Scale-Up Project and initial test work in the London Borough of Hackney (see Introduction). Sites were asked to identify existing meeting structures for addressing EFH. Excluding meetings associated with statutory processes, such as child in need meetings, over 20 multi-agency forums were identified. These included missing and child exploitation meetings, vulnerable adolescent panels, violence reduction meetings and multi-agency risk assessment conferences. To streamline the number of forums designed to address EFH, six sites introduced or adapted existing meetings to provide oversight of multi-agency responses to EFH. What distinguishes these meetings is a specific focus on Level 2 CS – work around peer groups, schools and neighbourhoods – as well as Level 1 work with children and families – affected by EFH. This means that they not only address EFH at an individual level but focus on intervening in contexts beyond the home where EFH occurs.

In six sites, 11 new CS-informed multi-agency meetings were identified. Meetings operate at three levels: strategic (n=2) to identify overarching themes and trends informing interventions with individuals, groups and locations; operational (n=7) to address harm outside of the family, including specific contexts such as peer groups, locations or schools; and individual planning (n=2) to address the needs of individuals/groups of young people. Most were chaired by social care or co-chaired by social care and the police; some were chaired by adolescent services or Community Safety. At an operational level, four out of seven addressed most forms of EFH; only one included radicalisation.

Methods

Data collection

For the purposes of this chapter, and to create an in-depth understanding of how such meetings address EFH, a total of 16 operational meetings were observed across three sites (see Table 10.1). Observations were not audio-recorded but based on contemporaneous field notes that aimed to capture discussion verbatim between participants. Researcher reflections were recorded separately, although included in final analysis to illuminate themes (Spradley, 1980).

Due to COVID-19-related restrictions, all meetings were observed online between October 2020 and June 2021. Ethical approval was granted by the Institute for Applied Social Research (IASR) ethics panel at the University of Bedfordshire (and reapproved at Durham University), and consent was provided by practitioners to observe and record notes to support learning and development.

Table 10.1: Number of meeting observations by site

Research site	Number of observations
Site 1	4
Site 2	6
Site 3	6

Analysis

Each observation was given an RAG rating (red, amber or green) for the meeting's alignment with the four domains of CS. The RAG rating assessed the degree to which each meeting 1) targeted the context of harm; 2) maintained a child welfare focus; 3) engaged partners, specifically non-traditional partners; and 4) identified clear objectives or actions (Firmin, 2020). Following RAG rating, an additional question was posed of the data focused on the degree to which the voices of young people and family members were included.

Profile of participants

A total of 264 professionals attended the meetings, primarily (90 per cent) from traditional safeguarding partnerships, most notably (40 per cent) from children's social care (CSC) and the police. A small proportion were from non-traditional services such as the fire service. Discussions covered 106 young people (aged between 12 and 18), including between ten and 20 peer groups and ten and 20 locations. Most young people discussed were young men; only nine young women featured in discussions, including two peer groups of three young women. Ethnicity was not specified for 63 per cent of young people. Where it was specified, 37 per cent were identified as Black British or of mixed heritage.

Findings

Table 10.2 outlines the RAG rating of each meeting by site and domain. Across the 16 meetings, the balance is towards amber. This means that practice was developing but further work is required to fully meet the CS domains. Site 2 (panels 5–10), which had the most long-standing meeting, achieved either green or amber alignment with half of the domains. This was the only site where a meeting was assessed as fully meeting all the domains of CS, including capturing the voice of young people and families.

Extra-familial harm meetings
Domain 1: Target

To be rated as green, contextual dynamics were consistently discussed by meeting members. Site 2 was the only one to have been rated as green (four out of six meetings) for the domain of target. The site had developed a meeting referral form to support practitioners to explore risks, strengths and interventions across each context identified as associated to EFH. In these meetings, contexts were reviewed for each individual young person using a 'context grid' which reflected the structure of the referral form and included

Table 10.2: Site red, amber or green rating by Contextual Safeguarding domain

Site	Target	Welfare	Partners	Actions	YP voice
Site 1	Amber	Green	Amber	Amber	Red
Site 1	Amber	Green	Green	Red	Amber
Site 1	Amber	Green	Amber	Red	Red
Site 1	Amber	Green	Green	Amber	Amber
Site 2	Amber	Amber	Amber	Amber	Red
Site 2	Green	Amber	Amber	Green	Amber
Site 2	Green	Green	Green	Green	Green
Site 2	Green	Amber	Amber	Amber	Green
Site 2	Amber	Amber	Green	Amber	Amber
Site 2	Green	Green	Green	Green	Amber
Site 3	Amber	Amber	Green	Amber	Red
Site 3	Amber	Amber	Amber	Amber	Red
Site 3	Amber	Amber	Amber	Amber	Amber
Site 3	Amber	Green	Amber	Amber	Green
Site 3	Amber	Amber	Amber	Amber	Amber
Site 3	Amber	Green	Amber	Amber	Amber

child/young person; home/family; peers; school/education; neighbourhoods and locations. Where referrals were well developed prior to the meeting, discussion was more succinctly focused on the context of harm, identifying known as well as unknown features: "The concern relates to CSE related to the peer group [of three young women]. These young women are being exploited by unknown/s and YP2 appears to being coercive by YP1 into participating in CSE. However, we have less information YP3 who is new to the [area]" (Meeting 10). A focus on peer group dynamics was notable, not only for any peer groups discussed but also in relation to individual young people. Typically, discussions focused on peer relationships and recognised both strengths and potential risks, for example, "what do we know about his peer group, what strengths or risks, is there further detail on who is pulling him out of the home?" (Meeting 6), understanding the positive: "protect the friendship, if possible, rather than disrupting it" (Meeting 5).

Where meetings were rated as amber, there were clear attempts to target the wider context. In Sites 1 and 3, this was most readily identified by the inclusion of standing agenda items regarding locations of concern, sometimes referred to as 'hotspots'. At the time of the observations, both sites were in the early stages of developing their approach to place-based safeguarding interventions, including piloting social care-led location assessments in Site

3. Location assessments aim to develop location-specific plans to address young people's risk of criminal and sexual exploitation; a location might be supported accommodation, a road or a city centre.

However, within amber-rated meetings, the focus on contextual dynamics tended to be more inconsistent, with discussion beyond the context of individual child or young person more limited. At times, discussion was marked by fact finding and clarifications, with requests for more "information", "intel" and "further digging" the most notable actions. This in part reflected recording practice that was individualised rather than sensitised to contextual thinking, meaning that, for example, links between young people were missing or mentions of wider context of concern absent.

Domain 2: Legislative framework

A focus on child welfare was evident across sites, with half (eight out of 16 meetings) rated as green. This manifested through discussion and appropriate challenge between partner agencies. In this example, work was undertaken with a school to support them to understand EFH and the head teacher was "persuaded" not to permanently exclude a young person who had brought a knife into school due to concerns about their increased vulnerability in the community. Instead, the school provided the young person with additional "pastoral care" and was in the process of "undertaking a Contextual Safeguarding assessment" (Meeting 13).

Site 1 was the only one to be rated as green for all four meetings observed, reflecting a "level of openness from practitioners that challenged the systems and roles that professionals play" which can "create problems for young people" (Researcher notes, Meeting 1). Within these meetings, there was a consistent focus on the emotional wellbeing of young people, recognising trauma experienced and coping strategies adopted, even if harmful, such as use of drugs and alcohol or serious youth violence.

The practice-shaping role of the chair was crucial in terms of challenging direct practice with young people themselves. In the following discussion from Meeting 6, a young man (17) who was missing was stopped by the police from a different area in an unregistered vehicle with an adult with previous arrests for drug dealing. The young person had also been arrested previously for possessions of drugs and, in a separate incident, had received a stab injury. When arrested, he reported that he was wearing a stab-proof vest and being "threatened with firearms and told to follow instructions".

The CSC chair explored police practice regarding criminal exploitation, asking: "would [the] young person be understood as being likely to be exploited, given the fact that [they were] missing for a long period?" The police recognised that "in an ideal world, we would have realised that this young person was missing as well as wanted on bail. Instead, the young person was seen as close-ish to being an adult and seen as someone wanted on a warrant". An immediate action was noted to make a referral to the National Referral Mechanism (NRM). This example underlines how the meetings enabled exploration of different agency perspectives on risk and, importantly, understand young people as children – rather than criminals – whose behaviours might be influenced by, in this case, the adults who are exploiting them.

In meetings rated as amber, while there was recognition of harm experienced by young people, tensions were noted regarding differences in statutory thresholds. For example, one young person was assessed as at risk of significant harm due to a series of missing episodes and exploitation associated with their peer group. However, the children's safeguarding team were not in agreement and argued that the extra-familial risk did not reach the threshold for child protection (Meeting 7). An action was made by the chair to raise with management of the safeguarding team outside of the meeting. In other instances, there was an initial reliance on "disruption activities" by the police to target groups where socially unacceptable behaviour was reported, with welfare concerns and school engagement a secondary priority.

Domain 3: Partnerships

Domain 3 refers to the degree to which partnerships are developed with individuals and sectors with responsibility for the nature of extra-familial contexts. These might include parks and recreation, shop or hotel owners or those involved in the night-time economy. Most meetings (ten) were rated as amber, reflecting that 90 per cent of meeting participants were made up of more traditional safeguarding partners: children's social care, youth services, the police, education and healthcare. Across sites, over-representation of traditional safeguarding partners was a limitation of the meetings and served to preclude perspectives that may have provided a different – and possibly competing – understanding of what was known or unknown about what might be happening for the young people discussed.

However, in meetings rated as green, there were conversations about how best to engage with local people and business owners to increase community guardianship – that is, adults who spend time in the community and can play a safeguarding role. In an example from Meeting 4, there was an extended discussion about how best to "raise awareness" with the wider community to promote children's safeguarding as "everybody's responsibility". The idea of a "public campaign" was raised to "effectively engage with local people and business owners", providing them with the skills to "recognise the signs of exploitation of young people". In Meeting 13, plans were discussed to pilot restorative approaches with residents and young people to address a breakdown in community relations related to behaviours identified as socially unacceptable, including drug dealing, violence and hate crimes.

Young people or parents were not invited to the meetings; hence, it was the responsibility of professionals to present their wishes and feelings in their absence. This varied across the meetings and challenges were noted regarding relationships between professionals and young people. Sometimes, this was because there were difficulties in building trusting relationships due to frequent missing episodes, meaning direct work with the young people themselves had been limited. At other times, "non-engagement" with services was noted, although not necessarily explored as to why this might be the case, or what other opportunities practitioners might have to build engagement with the young person/people; in some cases, "non-engagement" appeared to be used as a proxy for young people's views about service provision. There were some examples of considering the safeguarding capabilities of family members, such as how best to work with an uncle who had "successfully exited a local gang" to support a young person at risk of criminal exploitation (Meeting 9). For the most part, however, understanding of the role of family members as safeguarding partners was underdeveloped.

Domain 4: Outcome measurement

This domain refers to processes for monitoring the outcomes of success in relation to contextual as well as individual change. This was difficult to evidence given one-off meeting observations, where new individual young people, locations or peer groups were being discussed. In other words, it is difficult to comment on change over time in relation to contexts where harm might be occurring. It is possible to comment on actions. In Site 2, where half (three out of six) meetings were assessed as green, degree of risk associated with each context was weighted and actions to address harm experienced by young people prioritised accordingly. In the two meetings rated as red, researchers were unclear about "what objectives were set to target the context of harm". Such meetings were described as reflective, generating multiple perspectives about what was "underpinning the harm young people were experiencing" but "discussion to consider interventions limited" and actions noted as "piecemeal" (Researcher notes, Meeting 1).

Across the three sites, most meetings (11) were rated as amber, reflecting an over-reliance on tasking practitioners to collect more information, make a referral or convene another meeting rather than "actions targeting contexts" (Researcher notes, Meeting 16). On balance, actions related to interventions focused on the welfare of individual young people. In part, this reflected the traditional background of safeguarding agencies represented. In this example from Meeting 5, a young person (16) had been targeted by two rival gangs. Over the past four years, he had been repeatedly robbed and threatened outside his home. The response from housing was focused on moving the family to protect their safety. Actions at Level 1 were focused on the mental health needs of the young person, such as referral to clinical services, but actions at Level 2 to address the harm experienced outside the home were limited to further information gathering about known associates. This was recognised by the CSC chair as problematic: "I do think that we will have failed as a system if we move the family rather than dealing with the source harm". However, no further actions were identified to make this a reality. In this instance, seeking sources of community guardianship may have enabled the safeguarding system to develop a more robust CS response to the EFH experienced.

Voices of young people

Although young people were not invited to meetings, there were examples of professionals advocating for their perspectives, needs and rights. In this example, the professional network expressed serious concerns about a young person (16) in care who was at risk of criminal exploitation, serious youth violence and had ten missing episodes. This young person had significant learning needs and had experienced the recent bereavement of a parent. Much of the early discussion had focused on clarifications and fact finding, including possible connection to a shooting.

These discussions were tempered by an intervention from a psychologist, who highlighted the impact of trauma on this young person and how professional activity had the potential to reinforce trauma without addressing his needs. They cautioned against task-based practice and the search for facts about wrongdoing:

> 'I think it would be helpful to give an overall view of where the young person is at. He is an adolescent, therefore his brain is developing; he will be working more off the emotional bit of his brain and risk taking is far more prevalent than the frontal lobe – planning, problem solving and executive function. He's also experienced the sudden death of [parent], and experienced significant difficulties in his family [reference to being in care]. There has been trauma upon trauma for this young person for many years. He feels like that he is seeking, searching for something and if we keep focusing on all the wrong things he is doing, we are giving him the wrong sort of attention, we could get sidetracked with all of this activity and forget him.' (Meeting 8)

Such interventions within multi-agency meetings highlight the importance of holding the child in mind. They provide a powerful reminder of how trauma impacts young people's attachment experiences and the responsibility of professionals to move beyond a focus on individual children to surfacing solutions that serve to intervene in contexts where harm occurs.

Multi-agency panel meetings: some reflections

Multi-agency panel meetings have the potential to target the social conditions of abuse, shifting thinking and practice beyond the home into the contexts where harm occurs. Across meetings, a focus on child welfare was notable, with attention paid to addressing the long-standing trauma that many of the young people had experienced. Challenges were observed, including that meetings could be marked by information sharing and fact finding. This was sometimes at the expense of curiosity about what might be happening within a context, whether for a young person, peer group or place of concern. This in part reflects that information represented at meetings can be insufficiently contextualised. It also reflects the complexities and uncertainties about what might be happening within contexts beyond the home. This underlines the importance of involving the wider partnership, including young people and family members with both the knowledge and interest in increasing community safety.

While all sites are continuing to develop and embed CS, five features of multi-agency meetings were identified in data presented in this chapter that may support effective multi-agency working in future stages of implementation:

- making a good quality referral – taking context into account when making a referral to multi-agency panel meetings;
- effective chairing – the role of the panel meeting chair in ensuring a contextually informed approach;
- collaborative working – how to work together to maintain a child welfare focus as a partnership;
- involving young people and their families – assessing how the views of young people and families are represented at meetings; and
- beyond talking and tasking – balancing Level 1 and Level 2 responses to actively change extra-familial contexts.

Referrers operate at the boundary between young people and families and other professions and organisations. They collate information into referral documents that convey the views of young people and family members to other professionals, taking account of the wider context within which harm may be occurring. While sites have developed different processes for making referrals, most have identified an initial point of contact whereby referrers can discuss their concerns and determine whether a referral is suitable for discussion at such a forum. This provides an opportunity to tease out contexts of concern through the conversation and explore the relational dynamics between professionals and young people, families and their communities.

A focus on child welfare is a core feature of multi-agency meetings. Meetings are generally chaired by CSC with the police or youth services.

The role of the chair(s) is critical to shaping discussion and engaging – and sometimes challenging – partners appropriately when necessary. Such discussions may surface tensions regarding statutory thresholds, with the chair(s) opting to discuss decisions outside of the meeting to ensure that young people's needs are addressed. They also challenge professional perspectives within meetings, focusing on the nature of direct practice with young people. This includes challenging practice that could be characterised as 'adultification' or criminalisation of young people at risk of exploitation.

Working in partnership is fundamental to safeguarding children and young people. Given there are many unknowns regarding the social conditions of abuse, this can create heightened levels of anxiety among the professional network that may need to be managed within the group. If not, such anxieties can lead to practice that is more process-driven to ensure that procedures are followed rather than focused on creative solutions. Swiftly fostering a sense of a safeguarding community – that is, a shared sense of responsibility for safeguarding – may help contextually informed decision making. Including non-traditional safeguarding partners such as café and shop owners or night-time economy workers may support development of interventions focused on the conditions of harm. These might include offering places of safety to young people when feeling threatened, thereby building the safeguarding community beyond the context of multi-agency meetings.

One of the primary benefits of multi-agency panel meetings to address EFH is support for practice, offering practitioners the opportunity to think through safety concerns and the complex interplay between different contexts. This is dependent on the acknowledgment that however much information is gathered, this cannot 'complete' the picture about risk to children in the community or provide certainty about what action to take. Rather, such meetings provide a pivotal practice forum to support practitioners adopt a position of 'authoritative doubt' by enabling them to reflect on what they are doing together as a partnership to safeguard children (Mason, 1993).

Holding a position of 'authoritative doubt' involves exploring ideas about what young people might be experiencing. Drawing on systemic social work practice, this can be supported through use of hypothesising (Lewis et al, 2022). Hypothesising enables practitioners to generate multiple perspectives about what might be happening within a context. Hypotheses are then used to test out different ideas with young people and their families to get their perspective (Brown, 2019). This might include reflecting on why peer dynamics had emerged and what such relationships gift young people living in challenging circumstances. This facilitates the voice of the child or family to be 'present' within the professional conversation as hypotheses evolve through feedback from young people and family members about their wishes, feelings and interactions.

Giving space to hypothesising has the potential to balance Level 1 (contexts around the child and family) actions and Level 2 (work around peer groups, schools and neighbourhoods) responses to EFH. This may support practitioners to explore solutions outside their normal ways of working, for example, at a community level, piloting a scheme to develop the confidence of women who are sex working to share their concerns with safeguarding agencies about young people they suspect are being exploited in the area, while, at the same time, receiving support themselves (Bostock, 2021: 42). In this way, such meetings have the potential to move beyond 'talking and tasking' and ensure that actions really are 'actions' to intervene in contexts of concern rather than tasking practitioners to gather more information.

Conclusions and implications

Multi-agency panel meetings to address EFH are an integral part of the safeguarding landscape. They help practitioners focus their attention beyond the home, challenging the safeguarding partnership to think and respond differently to the harms that young people are experiencing. What is unique about the meetings observed is their focus on Level 2 responses, providing the forum for commissioning work around peer groups, schools and neighbourhoods. In this way, their reach is far beyond the meetings themselves, drawing on the expertise of partners working in the community to identify creative solutions to what are often highly complex situations. This is dependent on the wider political commitment to place-based solutions to intransient problems, as noted in earlier chapters in this book (Chapters 2 and 3, for example). These include poverty and poor housing, education and employment and ensuring that local community resources, such as mental health and youth services, are funded in a way that enables flexibility of approach, reaching out to young people in the places that are meaningful to them, whether the park, seafront or city centre.

PART IV

Domain 4: The outcomes the system produces and measures

PART IV

11

Developing outcomes measurements in Contextual Safeguarding: explorations of theory and practice

Jenny Lloyd and Rachael Owens

Ask any parent, or child, what a good outcome for a child would be and they are likely to talk about being 'happy' or 'healthy', 'having friends' or access to the things they need. Ask someone working in a quality assurance team in children's social care what a good outcome for a child could be and you could get the same answers, but you might also hear them talk about re-referral rates, missing episodes and offending of looked-after children. Trying to identify outcomes and outcomes measures in social care is challenging. It brings together a need to quantify the often unquantifiable within a context of having to demonstrate cost-effectiveness and efficiency (Hood, 2019; Clapton, 2021). So what happens, then, when you add measuring outcomes for contexts – like a park or school – to the mix? Ask any parent, or child, what a safe context for a child would be and they might first ask you what a context is. They might then talk about feeling safe in the community, having kind and loyal friends or schools where teachers care about the students. Ask someone working in a quality assurance team in children's social care what a good outcome for a context could be and they might struggle to answer. Perhaps where this chapter falls in this book (towards the end) is a good representation of where outcomes have fallen within the work of CS to date. Outcomes, as the name suggests, have been seen as *coming out of* and not a target *to get to*. Without a clear goal in mind, we are limited in our ability to design responses that seek to get us there. This means that CS work is often enthusiastically geared towards the *who* and *what*, not the *why* and *how*.

We – Jenny and Rachael – feel underqualified to be writing a chapter on outcomes. But we have found ourselves – or Rachael has at least – pulling on our proverbial wellies and trudging into the swampy lowlands of developing practice in this area (Schön, 1983). We have found that while theoretically we can articulate what we might mean by contextual outcomes, what that means in practice, and how we set about doing this, can be quite different. In this chapter, we dig into the questions of what we mean by a safe outcome for a context, but in an effort to be transparent, we discuss the challenges we have found in doing this in practice. To do this, this chapter is formatted to reflect the divide between the theoretical insights of the 'ivory towers' (written in the left-hand column) and the realities of trying to do this in the 'swampy lowlands' of practice (written in the right-hand column by Rachael). We begin with an overview of the literature on outcomes in social care and community safety, before tackling the question of outcomes for CS.

Outcomes in children's social care

Statutory guidance and local safeguarding policies are awash with the language of 'achieving better outcomes for children and young people'. Yet despite the pressure and requirement for social care to be able to demonstrate measurable outcomes for children, there is little by way of specific and measurable outcomes that can be used (La Valle et al, 2016). Here, we focus on child-level outcomes, that is, outcomes used to measure the experiences of individual young people (often measured through assessment), as opposed to system outcomes that are reported to the Department for Education (for example, numbers of looked-after children). *Working Together* (HM Government 2018b), England's statutory policy for safeguarding partners, presents three assessment domains covering a child's developmental needs, parenting capacity and family and environmental factors of healthy child development in their assessment triangle, but not the specific details of what or how these can be measured. As Holmes et al (2016) note, while Ofsted's standards for achieving a rating require 'measurably improved outcomes', the outcomes themselves are not specifically detailed or consistently measured against. Studies into the relationship between Ofsted ratings of different local authorities and better or worse outcomes for children have found no relationship between the two (La Valle et al, 2016), with those achieving better Ofsted ratings being those that often meet their statutory requirements, for example, the proportion of assessments completed within statutory timeframes, rather than child-level outcomes related to children's wellbeing (Wilkins and Antonopoulou, 2020).

Evaluations into responses to EFH, such as the Department for Education's Children's Social Care Innovation Programme (Department for Education, 2022), provide insights into the types of outcomes measures that could be used. For example, evaluations into programmes tackling CSE or adolescents facing complex risks detail the outcomes measures used (some of these are detailed in the next chapter). Looking across evaluations highlights that while there is some evidence of contextual approaches such as improving guardianship through relationships in these frameworks, on the whole, emphasis is overwhelmingly placed on individual changes for young people. For example, the Safer Steps programme for girls experiencing CSE aimed for outcomes such as girls being at reduced risk of CSE, having improved emotional wellbeing, making positive choices and having improved relationships with project staff (Williams et al, 2017). Similar outcomes are framed for other programmes, where the focus overwhelmingly falls on individual-level outcomes such as 'reduced criminal severity' and 'risky behaviour reduced' of young people (Blower et al, 2017). Not only do some of these run in conflict with the values which underpin CS – for example, we remain critical of discourse that places emphasis on the 'risky behaviour' of young people – but these reports also highlight the complexities of measuring such changes.

Measuring child-level outcomes in social care for any child is fraught with challenges: the broad scope of possible factors and the question of who defines what is measured (Forrester, 2017), what and who is prioritised (Clapton, 2021) and how the act of measurement alters what and how services are provided (Hood, 2019). And while it is, of course, important to engage children and families in the process of setting outcomes, there are challenges in finding agreement between young people, parents and practitioners of what the problem is and developing shared measures of success (Forrester 2017; Forrester et al, 2019). For young people that are being exploited, it may often be the case that they do not agree with the risks identified by practitioners and parents and the response needed (Pearce, 2007). Outcomes measures make several assumptions about the services delivered and the impacts these have. Services which young people talk about as being beneficial to them often struggle to identify and measure change in ways that relate readily to the world of outcomes (Harris, 2014).

When funding is predicated on identifying certain measurable criteria, it should not be surprising, then, that we start having services designed almost entirely around commissioning arrangements (Milbourne and Cushman, 2013), for example, short funding streams where organisations are required to demonstrate that they are working with the 'right' cohort to provide demonstrable change to often pre-defined outcomes by funders. In a climate of reduced funding opportunities, services are often guided down a discursive route where they must shout the loudest about how they tackle the pressing issue du jour for the least amount of money. We know of organisations who, to meet the requirements of their funders, have required those using their services to narrate their experiences in a particular way, for example, one which might show them as 'gang-involved' even if that may not be the case in order to access the services they need. There are clear ethical implications for providers and those that use services through this process. Perhaps we didn't have such a problem with gangs and county lines until the Home Office started providing funding for just that (Wroe, 2019).

Measuring outcomes is not only, then, about what changes happen for young people but the context in which those changes are made.

The What Works for Children's Social Care (2021) centre's outcomes framework nestles individual child and parent outcomes between outcomes that promote the rights of children and families and those that improve organisational factors. La Valle et al's (2016) framework provides a detailed overview of outcomes, indicators and data needed to measure outcomes in children's social care services. Crucially, this framework centres on four key aspects: the conditions and culture of children's social care services created by leaders, reaching the right children and families with the right support, relationships that value children and families and ensuring children are safe where they live in their homes and communities. Overarching this is the need to understand the socio-economic and cultural context, the corporate commitment to, and support for, children's social care services and the role of other agencies. While La Valle et al (2016) situate outcomes for children and families within wider systemic structures, the outcomes themselves are overall focused on change for people rather than for places. Defining outcomes for contexts themselves may require going beyond those for social care to partners that work in contexts beyond the home, such as Community Safety.

Outcomes in Community Safety

In Chapter 5, Joanne Walker and Carlene Firmin outlined some of the ways in which Community Safety is aligned to, and distinct from, CS. In some respects, Community Safety outcomes may be better aligned to CS. Community Safety outcomes, underlined by partnership commitments and priorities, often relate to tackling forms of harm more traditionally associated to EFH and within places beyond the home, such as neighbourhoods. These outcomes can range in scale from the individual level of a 'victim' (fewer victims of violence), harm within groups (volume of group offences) to the scale of the neighbourhood itself (people feel safer) (Tower Hamlets, 2021). Community Safety outcomes also often include those beyond those directly impacted by crime – such as victims and instigators – to the broader community, including commitments to increase perceptions of safety and confidence in partner responses.

While aligned geographically and ecologically with CS, Community Safety approaches may not be so theoretically. As outline in Chapter 5, following the Crime and Disorder Act 1998, the focus of Community Safety partners expanded from the narrow police-led focus on crime prevention to the broader remit of 'community safety'. This movement saw a shift towards focusing on 'pre-crime', attempting to stop crime before it happens. The language of 'antisocial behaviour' and the commissioning, policy and practice responses resulting from this can be seen as a movement to focusing on behaviours of (young) people which are not 'yet' criminal but considered to be determiners of potential future crime (Zedner, 2007). Secondly, Community Safety approaches are underpinned by theoretical approaches that predominantly target the *behaviours* of individuals. The dominance of situational crime prevention (Clarke, 1997), underpinned by rational choice theory (Cornish and Clarke, 1987), has resulted in responses which focus on 'designing out' crime through environmental design but do little to increase feelings of safety or consider broader social, cultural and systemic factors behind crime and safety (Pain, 2000). For example, public campaigns providing female university students with personal safety alarms might reduce an attacker pursuing a sexual assault (due to the knowledge that women may carry alarms) but will do little to tackle the patriarchal norms underpinning assaults or the victim blaming that may ensue. Responses of this nature are sharply focused on the behaviour of those that might commit crime – but haven't done so yet – through interventions such as 'target hardening' (making it harder to commit crime, for example, by adding a lock) or awareness raising. For example, 'education and awareness for young people carrying weapons' (Isle of Wight Community Safety Partnership, 2016) would be seen as an attempt to target those who are considered at risk (young people), through training that focuses on changing their possible behaviours (carrying a weapon), via education which (presumably) highlights the detrimental effects of doing so.

While outcomes in Community Safety provide an insight into opportunities to measure outcomes for places, it is worth noting that some of these approaches can be seen to undermine child welfare and contribute to the criminalisation of children. For example, focusing on intervention before crime has been seen to 'net widen' and increase the number of young people receiving institutional disposals (Bottoms and Kemp, 2017). As we have seen in Chapter 5, if Community Safety approaches do not prioritise the welfare of children, they may undermine the overarching goal of CS and its core values. While Community Safety may give us a sense of how to measure outcomes beyond individuals, the outcomes they strive for may undermine the goals of CS as well as measure behaviours over and above social conditions. We are left with the question, then, of how to measure outcomes in a way which focuses on the social conditions of harm, and not just on individual behaviours in contexts. In the following section, we consider outcomes for CS, in theory and practice.

Outcomes for Contextual Safeguarding

Within the Scale-Up Project, sites grappled with how to implement the fourth domain of CS – measuring the outcome of changes made within a context to bring about safety for young people. That this has been challenging is understandable: assessing and responding to harm in a context to alter the social conditions of harm is new and challenging enough, without adding in the need to demonstrate the extent to which these have contributed to safety for young people. Added to this is the complexity around what exactly is being measured. As discussed, within children's social care, outcomes are measured for individual children (for example, through care plans and so on) and at a system level (for example, fewer looked-after children overall). Measuring outcomes in CS involves working at both the individual and system levels, although these do not map neatly across. For example, in CS, we might want to measure whether an individual young person feels safer in their context (that is, via a child protection process), whether a context is safer for particular young people who interact with that context (that is, via a targeted Level 2 context response) and, potentially, once targeted work has been completed, whether future children who also interact with that context are safe there (that is, via detached youth work). Thinking about an equivalency for the system-level outcome of 'fewer looked-after children', it may also be desirable to measure the extent to which an embedded CS system sees a reduction in EFH contexts where young people experience high-risk levels of harm.

However, in saying this, it's important to acknowledge the distinction between what we want for young people and contexts versus what can actually be quantified and measured. We recognise that not all of the former *can* be measured. This is because measurement introduces requirements to be specific, to think about the validity and reliability of the approach. Consequently, our task is to come as close as possible to measuring the outcomes we want to see by considering what could provide a reasonable indication of these, while acknowledging that this is only a part of what might be going on in a context. Our aim is to understand at a local level if we are making an incremental difference in that place at that time, rather than any claims to universal truth about 'what works'. This is inherent in the emphasis on context and to act otherwise would be to deny the complex interactions and factors that make up a particular place.

This is, therefore, a complex undertaking and needs careful thinking. On the other hand, CS champions (practitioners who have received training on CS that are developing contextual practice nationally) have felt a growing sense of urgency to be able to account for the new work they are doing. There is a need to be able to effectively 'tell the story' in such a way that those more removed from the work – and, crucially, responsible for its continued resourcing – can understand and justify. Within a context of diminishing resources and a commissioning culture focused on targeting things that 'work', champions have found themselves in need of robust frameworks that

Developing outcomes measurements in Contextual Safeguarding

Figure 11.1: Contextual Safeguarding neighbourhood assessment triangle

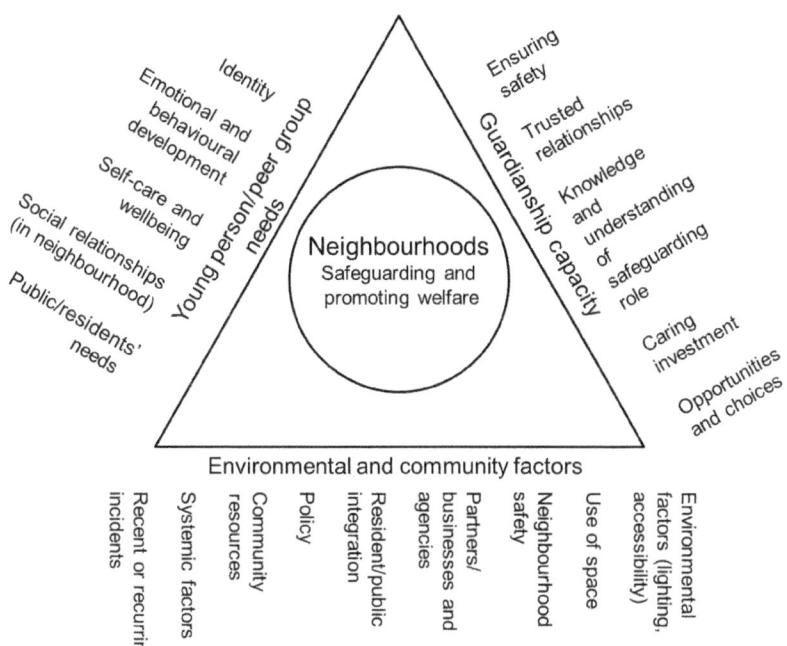

will support the continued development of creative and innovative work, but which do so in a way that is in keeping with the values with which that work has been undertaken.

Kelly Shannon, a Scale-Up champion for Swansea Children's Services, decided to take up the challenge. Kelly leads a team who oversee and undertake context assessments and has also helped to shape a new multi-agency pathway for contexts of harm. She was joined in this work by Jess Myden, who manages the Quality and Improvement Service. In the following section, we discuss the 'theoretical' requirements of the outcomes framework she has developed against what this meant in practice. In providing a description of this work, we have tried to illuminate its realities and challenges and provide food for thought for those that may be developing their own frameworks. While reading from left to right suggests that the 'theory' on the left has informed the 'practice' on the right, it has been an iterative process whereby it has been the practice that has allowed us to grapple with questions which we now explore on the left. We recommend reading each section of text per theme (in theory and practice). We have included in Figure 11.1 the neighbourhood assessment triangle for ease. It is one of the three context assessment triangles drawn on by the Swansea team during this process.

Theme	In theory	In practice
	In developing contextual outcomes, several principles have emerged.	
Focusing on contexts not individuals	Firstly, when designing contextual outcomes for Level 2 (responses to contexts), we start with outcomes that assess changes to contexts, and not changes to individual behaviour. This might seem simple or obvious, but what we mean by this is that we are interested in changes to places and peer groups which affect the experience of all young people who spend time within them and change the dynamics within those spaces which may influence the harm that occurs.	When we started this work, the only things we had to draw on were existing measurements which related to individual young people – for example, 'young person's behaviour has improved so they are no longer at risk of being excluded from school'. We realised that these would not tell us what we needed to know about the changes made within a context. We set about developing new measures which would do that – so, in the previous example, the equivalent measure might be 'the school has reduced numbers of exclusions'.
Setting outcomes linked to good quality assessment	Outcomes should aim to measure changes to the social conditions of abuse. What we mean by this is considering the underlying causes of harm which go beyond trying to modify the behaviour or choices of young people. The context assessment triangles (Figure 11.1) were designed to support practitioners to identify young people's experiences in different contexts with relation to the role of guardians and the environmental and community factors which may be facilitating or mitigating harm, providing a broader exploration of what harm in a context means. Any CS outcomes measures therefore need to be part of wider approaches which assess contextual factors in relation to young people's safety and can link back to this at the end. Outcomes need to relate to the assessment of harm for that specific context and be grounded in the reality of young people's lives. CS requires practitioners to move away from relying on traditional responses and therefore traditional measurements. This necessitates a radical reorientation of safeguarding theory and practice. Relying on existing measures won't be sufficient for creating contextual safety.	We realised that it was important for outcomes to be defined at the point of when responses/ interventions are being planned. This then led to a realisation that an outcomes framework needs to also link to the assessment of the context, and this would give us a clear rationale for those goals. Swansea had developed a context assessment tool, based on the contextual assessment triangles. Kelly and I worked to consolidate the indicators into a set of goal statements which we hoped would be relevant to any context assessment. For example, one of the indicators on the triangle is 'identity', with a supporting question in the guidance for assessing this, which is 'how does the young person/peer see themselves?' Kelly and I then thought about how this might be phrased as a desired outcome or goal statement and decided on 'young people have a positive identity within the context and think positively about themselves'.

Developing new ways of collecting data	It is important to be mindful that in the absence of available data on EFH, it may be compelling to draw on available data. However, in most authorities, for EFH (where data is not routinely recorded in social care), available data is often held by police and crime partners, and therefore may represent structural biases inherent in these organisations, such as the over-representation of Black boys in the local profiles of 'gang' membership (Williams, 2018). Therefore, development of outcome measures in CS should involve critical reflection on how existing data sets are used. At the core of this work is respecting the rights of young people to know when they are included in data and how this is being used.	One of the challenges we faced was how to align this work within the wider data reporting work of the Local Authority. To understand this better, Kelly and I met with Jess. Jess had been asked by the Head of Service to develop a quality assurance framework for the CS work in Swansea that would replicate a similar data reporting process, as is currently in place for child and family work.
Keeping values at the centre through collaborative critical reflection	What we have learnt over the last three years is that, while those undertaking CS approaches have often held the four domains clearly in mind as they develop responses, this hasn't been enough to sufficiently bring the values inherent in the CS framework into this work. We have learnt that the values need to be an explicit feature of the work. The way in which these are applied is through regular critical reflection and evaluation. For example, collaboration is an essential value of CS. We mean this both in collaboration with young people but also in recognition that this work can't be done alone; you need a range of views and ideas to really interrogate the ethics of a plan. The same principles need to be applied in the development of outcomes measures, whereby critical reflection on the implications for young people are kept front and centre.	Developing a new framework like this is complex work. We realised there was great value in having the three of us together, able to hold on to the different strands that were important to integrate into the framework. So while Kelly could help us to stay focused on what was realistic in terms of practice and Jess had an eye on the expectations of the wider reporting mechanisms and what was possible there, I could help to keep the work aligned with the domains and values of CS. Part of this was recognising that there are aspects of practice as usual that CS does not want to replicate and things that we did want to characterise the work. In particular, we were in agreement about promoting the rights of young people when it comes to data sharing. So it was important that we did not default into producing large data sets about the activities of young people – particularly with a criminal lens – which would compromise these values.

Being realistic about what you can test	CS is about developing new practice such as assessments and responses to schools and peer groups, which was not something that has traditionally been required of the social work role. At the same time, however, we acknowledge that we need to operate within the parameters of the existing system and take a realistic approach. This is especially true at this point in the development of CS in relation to developing outcome measures. Our learning about CS development has taught us that starting small and learning iteratively is far more likely to be successful than launching something very ambitious but which turns out to be too cumbersome for the system to accommodate.	It was for this reason that we decided that once we had a draft framework in place, the best way to proceed would be to run a short pilot with four live cases. In the pilot, we would work together on how to define the measure for each of the goals – asking ourselves, how will we know if this has been achieved? Before beginning, I analysed the measures we had developed in a hypothetical scenario. The idea was to test and refine these categories so that they could be scaled up. The pilot was also intended to understand the resource implications of measuring outcomes in this way.
Distinguishing outcomes from outputs	In setting outcomes for contexts, it is important that we stay focused on measuring outcomes and not *outputs*. There can be a temptation to take activity undertaken as part of service delivery (an output) as an outcome measure. An example of using an output as an outcome measure might be taking the number of programme sessions delivered to young people as an indication of success. While this is tempting, the problem lies in trying to use something as a measure which is based on service priorities rather than the safety of the young people affected.	In the course of doing this work, we had to keep defining and redefining the parameters of what we were trying to do. One of the strongest pulls was towards using safeguarding activity (that is, the number of young people who have attended a programme) as a measure of the work, rather than a goal of the work (that is, that young people are now safer in the area). We also grappled with how to measure some of the aspects of CS which focus on the activity of adults (that is, guardians) or services (that is, changing policies). If increasing guardianship was a goal of the work, and there was evidence of a shift in the availability of trusted adults in a context, was this a measure of the work? We realised that it was hard to know if a context was indeed safer and that having measures on all three sides of the triangle combined (what young people say, increase in guardianship and observable changes in an environment) would be the most sensible way to go.
Refining and reflecting using the context assessment triangles	Our work has shown that in the context of innovation, there can be a temptation to overly focus on practice activity as the measure of CS success. This is particularly the case if the activity is new and there	Given, then, how challenging this is, we also realised that the framework we were developing could not address whether CS 'worked' in the sense of evaluating the wider approach and neither

Refining and reflecting using the context assessment triangles	is a wish to celebrate the success of something which extends practice as usual. The important thing is to have a rigorous and critical approach which keeps returning to the question of whether the measure can indicate improved safety for young people. This is a refining process that requires reflection and collaboration, as discussed. Measures need to reflect a combined focus on a) the experience of young people, b) guardianship capacity and c) changes in the environment.	could it disaggregate within a contextual piece of work what exactly had made the difference. The possibilities for this new framework lay in building on the assessment and response skills that the Swansea team had developed and to orientate those towards measuring outcomes. For example, where a survey with young people had been used to assess safety in a school, it would then be possible to return to that school with a modified survey to find out if changes had taken place. This could then be thought about alongside changes made to the guardianship and observable changes in the environment to build a strong picture of improvements in the context, acknowledging that it is always a changing picture and there will be many more things going on that cannot be measured in terms of the changes we want to bring about.

Conclusions

Where do we go from here? One of the things that has become apparent through the Scale-Up Project is that measuring outcomes is a pivotal part of the project, but it remains underdeveloped. As with every aspect of practice development in creating CS (for example, developing context assessment tools), developing outcomes measures is a slow, iterative and collaborative process that is messy and requires relationships where there is the ability for critical reflection. It has taken us until now to understand what we don't know about outcomes. Where we have reached is having a clear vision for a process for doing so that follows the method of the Scale-Up. This involves piloting, refining, testing and re-refining. We have learnt that the imminent focus is on having a robust set of categories to guide us in setting outcome measures for specific cases. Working through this process will allow us to interrogate the range of measures that can be drawn upon in an outcomes framework. We want to stay close to practice and the values of CS with an awareness that there are a lot of pitfalls that we want to avoid. Several challenges remain in the structures of children's safeguarding systems which are not unique to CS but are implicated in this outcomes work. We note a number of these here.

Firstly, we don't yet know enough about effective responses for contexts in order to be able to measure their outcomes in the first place. We've made significant moves in this area over the last three years, as will be shown in Chapter 13, but questions such as how to intervene in the dynamics of peer groups or tackling the normalisation of sexual harm in schools require further exploration, not to mention the systemic and structural causes of harm which we have seen throughout this book.

Secondly, the terrain of what is encompassed within 'extra-familial harm' is very broad: from online abuse and criminal exploitation to group-based self-harm and sexual harassment. Likewise, as we explored in this chapter, the questions of, 'what is a safe peer group?' and 'whose assessment of risk counts?' are complex. This is why we rely on a triangulated approach that draws on young people's safety, guardianship and environment and community features. There is work to be done to understand the social conditions of various harm types – both in terms of what they have in common and how they differ. It is important that, as contextual assessments and outcomes frameworks develop, they reflect the available evidence on the conditions that facilitate different forms of harm to support a nuanced and sophisticated approach to what is meant by changing the social conditions of harm.

Thirdly, to do this work well, we need to create the environments and structures that acknowledge, value and facilitate adults engaging with young people. Speaking and talking with young people is essential. There are no shortcuts for this. This challenge is not unique to CS, but it provides us with a point in time to consider how we bring in young people's voices into all parts of the child protection system.

Fourthly, commissioning and funding arrangements for responses still narrowly focus on individual behaviours and shape service delivery. Until those that fund the work are oriented towards funding a system that targets the social conditions of abuse and take a reasonable and proportionate approach to reporting on this, given how new this practice is, this work will be limited.

Fifthly, the current lens of inspection frameworks remains focused on individuals. While there is some movement towards considering contexts within inspection frameworks, the impact inspection has in creating a climate of anxiety (Hood and Goldacre, 2021) means that the kind of nuanced innovation we advocate for is very hard to sustain. In many places, the pressure to perform often outweighs the creativity and risk taking that is required of this work. Joint to this are other challenges that are not unique to this issue but definitely effect its ongoing progress, such as how current data management systems are focused on individual young people, and reporting requirements for funders and inspectors reflect this.

Finally, in ending, we want to caution a word of warning. While we have argued that outcome measures are vitally important to the development of CS, we also note that there are dangers inherent in taking this forward. These are around the reductionist approach that can infiltrate this type of work. Relationships are fluid and multiple-faceted. They should not be measured or deployed instrumentally or mechanistically. With this in mind, we need therefore to acknowledge that measuring outcomes within the terrain is not an exact science. While we can make strides towards clarifying outcomes, as we do this, we need to make space for, and value, the messy, iterative and complex nature of life that is reflected in this work.

12

Counting children and chip shops: dilemmas and challenges in evaluating the impact of Contextual Safeguarding

Michelle Lefevre, Paula Skidmore and Carlene Firmin

Introduction

As has been explained in Chapter 11, whereas conventional safeguarding responses are centred on individual young people experiencing extra-familial risks, and their families, CS approaches seek to harness the potential of social care practice and systems to target additionally the social conditions and associated contexts where EFH occurs. Lloyd and Owens in Chapter 11 have outlined the extended set of outcomes that this innovative approach aims to achieve. We move now in this chapter to consider how organisations and safeguarding networks might measure the different kinds of impact produced by systems designed on CS principles. In particular, we explore how research and evaluation needs to not only ascertain the service experiences and outcomes for individual children considered to be at risk (what CS terms Level 1 professional responses – see Introduction), but whether risky extra-familial contexts themselves become any safer as a result of Level 2 responses.

One example of this would be where two young people were approached and groomed for exploitation when hanging around outside their local chip shop. Measures would be needed not only of whether the safety of these two young people individually had been enhanced through professional intervention but of whether the chip shop and its surroundings had become a safer environment as a result of the CS approach. The impact of the latter is potentially much further reaching, as safety might be created around multiple young people socialising in that setting, and over an extended time period. Effective evaluation, as a result, must cover the impact of both levels of CS response.

To explore the implications of this, we draw on three separate studies that we (the three chapter authors) have previously conducted, which took rather different approaches. We discuss the reasons for taking the particular approach on each occasion, some of the complexities encountered and what insights the work offers for what is both *possible* and *meaningful* to measure when researching the impact of CS systems.

Starting from scratch: evaluating a whole-system change

CS began as a theory – a hypothesis based on the research of Firmin et al (2016) that had revealed how professional responses to harms such as exploitation during adolescence needed to recognise and address the peer and environmental risks and relationships that lay beyond the family and home. Their proposal that CS theory could act as the basis for development of a new, complementary safeguarding system, which moved beyond individualised solutions, captured the imagination of Hackney Children and Families Services. Hackney's successful bid in 2017 to the Department for Education's Children's Social Care Innovation Programme, in partnership with a range of local agencies and community stakeholders across the borough, plus Firmin and her colleagues, led to the development and pilot of a full-scale CS system.

Two waves of independent evaluation were also funded by the Department for Education, which set the parameters for what was to be studied and measured. As evaluators, we needed to employ a diverse and extensive range of methods and tools to cover the priorities of both the funder (child-level outcomes and cost-effectiveness) and the local authority (the feasibility of a new CS system for responding to extra-familial risks safely and efficiently). As the Hackney pilot was the first time that CS had been concretised, the initial programme of work included substantial design and experimentation regarding systems, tools and procedures as the theory was interpreted for the specific conditions and needs within that borough.

Embedded action research internal to Hackney was ongoing through this period to identify system requirements and provide iterative feedback on whether structures and tools were fit for purpose. While the embedded researcher tracked and supported the development of the new system, our focus as external evaluators was on whether there was any *impact* on practice and, if so, what *role* the new system components played in this. For example, did the new IT system automatically prompt staff to consider and record risks posed by a group of young people, or connected to a specific environment? Did the new tools guide practitioners to conduct rigorous assessments of a peer group, gang or location in a consistent way, just as they would when there were concerns about an individual child or young person?

Such aspects of our external evaluation primarily concerned 'process change' – necessary shifts in organisational and interagency policies, procedures, cultures, skills and practices as a service moves from one kind of configuration to another (Young Foundation, 2012). Process change is an integral component of an innovation project's 'theory of change', representing some of the steps which take a new practice model or service from hypothesis to development to change to impact. The theory of change underpinning the evaluation of the Hackney pilot is set out in Figure 12.1. This illuminates how a range of measures is necessary to indicate whether and how the necessary processes are in place that will result in staff having the self-efficacy and capabilities to respond effectively and ethically, such that young people, families and communities feel the difference, and that there is an objectively demonstrable improvement in outcomes for young people.

Surveys and interviews enabled us to identify how confident practitioners felt in working with risks beyond the home and whether/how they thought it was changing their practice. Analysis of case file assessments, plans and reports enabled us to track whether extra-familial risks were starting to be routinely recognised, assessed, planned for and recorded, and whether documentation reflected a more sophisticated and child-centred understanding of young people's agency and rights. Such measures told us about both the level to which the new system was embedded *and* about the kind of impact this was having on practice.

The project's theory of change assumed that such improvements in practice would enhance young people's and parents' experience of being involved with children's social care and, ultimately, that there would be improvements in the extent to which young people *felt* and *were* safer in respect of risks beyond the home. The funder's interests were concentrated here: was there clear evidence that the new CS system had had a discernible impact on safety and welfare outcomes for young people (if compared with the previous approach and with systems in other comparable local authorities)?

Given that CS seeks to improve service experiences and outcomes not just for young people at highest risk involved with children's social care (Level 1 CS) but young people more widely in community 'hotspots' of extra-familial risk (Level 2), we needed to hear from across both groups. In addition to aiming to interview young people subject to child protection plans, and their parents, we conducted focus groups with young people in schools and youth clubs to learn about their experiences of risk and community safety in the area. We completed standardised measures with young people in schools to learn whether there had been changes in their wellbeing, coping and sense of community integration and safety following CS community interventions. Quantitative analysis was undertaken of the statutory data returns (Child in Need Census and SSDA 903 data) that every local authority provides to the Department for Education, comparing Hackney's administrative data before and after CS with three other local authorities', to ascertain whether there were appreciable differences in service response and child-level outcomes when CS was not in operation. We also captured comparable data in another local authority to provide some insight into how risk and safety were experienced similarly or differently there.

By the end of the first wave of funding in 2020, our evaluation was able to identify that substantial progress had been made in designing and

Counting children and chip shops

Figure 12.1: The theory of change for Contextual Safeguarding in Hackney

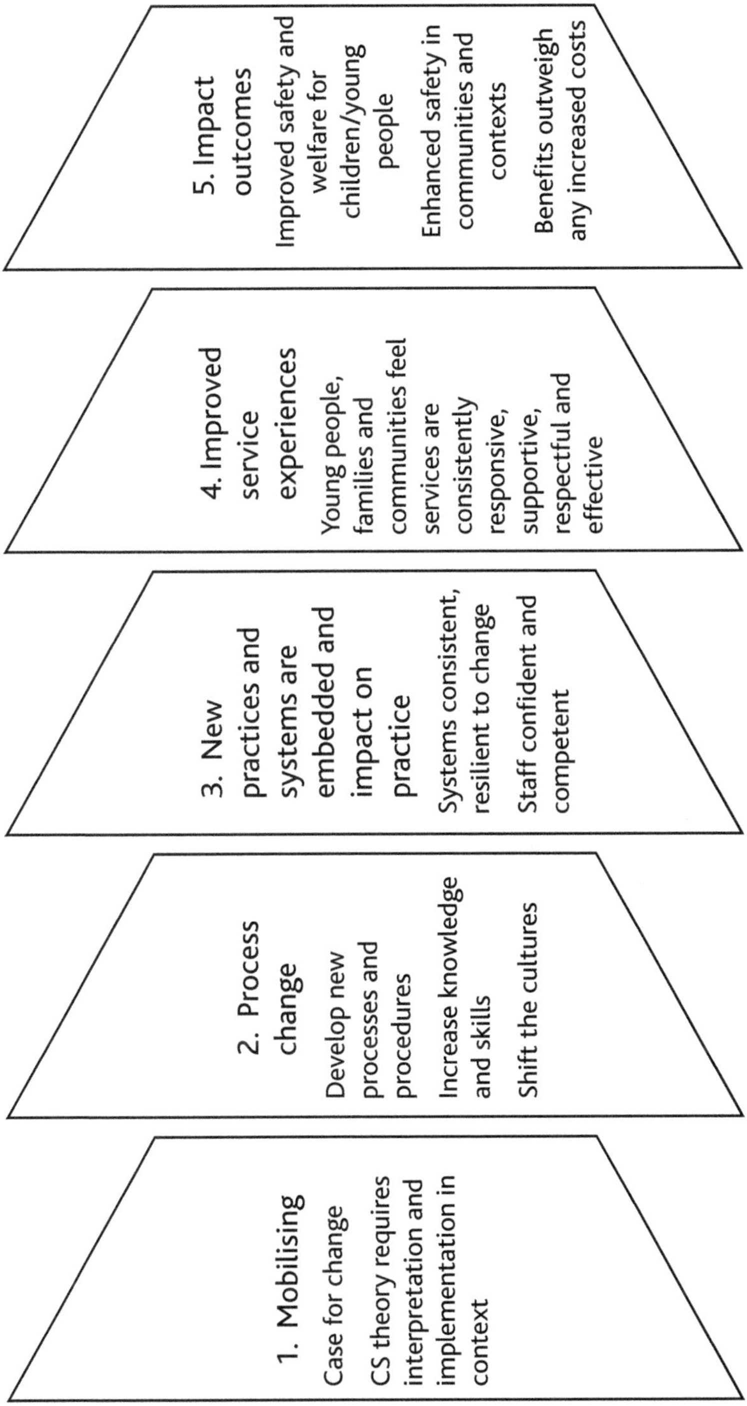

1. Mobilising
Case for change
CS theory requires interpretation and implementation in context

2. Process change
Develop new processes and procedures
Increase knowledge and skills
Shift the cultures

3. New practices and systems are embedded and impact on practice
Systems consistent, resilient to change
Staff confident and competent

4. Improved service experiences
Young people, families and communities feel services are consistently responsive, supportive, respectful and effective

5. Impact outcomes
Improved safety and welfare for children/young people
Enhanced safety in communities and contexts
Benefits outweigh any increased costs

163

implementing a feasible safeguarding system focused around extra-familial risk that complemented the existing and ongoing system for working with harm within the family home. However, while we could see that CS had the potential to positively influence practice, demonstrable improvements in neither service experiences nor outcomes were yet apparent. Drawing on our Theory of Change, we would suggest that, at least in part, this was because the new system was not yet embedded. Aspects were still under design, and new processes not yet uniformly in place; hence, young people and families were not yet consistently on the receiving end of new service processes. Our conclusion was that unrealistic funder timescales meant we were looking for observable evidence of positive effect too soon.

Additionally, seeking objective impact outcomes from a programme of change focused primarily on design and implementation may not be the right approach. Quantitative system pattern and outcome data may provide broad insights into the progress of referrals and interventions with children who have had particular experiences or services, but these are often limited by data error and bias, so patterns in data cannot be readily interpreted. For example, clear differences could be noted in recording practices within Hackney over time, and between Hackney and comparator local authorities, including regarding how risks were classified. Any decrease over time in the numbers of young people on protection plans due to exploitation might not reflect enhanced safety for young people, but rather be an artefact of how risks were categorised or recorded differently within IT systems, or reflect professional inadequacies within the interagency system regarding identifying or responding to young people at risk. For example, an improved or superior system might potentially put *more* young people on protection plans.

Conversely, although increased numbers of protection plans in a local authority over time might reflect how the service had become better at working with extra-familial risk, they might alternatively or additionally be indicating higher levels of EFH in that area. For example, during this evaluation, the prevalence of serious youth violence, particularly knife crime, rose in Hackney. Here, the benefits of looking at what is happening in comparable local authorities comes to the fore: we were able to identify that there were similar trends across other London boroughs. We were then able to speculate as to whether wider factors such as poverty, social inequalities and policies of austerity were playing a role in these trends.

The question of whether CS offers value for money is now being considered in the latter stages of our second wave of evaluation. The funder is keen to know if the new CS system costs more than what went before, and whether such costs can be justified because of the benefits it brings. It can be anticipated that there are likely to be higher costs, as Hackney is doing more than it did pre-CS to address extra-familial risk. However, it will be tricky to determine how much of the increased costs relate specifically to the introduction of

CS, and what stems simply from dealing with the ever-escalating nature of emergent extra-familial risks such as 'County Lines'. We aim to gain some insight into this by comparing data with other comparable local authorities which do not utilise CS but do still work to address extra-familial risk.

If we find that CS is more expensive than alternative systems, then it will be important to establish whether and how such costs can be justified on the grounds of value for money. Clear justification could be provided if there were tangible impact outcomes, for example, with reductions in young people involved in criminal or sexual exploitation. Even without such evidence, an ethical argument might still be built if young people and their parents are able to tell us that they feel safer in Hackney and/or that they feel helped, supported and respected when involved with children's social care and related organisations. It might be difficult, if not impossible, for a clear linkage to be drawn between such positive service experiences and the future absence of, for example, adverse mental health or involvement in criminality, but a robust theory of change could be able to make a persuasive case of benefit that would justify the scaling and spreading of CS.

Examining system capabilities not individuals

As explained in the introductory chapter of this book, from 2019 to 2022, funding from the National Lottery Community Fund was used to test the embedding of CS in five local authorities (test sites) in England and Wales: Bristol, Kent, Knowsley, Swansea and Wiltshire (testing also took place in four London boroughs). The project was divided into three phases.

The first phase examined how test sites were responding to EFH and identified elements of the sites' systems that required revision to better align with the CS framework. During the second phase, sites piloted elements of the proposed system change and reflected on whether it was feasible to scale and sustain that change. The third and final phase involved developing and implementing a plan to embed lessons from the pilot phase, and therefore the CS framework, into the sites' systems.

As detailed in various parts of this book (Chapters 4, 5 and 10), data were collected during each phase using a range of embedded and qualitative research methods. The ways that practitioners and managers framed and responded to EFH were evidenced through observations of professionals' meetings, reviews of young people's case files and analysis of completed assessments and plans for groups and contexts. Professional reflections on each phase were gathered through both focus groups and interviews, as well as regular meetings with each site's single point of contact with whom researchers worked to co-produce action plans. Researchers also captured strategic developments in each site through ongoing analysis of the local policies and procedures that scaffolded the developing local response.

Contextual Safeguarding

Figure 12.2: System review red, amber, green rating tool for Domain 1

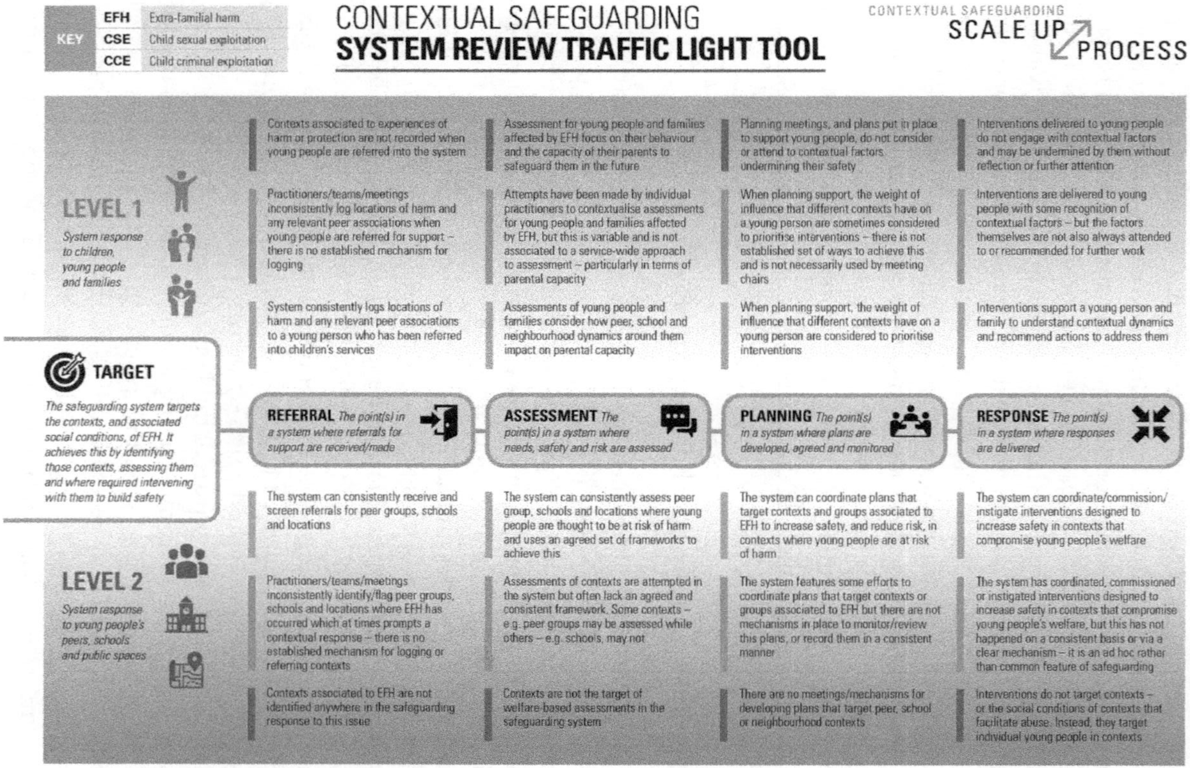

CONTEXTUAL SAFEGUARDING
SYSTEM REVIEW TRAFFIC LIGHT TOOL

CONTEXTUAL SAFEGUARDING
SCALE UP PROCESS

KEY
- EFH — Extra-Familial harm
- CSE — Child sexual exploitation
- CCE — Child criminal exploitation

TARGET
The safeguarding system targets the contexts, and associated social conditions, of EFH. It achieves this by identifying those contexts, assessing them and where required intervening with them to build safety

LEVEL 1
System response to children, young people and families

LEVEL 2
System response to young people's peers, schools and public spaces

---

REFERRAL The point(s) in a system where referrals for support are received/made

- Contexts associated to experiences of harm or protection are not recorded when young people are referred into the system
- Practitioners/teams/meetings inconsistently log locations of harm and any relevant peer associations when young people are referred for support — there is no established mechanism for logging
- System consistently logs locations of harm and any relevant peer associations to a young person who has been referred into children's services

- The system can consistently receive and screen referrals for peer groups, schools and locations
- Practitioners/teams/meetings inconsistently identify/flag peer groups, schools and locations where EFH has occurred, which at times prompts a contextual response — there is no established mechanism for logging or referring contacts
- Contacts associated to EFH are not identified anywhere in the safeguarding response to this issue

---

ASSESSMENT The point(s) in a system where needs, safety and risk are assessed

- Assessment for young people and families affected by EFH focus on their behaviour and the capacity of their parents to safeguard them in the future
- Attempts have been made by individual practitioners to contextualise assessments for young people and families affected by EFH, but this is variable and is not associated to a service-wide approach to assessment — particularly in terms of parental capacity
- Assessments of young people and families consider how peer, school and neighbourhood dynamics impact on parental capacity

- The system can consistently assess peer group, schools and locations where young people are thought to be at risk of harm and uses an agreed set of frameworks to achieve this
- Assessments of contexts are attempted in the system but often lack an agreed and consistent framework. Some contexts — e.g. peer groups may be assessed while others — e.g. schools, may not
- Contexts are not the target of welfare-based assessments in the safeguarding system

---

PLANNING The point(s) in a system where plans are developed, agreed and monitored

- Planning meetings, and plans put in place to support young people, do not consider or attend to contextual factors undermining their safety
- When planning support, the weight of influence that different contexts have on a young person are sometimes considered to prioritise interventions — there is not established set of ways to achieve this and is not necessarily used by meeting chairs
- When planning support, the weight of influence that different contexts have on a young person are considered to prioritise interventions

- The system can coordinate plans that target contexts and groups associated to EFH to increase safety, and reduce risk, in contexts where young people are at risk of harm
- The system features some efforts to coordinate plans that target contexts or groups associated to EFH but there are not mechanisms in place to monitor/review this plane, or record them in a consistent manner
- There are no meetings/mechanisms for developing plans that target peer, school or neighbourhood contexts

---

RESPONSE The point(s) in a system where responses are delivered

- Interventions delivered to young people do not engage with contextual factors and may be undermined by them without reflection or further attention
- Interventions are delivered to young people with some recognition of contextual factors — but the factors themselves are not also always attended to or recommended for further work
- Interventions support a young person and family to understand contextual dynamics and recommend actions to address them

- The system can coordinate/commission/ instigate interventions designed to increase safety in contexts that compromise young people's welfare
- The system has coordinated or instigated interventions designed to increase safety in contexts that compromise young people's welfare, but this has not happened on a consistent basis or via a clear mechanism — it is an ad hoc rather than common feature of safeguarding
- Interventions do not target contexts — or the social conditions of contexts that facilitate abuse. Instead, they target individual young people in contexts

166

As sites moved from one phase to the next, a 'system review' exercise was undertaken. System reviews were facilitated by the project lead and tracked each site's progress. Prior to each system review, data collected over the preceding phase was drawn together by the research team and plotted against an assessment framework comprised of the following intersecting factors:

- two levels of implementation: the site's response to young people affected by EFH (Level 1), and their response to contexts associated with EFH (Level 2);
- the four domains of the CS framework: the site's ability to target the social conditions (and associated contexts) of EFH (Domain 1), through the lens of child protection and child welfare (as opposed to Community Safety) (Domain 2), in partnership with those who can create safety in those contexts (Domain 3) and measuring its impact contextually (Domain 4); and
- four points of local safeguarding systems: where young people/contexts are referred for support (1); assessed (2); have support plans developed (3); are responded to (4).

Researchers worked to 'RAG rate' (red, amber, green) the site's performance in this intersecting framework, asking whether, based on the data collected, each part of the site's system was:

- yet to evidence any progress towards alignment with CS (Red);
- making progress towards CS, but was inconsistent (Amber); and
- fully aligned with an identified CS (Green).

Figure 12.2 shows the section of the RAG rating tool applied to Domain 1 of the CS framework. For each part of the system, and at both Levels 1 and 2, the research team could consider whether the data collected suggested the site was performing at Red (the description furthest away from the central point of each domain), Amber (the description in the middle of the three levels from the central point of each domain) or Green (the description closest to the central point for each domain) in their ability to target the social conditions of EFH.

The Case study illustrates how this tool might be used to assess the alignment of a site's approach to referrals for young people and contexts affected by EFH.

Case study

A young person, aged 15, is referred to children's social care due to concerns about them being sexually exploited in their local area.

At the point this young person is referred into the system:

- the contexts (a park and high street) where they are being exploited are recorded and considered (Level 1, Domain 1 – aligned);
- a child welfare lens is adopted and professionals consider whether they are at risk of significant harm (Level 1, Domain 2 – aligned);
- they were referred for support by their school, who was contacted by staff at the local park who were concerned about her welfare (Level 1, Domain 3 – aligned);
- contextual concerns about safety of young people in the park and the high street nearby are recorded – paperwork used to record referrals has been amended to accommodate this; this enables practitioners to revisit contextual factors later in the process of support and see if the park or high street is any safer as a result of the response offered (Level 1, Domain 4 – aligned).

When professionals in the site attempt to make a referral about the park and high street where this young person is being exploited:

- a form and process has been created to accept referrals for these contexts (Level 2, Domain 1 – aligned);
- referrals about the park and high street to date have largely been made to police and Community Safety partners following complaints related to crime and ASB rather than to social care (Level 2, Domain 2 – not aligned);
- criminal justice partners currently dominate referrals for the park and high street – there has been minimal engagement with young people and residents who use those spaces (Level 2, Domain 3 – not aligned);
- concerns about the park and high street are currently based on data related to ASB, and so the system is more likely to measure a reduction in crime in these contexts – rather than as an increase in young people's safety (Level 2, Domain 4 – not aligned).

In this example, the site's approach to receiving referrals about EFH is largely aligned with the CS framework when responding to young people affected – but less aligned for contexts where those young people come to harm.

The results of the initial RAG rating exercise were shared with site representatives at system reviews, where they offered reflections on the results and filled in any gaps. Researchers then used this input to make a final assessment of that site's performance against the CS framework at that point in the project. Tables 12.1 and 12.2 illustrate the RAG rating for one of the Scale-Up sites at the point of the first system review (post the initial review of the site's response to EFH in 2019), and at the point of the second system review (post the pilots in 2021).

The system review method enabled researchers to track site progress at a macro level. Micro-level data was required to achieve this. The data set featured detailed knowledge that was essential for evidencing site

Table 12.1: Red, amber or green rating of Site X in 2019

	Referral	Assessment	Planning	Response
Domain 1	Red	Amber	Amber	Amber
Domain 2	Red	Red	Amber	Amber
Domain 3	Red	Red	Red	Amber
Domain 4	Red	Red	Red	Red

Table 12.2: Red, amber or green rating of Site X in 2021

	Referral	Assessment	Planning	Response
Domain 1	Green	Green	Amber	Amber
Domain 2	Green	Green	Green	Green
Domain 3	Green	Green	Green	Green
Domain 4	Green	Green	Amber	Amber

performance, for example, language used in Child and Family Assessments or the approaches recorded in numerous observations of professionals' meetings where plans were being agreed. Researchers pulled these individual pieces of data together (micro evidence) into a system review framework to offer a macro framework analysis of the *system capability* for each site. In respect of Site X previously mentioned in 2019, for example, no aspect of their approach to referrals was aligned with the CS framework. By 2021, the data collected by the research team suggested that the converse was true.

System reviews didn't often surface detail about child-level, or even context-level, outcomes. Case examples were drawn upon to illustrate what the system was capable of achieving, but this was largely in terms of how it operated (not necessarily the impacts of those operations). As Chapters 11 and 13 chart, once CS has been established in a site (or at least to a degree) it is possible to begin documenting the impact of this operating model on the welfare of young people (and the contexts where they spend their time). After this point comes the question of scaling those impacts into a reportable fashion that can be collected at a population level.

None of this is achieved, or sought, by the system review method. Instead, system reviews have been employed to ask whether the service attempting to embed a CS approach appears to have achieved this – in respect of individual children, peer groups and other contexts of concern. If it wanted to, could it tell us the numbers of children and specific contexts that have been referred into the system due to EFH? Is it capable of assessing the needs of those children and contexts, developing a plan to create safety for each and mounting a response to individuals, groups and spaces that aligns with the principles of the CS framework?

While such questions appear somewhat distanced for child-level outcomes, they are arguably critical for thoroughly assessing the value of a system change exercise. As was noted with the Hackney evaluation discussed earlier, it is imperative to establish whether CS has been embedded in a system before the efficacy of that system (and therefore CS) can be examined. This is because CS changes an entire system – it isn't an appendage to an existing one. If we look at the child-level outcomes of a system, and we don't understand the capabilities of the system that has produced those outcomes, then we can't truly evaluate the efficacy of the approach that has been taken. If those working in a system say they are adopting a CS approach – and this is not questioned or examined – how does one know whether the outcomes produced by that system can be attributed to CS? As CS is an approach and not a model, some may think they are adopting it when they are not; and, as such, good or poor outcomes for children may be ascribed to CS when actually the system that has produced those outcomes is not aligned with CS at all.

The system review method offers us a way of establishing where a service/organisation has reached in its efforts to embed CS; outcomes of children and contexts can then be assessed in light of this progress. If this baseline isn't established, it may be difficult to ascertain whether the outcomes being surfaced are in any way attributable to the use (or absence) of the CS framework. In turn, this makes it difficult to evaluate the opportunities or risks that come with embedding CS into social care systems.

Measuring safety in contexts

From 2019 to 2021, a youth justice service based in the north of England implemented a pilot project within its prevention service which sought to identify and explore the relevance of adopting CS approaches to address serious youth violence. The pilot project delivery was led by a small team of staff from the youth justice service that included case workers, youth support workers and peer mentors, and was supported by a manager. An embedded researcher from the CS team worked to support the pilot implementation. This mirrored an approach that was already underway in a youth justice service in the south of England, where an embedded researcher spent time 'on the ground' with practitioners to help support the identification of CS in their service delivery. In several respects, therefore, this project was markedly different from the two outlined previously, both in scale and approach to a theory of change: it was based on the work of one small professional criminal justice team within a larger statutory youth justice service, it only involved one researcher and it was attempting to primarily support the first two steps of the Theory of Change model in Figure 12.1 – 'mobilising' and 'process change'. It was hoped that the project might be able to build towards the third step of 'embedded practice' and 'impact of practice' but, at the outset, the capacity to realise this was largely unclear.

The north of England service was attempting to work across numerous settings in order to develop preventive work around serious youth violence, a problem that had already been identified within the local district/area. The service offer was framed around the following key contexts:

- community/neighbourhoods;
- schools;
- young people/families; and
- peer groups.

Specific interventions were devised and implemented by the staff team and the embedded researcher role was to observe key staff meetings, multi-agency meetings and delivery activities in schools/communities; assess key documents; and work flexibly with the staff team to identify potentially useful tools to support any CS approaches being adopted. The embedded research work started six months into the delivery of the pilot, so work in one school and one community/neighbourhood had already commenced and was designed by the team, using information taken from the CS Network (a bespoke website of materials for practitioners to support development of contextual approaches).

By the end of year one of the pilot, the delivery in the one community/neighbourhood setting appeared to have worked well – the team were operating a weekly youth 'pop-up' provision on a Friday evening, primarily based around a sports provision, with opportunity for onward referral to additional sports activities. The model the team had used was clear: it identified and engaged key professional partners/other services; it was helping to build stronger guardianship with local business/other services in a location of identified need; young people had engaged and had been supported via the 'pop-up' who would otherwise not have been seen or provided with support; tentative work had commenced with peer groups through the pop-up, by staff and peer mentors. Alongside the delivery in the community/schools, the team had continued, through a case work model, to develop support and advocacy with individual young people and families already known to the youth justice service. This intervention was an area where the staff team struggled to initially see how they could 'do' CS through that delivery, so it was an area identified for development in year two.

The start of year two of the pilot involved the team working to more substantively and clearly develop some key elements of CS within their work, alongside the researcher. A second community location had been identified using the same model as for the first and this was supplemented with additional community-based activity by the team to identify potential needs and ways to promote local guardianship. This included 'on-the-ground' mapping work and observations in the locality, speaking with local businesses and other public services to build a picture of safeguarding needs and potential intervention 'hotspots'. In this way, the learning from year one was strongly utilised in the further development of community-based contextual work by the team.

Schools were one area of work by the team where a different approach was needed. As the development of the work in the first secondary school setting in year one had been less successful overall, the researcher had worked with the staff team to try and identify the reasons for this, in order to approach the second school location differently. It emerged that, in the first school setting, the school management had been resistant to enabling a 'whole-school' contextual safety audit to take place and, specifically, did not enable youth justice staff to access the 'behaviour logs' as a starting point for this. Instead, the school itself had identified individual children/young people, who were then 'referred' for a contextual assessment with youth justice staff. With this approach, the school management had viewed the pilot more as a 'targeted intervention' to be carried out as part of an overall school behaviour policy, primarily within the on-site alternative provision unit, rather than to scrutinise the dynamics of the school's approach to students' behaviour as being a significant context in and of itself.

The work in school settings was subsequently reviewed and conclusions reached about how to develop a different approach within an alternative secondary setting, as well as potential early engagement with a primary school. In particular, the work of the youth justice team was framed very differently from the start in the second secondary school location, to avoid these previous problems. In year two, then, it became possible to build and implement a contextual safety audit in the second school, albeit with some significant COVID-related restrictions. In this way, the team successfully overcame the difficulties they had encountered in the first school setting and were able to bring a clearer CS approach into building their direct work with the second school location.

By the start of year two, the youth justice team had completed some useful and interesting work that showed the potential of adopting a 'contextual lens' within their 'usual' prevention model of '1-2-1' intervention work with young people. The team was beginning to frame its thinking differently – moving away from seeing themselves simply as individual professionals who, for example, managed a caseload of young people to be worked with on prevention of youth violence, or went into a school to deliver sessions about knife crime. Supported by the embedded researcher, the team had instead begun to identify how they could draw on some of the specific ideas from

CS to actively effect change in a place/location (alongside multi-agency partners) and potentially with a whole group of young people – and how they could do this *as an interconnected team*, not just as individual professionals. It was at this point the whole team began to grasp the required shift in focus; within one team meeting, a professional commented, "so, you want us to count the chip shops, not just the children?", as a way to identify the possible impact of the community-focused CS work.

Although this approach subsequently brought some challenges – notably, how to monitor and represent the impact and outcome of the on-the-ground intervention with a 'chip shop' and not just 'the child' – the team were becoming clearer about the necessity and value of a shift in practice. Sadly, it was at exactly this point that the effect of the COVID-related shutdown in the UK was felt very strongly within the pilot work and almost all key aspects of the direct delivery were halted, especially community and school settings as well as direct work with groups of young people.

Conclusions: What is possible *and* meaningful to measure?

The title of this chapter raises the question of what can, or should, be quantified and measured when evaluating the potential effects of a CS system. The three studies described earlier took very different approaches to scrutinising how different aspects of new interagency systems and interventions had improved practice, enhanced the service experiences of children and families, addressed contexts of concern and increased safety for young people. Collectively, they highlight a number of potential benefits and limitations regarding the kinds of data that might be collected to measure impact, and challenges for the interpretation of this data in future evaluation of CS.

A clear Theory of Change (ToC) is beneficial to establish at the outset of CS system implementations and associated evaluations, as a ToC requires the mapping of the mechanisms by which changes are expected to occur within a specific context – and the CS framework will *always* require a bespoke tailoring for an area's unique geography, culture, challenges and resources. The ToC not only directs subsequent planning but enables the stages of implementation to be tracked and orients evaluators towards data that might establish whether process change, intermediate goals and end outcomes have been achieved. The question of attribution is central in any evaluation: what level of confidence can there be that a new CS system is responsible for any documented effects rather than other external factors (Mayne, 2008)? Hypothesising what the data might indicate had the new CS system not been implemented ('judging the counterfactual') is also central to this contribution story and comparisons with data in sites without a CS system could be invaluable here (Preston et al, 2021: 239).

Of course, it is essential to establish whether a CS system has been properly embedded before it can be known whether and how a new approach has improved outcomes. This requires a detailed review of system capabilities and resources and analysis of whether staff are confident in operating CS principles and practices throughout the service, and at its interface with partner agencies – such as via the method described in this chapter. Unless and until a service is fully embedded, any data on impact are meaningless. However, learning from the two rounds of funding from the Children's Social Care Innovation Programme (Sebba et al, 2017; McCracken and FitzSimons, 2020) suggests that the kind of transformation in social care systems and operations that CS demands take a long time to design and implement, let alone embed. Perhaps evidence of impact should not be expected until at least three to five years after a new CS system is consistently operating as 'business as usual' (Preston et al, 2021)?

Such extended timelines will, of course, have implications for project plans and timelines, and may contravene commissioners' expectations. In our experience, funders are often extremely reluctant to extend deadlines, despite compelling arguments regarding why implementation needs to take longer than initially envisaged. In respect of the ongoing follow-up evaluation in Hackney, the initial reluctance to extend to what we felt was a meaningful research timescale was communicated to us as the necessity for government to roll out promising new approaches as quickly as possible, for the benefit of services and families. The potential value that might then accrue from a truncated timeline is easy to appreciate, but there are, of course, risks in implementing a new approach whose design has not yet been decisively tested and in the absence of evidence for its efficacy (Seddon, 2008).

Finally, these three studies indicate that approaches to research and evaluation must themselves move beyond conventional measures. The challenge is not only whether a particular service is able to capture certain kinds of data but whether that data can meaningfully offer insight into the central questions posed by an evaluation. It is clear from our analysis in this chapter that both individual children and contexts such as peer groups, schools and chip shops *count* (matter) and should *be counted* (enumerated) to measure changes in places, groups, communities and other contexts, as well as improvements in the safety and wellbeing of individual young people experiencing EFH.

13

Gather round: stories that expand the possibilities of Contextual Safeguarding practice

Rachael Owens

'But what do we do next?' It had become something of a CS 'sixty-four-thousand-dollar question'. I was a practice development manager with the recently formed CS team in Hackney, and I'd been invited into a meeting to think through the implications of a social work assessment. As we talked, it became clear that for the young person we were there to consider, his experiences of harm outside the home were much more 'significant' than anything going on at home. This was a young person who had been excluded from school, and felt too scared to travel to the Pupil Referral Unit where he was now meant to go. In fact, for the past week, he had been too scared to leave his home because his friend had been violently attacked just outside his home and this young person thought the same would likely happen to him. The practitioner presenting the case had drawn on new prompts in the Child and Family Assessment (developed through the new CS approach) to think more broadly about the young person's life outside the home. Using this information, she drew on a flip chart paper a rough context weighting tool (a way to consider which context has the most pressing issues), which made the situation even clearer – the problem was not at home. Not only that, we realised that just working with him on his own would do nothing to change his neighbourhood, peer group and school environment – the contexts where he was experiencing harm. But what kind of social work could be done to change these contexts so that he, and his friends, could be safer? What role did youth workers have in this and was it even possible to address things like sexism, poverty, racism – the underlying structural reasons behind the issues we were discussing? These felt like huge, and at times quite overwhelming, questions. Alongside this, there were internal pressures coming from within the organisation, with senior managers wanting assurances that doing something different, and not focusing on family dynamics and parental capacity, was going to be 'worth' the extra time and cost. So what were we to do next?

That was three years ago. Up to that point, CS researchers had partnered with practitioners to create processes which, by and large, mirrored traditional safeguarding practice with families to respond to EFH. Following the idea of assessment practices, we had taken the idea of a 'home visit' within traditional family social work and thought about what this might look like in extra-familial safeguarding. This had led to us adapting resources for observing, surveying and scoping the nature of harm in community settings and producing guidance for how this information could be weighed, analysed and used to inform a safeguarding plan that targeted those contexts. But the plans themselves were yet to be fully executed. As we started on the Scale-Up Project in April 2019, the answer to the 'but what next?' question was that we thought many things were possible. We looked to the pockets of examples, mainly from VCS partners, and wondered what it would look like if we could develop and embed these within a wider child safeguarding local authority system committed to implementing CS. If you will pardon the metaphor, the challenge seemed to be how we could move from responding to harm by picking off the menu of responses already available to us to developing a completely new set of dishes. This expanded menu might include some dishes that were new twists on existing options, but we knew we also needed some completely original inventions that incorporated ingredients we had never used before. How was this to be done? We realised that from now on, while we would continue to mirror practice as usual, delivering CS responses would also require a boldness and willingness to experiment in what would likely be a somewhat messy process. Enter nine more local authority sites willing to roll up their sleeves and enter the kitchen!

Gather round

This chapter tells the story of our journey from imagining that new types of CS responses were possible to seeing them take shape, and learning about the differences they can make. This is not a chapter on evidencing outcomes, as this is covered in Chapter 11. Rather, it is about showing, and to some extent showcasing, what we have seen and now know to be possible. For myself, during this time, I moved from a practice-focused role to a research-focused role, through a secondment with the CS research team. Here, I have been privileged to work closely with managers and practitioners from local authority partner sites. As we have thought together and teased out the next steps, I have been inspired and humbled by their courage, creativity and determination to do things differently. I don't mean to sound too sentimental, and I am aware that when a story is told retrospectively, there is always a danger of editing out less-than-perfect aspects of the process. There have been many challenges, and – although we may not have felt it at the time – these have proved invaluable in sharpening our understanding of CS, and the wider organisational, legislative and cultural challenges involved in its implementation. Social care is a context that includes, on the one hand, limited resources, constant internal restructuring and a competitive service commissioning agenda. On the other hand, it involves the reality of significant inequality and structural discrimination. All of these play a very important part in understanding the limitations of CS responses to EFH and what needs to happen if we are going to do better in future. The rest of this book documents, and is heavily informed by, such critiques and challenges that have arisen over the recent years in our research of CS. But, in this chapter, the focus will not primarily be on this.

Here, rather than thinking about what could be better, I want to think about what has been possible. In doing this, I am drawing on one of the key values of CS – namely, that we are 'strengths-based'. This means we are committed to a view of young people and communities which is about building on strengths, not pathologising and risk-centred. But it also points to our commitment to a hopeful outlook in relation to what is possible within the safeguarding system and, beyond that, into communities where young people spend their time. This means that despite the enormity of the task, we remain committed to creating child protection systems that can work with communities, so that these can become places that are good for all young people and where young people are safe from harm when they are with their friends, in school and going about their day-to-day lives. We believe it's possible that these systems, rather than only looking at what parents can do better, can work with parents as partners in respectful relationships so that they no longer alienate and create stigma (as we saw in Chapter 9). These are things we have long held as possibilities, but three years on, although we still have much to learn, we are much closer to knowing what this new system and community could look like in reality and how we can get there.

I have decided to illustrate this through stories. My vision for this chapter is that it will feel less like sitting in a lecture and more like gathering round a fire, where you are inspired by what you hear and excited about what tomorrow might hold. From the myriad instances of CS practice that took part during the Scale-Up Project, I have selected five and have turned them into semi-fictionalised, anonymised accounts which exemplify the innovation that has taken place. These are based on interviews, observations and focus groups with those involved, and are presented here as stories of hopeful practice. As a research team, we are excited by what these point to about the future of CS responses to EFH and we hope that they expand your horizons too.

One step at a time

Before I begin, a word of caution. There is danger that you might read these narratives and, misunderstanding the intention, attempt to replicate what is described here as closely as possible in your area. This is not my intention. Having said that, in one very specific way, we do encourage you to follow the examples here. This is the way that each story points to the fact that a good CS response follows from a good CS assessment or thorough understanding of the context and situation. Following this principle, every response will be uniquely tailored to its situation, meaning that what happens in one place cannot be straightforwardly replicated in other places. The fact that the CS team began its work by developing assessment resources underlines the importance of giving the assessment stage due attention. We must get as clear an understanding as possible of each safeguarding problem, within its specific context and as it relates to the safety of the particular young people associated with it, if we are to launch an effective response. There are no shortcuts for this, and we make assumptions at our peril. For example, it is not enough to map out a peer group or rehearse historic 'antisocial behaviour' issues on a housing estate, and then jump from these to a response (as we saw in Chapter 5). In the Scale-Up Project, those sites who had most success with their responses were committed to a structured and robust assessment process, which enabled them to have a deep and nuanced understanding of what was going on, what they needed to do and, as we discussed in Chapter 11, some sites also thought about how they would know if they got there. It is only by doing this that we are able, in the words of the first CS domain, to *target* the context of harm.

If this seems somewhat daunting, the first example is one which demonstrates how a CS assessment and response can be fairly small in scale, and can also draw on many existing practice skills – in this case, curiosity, care, relationship building, a judicial holding of risk and tenacity.

Rob knocked on Omar's door for a third time but knew it probably wouldn't do any good. He had been trying to see Omar for weeks but whenever he went round, he was never there. Omar was 17 and so it was understandable that he would be out and about, but at the same time, Rob was worried about him: he wasn't attending college and had arrived a few months ago into the UK unaccompanied. Rob felt that it would really help if he could just see Omar and talk to him, build a connection perhaps and find out what his hopes were for his future. Omar wasn't the only young person on Rob's caseload who he was struggling to engage. There was also Sam, who was also not accessing education and Rob generally had very little idea about where he was or what he was doing. One day, on his route home, Rob spotted Omar through the window of a barber shop. He stopped in his tracks and watched for a few minutes at Omar brushing up – so, Rob thought, Omar is working in the shop – that's interesting. A few days later, he discovered that, coincidentally, Sam was also working in the same barber shop. Questions started to ping in his mind about what the meaning of this could be. Rob had heard things about nail bars sometimes being used to exploit trafficked people – was there something exploitative going on here? But he didn't panic. Rather than jump to conclusions, he decided that actually he needed to know more. The barber shop, he realised, was in many ways like a family home – a context in need of assessment and potentially a response. So, over the next few weeks, Rob visited the barber shop. Realising it might be awkward to just go in and talk safeguarding, he had his hair cut and got to know those working there in as natural a way as possible. He talked privately to the barber shop owner about his interest in understanding how he could help Omar and Sam, particularly when it came to their educational hopes and plans. Over time, Rob came several times to see Omar and Sam at the shop and to speak to the owner. The barber supported Rob's interest in providing the boys with opportunities to develop and went on to arrange formal apprenticeships at a college for them, using their work in the shop as a placement. Rob realised that the barber was a very significant community 'guardian' for both young men – offering not only educational and employment opportunities but also social and familial relations as well. So, in this way, by working with the barber as a 'non-traditional partner' and working with, rather than against, Omar and Sam's choices, Rob built cooperation, trust and understanding, and in doing this, he bolstered the safety and support available to these young people.

Keeping the main thing the main thing

The barber shop example shows us the power of keeping the CS values central to practice. Being strengths-based and having a commitment to taking on the young people's perspectives, rather than imposing his adult viewpoint – which can be full of (often mistaken) assumptions – are both exemplified here by the practitioner 'Rob'. When we look across at the responses that Scale-Up sites tried, rather than stand-out techniques or approaches, what we notice is the quality of their commitment to young people. It might seem like an obvious thing to say, but the most successful CS responses are those led by people who *like* young people! These are practitioners who are invested in engaging young people and of seeing things from their point of view. They do not see a group of young people on a street corner as a threat but as people and citizens enjoying being together. So having this as your starting point and keeping this at the centre of any safeguarding response will serve you well. Next, we have an example of another safeguarding response which, although it takes place in a very different context – with a group of young people in a park – is similarly characterised by a positive view of young people and a respect for their rights and agency.

Penny is a children's services senior manager who often walked to work through her local park. She recalled how, during the COVID-19 lockdown, although they were meant to be indoors, young people started to gather in large numbers. She knew that the police were going to be concerned about breaking lockdown rules, but she was worried about risks of a different nature in the park. Youth workers had begun to hear about young people being criminally exploited there, and that this was causing different peer groups to be in conflict with one another. This in turn also led to reports of 'antisocial behaviour' from local residents of the park. Penny and her team were adamant that moving the young people away from the park was not the answer. At the end of the day, she said, it wouldn't solve anything because we've seen it happen before – it's not effective. So Penny had a job to do – not only with the police but also the local residents – to persuade them that it was better that they work together to make the park a safer place for young people to socialise there, rather than seeking to move them on. With support from the Youth Offending Service, Penny's team worked with the PCSOs to get them behind her plan to bring detached youth workers into the park. They also made friends with the local councillors, getting an invite to a ward meeting. When Penny and her team arrived, the mood was negative and fearful. Someone suggested they should remove the shelter in the park that young people often gathered under to keep dry and warm – surely that would get rid of them? But Penny and her team spoke up. Where else could the young people go to be together, if not in the park? Did they not have as much right to be there as anyone else? Surely the answer was to protect the young people who were, after all, just our local children a bit more grown up. The fact that Penny was a resident of the park herself helped her to model for her community what it was like to take a more compassionate and neighbourly stance towards the young people, even if they weren't known to them individually and sometimes did things that were annoying or frustrating. Just as with the PCSOs, the councillor and the neighbours listened and reciprocated. A councillor came up with a compromise – to use ward funds to move the shelter further into the park to reduce the noise of young people socialising. Penny's team were then able to deliver outreach youth work in the park, and in the process of facilitating that response, she had changed the minds and attitudes of two groups of people – the police and the local residents. They had gone from seeing young people as a problem to engaging much more with them as people, individuals and groups with needs and rights.

Being on the same page

When we first spoke to Penny and her team about their work in this park, it was the detached youth work that she focused on. But, as we listened more closely to what had happened in this response, we realised that the direct work was only part of the picture. Yes, it was important to build trust and understand what was going on with the young people in order to reduce their risk of exploitation. But this in and of itself would only partly alter the context of harm. In this situation, the 'social conditions' that contributed to the continuation of risk for these young people included a hostile and unsympathetic environment where a criminal and punitive attitude dominated over one concerned with the care and welfare of young people. So we came to understand that shifting the perspective of those adults associated with the park context was just as important as any work with the young people themselves. What comes through strongly when talking to Penny is the tone she used to talk about the young people. It wasn't that she was condoning the types of behaviour that the residents were complaining about but, at the same time, she wasn't ascribing adult motives to the young people or talking about them in that way. Yes, they were sometimes a pain but they were also children and needed to be given a break. More than anything, they were not to be feared. Thinking about what this reminded me of, it struck me that Penny showed the sort of partiality – you might call it love, in its broadest, most 'professional' sense – that you see parents show towards their own children, even when they really misbehave. It felt like, at the end of the day, Penny and her team had these young people's backs – they were invested in them; they really wanted the best for them. The response that the team delivered came from this place and that is what gave their work such momentum.

For Penny and her team to act out of care and kindness towards young people was one thing, but to persuade others to do the same, when they felt they had something to lose, was another. While trying to engage wary teenagers in conversations might come with its own challenges, trying to engage wary adults also takes a very particular type of courage. In the next example, we encounter a response in a school to reflect further on how changing the 'social conditions' (the environment, culture and 'rules at play') often involves working with adults as well as young people, and not always in the most obvious or expected ways.

Tamara and Vera had been scratching their heads for a long time, wondering what to do next. They had spent the past three weeks talking to youth workers, residents, social workers, police and Community Safety, trying to learn about the risks and harms faced by a peer group of young people. The group had been referred to a local EFH panel due to exploitation and substance misuse, and Tamara and Vera had been asked to draw on their skills as Family Group Conference (FGC) coordinators to consider what the equivalent of a 'family network' might be for a peer group facing harm outside the home, and then to invite this network to a community conference. Tamara and Vera had a lot of information, but what would be the right way forward? On the piece of paper in front of her, Tamara drew circles to represent each of the contexts where these young people spent their time, overlapping the ones where there was an interplay between the contexts. Looking at the neighbourhood circle, Vera wrote down that being in their local neighbourhood for hours and hours every day increased the young people's visibility as targets and made them vulnerable to being groomed into exploitation. 'But', Tamara said, 'what about the school?' She drew a circle to overlap it with the neighbourhood circle. In it she wrote 'not attending school'. In fact, most of the young people had very part-time school arrangements but even these hadn't been consistently applied for a long time. Rather than discounting this context (after all, they didn't go there, so where was the relevance?), Tamara and Vera dug further in. Inside the school/neighbourhood crossover, Vera wrote 'what would happen if they could be engaged by school?' Tamara and Vera looked at each other and realised that, actually, part of the picture for this peer group was their exposure to exploitative adults. If their exposure could be reduced, and their educational aspirations increased, this could change things considerably. Digging in further, Tamara and Vera thought about what was preventing school from being more assertive in their engagement with these young people. One of the reasons was a breakdown in school's relationship with children's services, which had led to a stalemate with little idea of how to move forward on either side. Perhaps addressing this could be a target of the response and shift things for this peer group? Yes, but was there anything else? Tamara and Vera thought again about this peer group. They all belonged to the same minoritised ethnic group – a group who had experienced racism within the local community. Could this also be playing a part? Recounting this to us, Tamara and Vera spoke about their dawning realisation – and discomfort – when this finally became clear to them. They realised that if the response was going to really address the social conditions enabling the harm, then it would need to include thinking with the school about why the rights and needs of this particular peer group were being overlooked. This was not an easy place to be. Tamara and Vera were used to holding FGCs where conflict and strong feelings were the order of the day, but they had never before facilitated a professional conference aimed at addressing inter-professional breakdown and racism. The motivation to press onwards came, though, from the realisation that a CS response was not about changing young people but about changing the environment to make it safer. This was a pivotal moment of clarity that drove them forwards into action. So, with that in mind, Tamara and Vera invited school leaders and Early Help to a conference, held along FGC lines. The first part of the meeting focused on restoring the relationship between agencies. Everyone was invited to share, and everyone was reminded that the focus of the meeting was safeguarding this peer group. Having Tamara and Vera as neutral facilitators helped both sides to overcome the difficulties and to agree to work together. The focus then shifted to the question of why this group of young people, from this ethnic group, were not accessing school provision. Tamara and Vera asked the group to consider whether racism could be at play. This was a delicate conversation, but Tamara and Vera's skills of preparation and relationship building leading up to the conference and in the conference itself really helped to minimise an atmosphere of blame. To their great relief, the school leaders took up the invitation to reflect on their own biases and assumptions towards access for these young people. The school suggested they attend training on structural racism and being anti-racist. As a group, with renewed interagency relationships established, they agreed that the youth services, who had positive relationships with the young people, would step up their engagement with them to hopefully facilitate the young people coming back into meaningful activity and education.

Holding the complexity

Looking at the responses presented so far, it is interesting to note how they unfold. There is often an initial plan – the first response – which enables other responses to take place. In the response mentioned earlier, for example, Tamara and Vera's scoping phase led to a conference. In some ways, the conference *was* the response, but it didn't end there – it enabled a plan to emerge, which triggered other responses that were facilitated by it. The crucial thing seems to be getting the initial response oriented around the welfare needs of young people, with a curiosity for understanding how the social conditions are impacting the harm. Once this course is set, then what needs to happen can follow. This is not meant to sound simplistic – it certainly is not – and it often involves understanding and working within multiple contexts to address the interplay between them. In the next example, we consider how this plays out within an individual child protection conference, where parents are brought more explicitly into the process of developing a plan for risk and harm outside the home.

Hana chairs child protection conferences. When her manager asked her if she would chair a new type of conference, where the category 'risk outside the home' would be used to frame the harm and response, she was intrigued. For a while, Hana had felt that the usual way of talking about significant harm, where most of the actions were for parents, didn't seem to work, especially when they were talking about harm happening in places that parents never go to and couldn't influence. Hana had teenagers herself and knew first-hand that it was their friends, and the wider world, that held the most sway for them. So the idea of the new category made sense to her, but she was still unsure about how much difference it would make to the responses that came out of the conference. The young person in question was Jaden, a 16-year-old boy who lived at home with his mum and younger sister. Jaden had been attacked in public places three times by a group of young people, causing him serious injuries. He was afraid to leave the house and, after one of the attacks had taken place at college, they had asked him to stop attending as they no longer felt able to keep him safe there. Jaden's mother was extremely worried for his safety but couldn't seem to get the support she needed. It did not take long for the conference to agree that Jaden was at significant risk of physical and emotional harm and that this was due to risk outside the home. When it came to the response plan, Hana was determined to change the focus from how things usually ran, but she nevertheless felt a pang of nervousness: would she be able to challenge and steer things round if they drifted into the familiar territory of 'what more Mum could do'? Taking a deep breath and armed with a thorough assessment setting out the four things that needed targeting if Jaden was to be safeguarded, she set off. Firstly, she asked, what could they do, in the short term, to enable Jaden to spend time with his friends outside his home? In response, Jaden, his mum, two of his friends and their parents (with some coordination support from Rani, Jaden's social worker) agreed to develop a plan for Jaden to regularly spend time at his friends' houses. They would choose times and days where there would be parents nearby for support, but they also agreed that they would stay in the background as much as possible, so that it felt as close to 'normal' as possible. Alongside this, the conference also agreed that Louis, a youth worker that Jaden trusted, would do some 'safety mapping' with him. This would involve Jaden working with a map of his local area and colouring them in 'green' or 'amber' according to whether he felt safe or relatively safe. Louis would then work with Jaden to increase his safety in the amber (and red) areas – by engaging local businesses and residents as 'guardians', for example. This was also included in the child protection plan. At this point, Hana felt pleased that the focus had broadened from just what Jaden's mother could do, but what about responses over the longer term that would prevent this from happening again? What they had so far was definitely not enough on its own. So she asked the conference to turn their attention to the instigators of the harm – the young people who had assaulted Jaden. These were young people whose names has been provided to services but who had not yet been engaged in any work. The conference agreed that the best route to disrupting this harmful behaviour was for youth services to partner up in a response. Youth workers and youth offending officers would seek to build trusting relationships with these young people and their parents. The aim would be to understand their needs and help them to access services. Although this type of response might have happened in different guises before, Hana had never seen anything like this on a child protection plan. The next focus of the conference was Jaden's college. The problem was not only that it was unsafe for Jaden to go, but that the college leadership felt powerless to make it safer for him. Hana felt that this was a significant issue, affecting not just Jaden but other young people too. She suggested that the college could be referred to the team responsible for safeguarding in contexts outside the home who could support the college to run an assessment to understand and address the factors undermining safety there. She asked for the outcome of this work to be shared at the next conference with a view to Jaden being able to return to college, once changes had been made. Finally, the conference looked at Jaden's reluctance to provide the police with further information due to fear of reprisals. In response to this, Louis offered to act as a link between Jaden and a named person in the police. Jaden said he might feel more confident to share information in this way if he was kept up to date with how any of his information was being shared and acted on. To end the conference, Hana thanked Jaden and his mother for their engagement, despite their having felt let down before. She felt much more hopeful that this was a new type of plan focused on supporting Jaden and building safety in multiple contexts.

Holding the anxiety

Each of the examples so far demonstrate how small changes in relationships, attitudes, resourcing, physical spaces and policies can each lead to large changes to the safety of young people. In the previous story, creating a new category of harm opens up a range of responses that might not have happened previously and certainly not under a safeguarding plan with statutory oversite. As well as safeguarding Jaden, the new structure also enabled the conference to extend the welfare principle to the young people who instigated harm, so that, rather than receiving a punitive response, they too could be thought about within a restorative framework, as children with unmet needs within their social context. What we also see this new category facilitating is Jaden and his mother engaged as equal partners in the work. However, while they are active agents in the change process, the conference structure underlines how responsibility for safety does not sit with them but is shared and overseen within a governance structure designed to ensure the safety of all children.

For these types of responses to happen, the practitioners leading the work need to be held within a supportive and reflective organisational system. They need a leadership and multi-agency culture that is comfortable with a degree of uncertainty and open to regular reflection. Practitioners who are dealing day to day with harm to young people often hold considerable anxiety and risk. They need regular and safe supervisory spaces where this can be thought about and 'processed' – that is, where feelings can be brought into conscious awareness, acknowledged and given respectful attention. When this happens, we have seen that new and creative responses are possible. In this last example, we see how, with sufficient freedom and support, safeguarding responses can develop across boundaries and new possibilities emerge.

There are many vans that might occasionally park on Higham Road, but for those who know it, there is one van that stands out. It belongs to an outreach service for sex workers. The van is a place open to the women to come for friendly conversation and a warm drink in the course of a night – a place of safety and support. Kat, who runs the service, has been going out with the van for years. She knows many of the women well. Often, they talk about the young people who also hang out on Higham Road and worry about if they're safe to be there. Up until lockdown, they were never sure of the answers to these questions, but then, when there was less of a buzz around the road, it became much easier to see that some young people were very vulnerable to being exploited there. So Kat was interested when she was invited to a multi-agency meeting to talk about the safety of young people on Higham Road. The meeting was led by social workers and attended by police, Community Safety and other charities who were also concerned about the safety of children in the area. 'We agreed to make a survey to talk to people who live and work in the area, including the young people, businesses, residents and, of course, the sex workers about their experiences of safety and risk on Higham Road,' explained Kat. 'And we realised, it came as quite a shock to some, but not to me, that in fact sex workers could – along with others – be a source of help and support for the young people.' For Kat, this process was part of a system change that was refreshing and new. This was the first time, she explained with a smile on her face, that professionals were open to learning from the wisdom of people who are usually overlooked and dismissed. Kat joined forces with the lead social worker, and they developed a programme for the women who use the van, to build on the concerns and interests they had in supporting the young people. 'We invited the women to see themselves as community guardians for the young people who hang out on Higham Road, and they responded enthusiastically,' said Kat. It was very important that anything they did was sensitive to the women's experiences and that their emotional safety was the most important consideration. 'The last thing we wanted to do', explained Kat, 'was to inadvertently re-traumatise the women with stories of exploitation that were triggering of their own experiences'. This meant that Kat took conversations very slowly, looking at the body language and cues of each woman. If someone was interested and wanted to know more, she was invited to be part of a programme to learn more about the signs of criminal and sexual exploitation in young people. Kat explained that the purpose was not to criminalise young people but ultimately to make it safer for them and for everyone who spent time there. Another important aspect in this partnership between the sex workers and the safeguarding partnership was a commitment by the partnership to building up trust and providing support. Once a month, for several months before the community guardianship programme began, a Child Sexual Exploitation social worker and a police officer would go out to Higham Road during the evening. Although their primary concern was the young people there, they also built relationships with the sex workers, giving out hot drinks and, if a woman felt unsafe, offering to drive her somewhere safer. The social worker gave out condoms. So when Kat invited the women to become community guardians, it meant that there was already a good foundation of trust in place for the women to share information if they were worried about any young people. As these relationships developed, it also led to more opportunities for the police and social care services to safeguard the women too, if they were in danger. Kat explained that while this was about the safety of young people, it also led to much more positive and respectful relationships between the sex workers and the wider community, which she says increased their sense of safety too. 'This is for the long term,' says Kat, something she hopes will have a positive impact in the years to come as understanding and respect grows between those who have, historically, been in suspicion of one another.

Leaving the story circle

These examples are a small slice of the work undertaken throughout the last three years in our Scale-Up test sites, and beyond. While we all have more to learn, particularly about how to measure this work over the long term, there is also much to celebrate about how leaders and practitioners have taken up the task of applying CS approaches, as they respond to risk and safety outside the home. If you are reading this and wondering where to start, here is a summary of key learning to get you on your way:

- Pilot new ways of responding where the stakes are lower: responding to very high risk in a way that is new and different can be very challenging. Practice wisdom so far suggests it's best to begin by responding to problems that come at the lower end of the risk scale and to set boundaries around the work. You can then reflect and learn, and then later scale up, but starting smaller will facilitate this process.
- Consider resources: some of the best responses have been possible within systems where there is agility when it comes to the deployment of resources. If all the funds are fixed within pre-existing programmes, it is going to be harder for you to try other things that haven't been done before. So it will service you well to secure some flexibility around funds at the outset, so that you're not bound by what's gone before and can be creative and responsive to the CS needs of young people.
- Draw on core skills and values: in many ways the work described here *is* new and different. Focusing primarily on the social conditions of harm rather than individual and family characteristics is new for social work and other professions alike. At the same time, the most successful responses are those which draw on existing values and skills. Building relationships, empathising, a commitment to social justice, listening to children and young people, analysing problems, finding creative and empowering solutions, having the courage and tenacity to see things through to make a difference – these are all at the core of good social work practice. Keep hold of this to support you through the uncertain and anxious terrain of developing new practice responses.
- Don't get overwhelmed and reach for shortcuts: working in the area of risk and harm to young people will always be anxiety-provoking. For this reason, we need to build in safe reflective spaces to learn from our feelings and avoid becoming overwhelmed or paralysed by the task. When we are overwhelmed, we can lose sight of important values about *how* this work should be done. It can be tempting to look for quick, technological or pre-existing methods that seem to offer simple solutions. But there are no shortcuts for doing thorough safeguarding work. Every context is different and deserves careful assessment and response planning, where young people's views and experiences are respected and taken seriously. Do everything you can to keep this at the heart of any CS response.

In ending, I would like to thank again all the people who have joined us in developing these, and many other, CS responses. We have learnt so much from you about what CS looks like in practice and are very excited about where things go next.

14

Conclusion: Creating societies where children can know love

Jenny Lloyd and Carlene Firmin

Have you ever been at a party standing with a stranger and they have asked you the predictable question 'so what do you do for a living?' If you are reading this book, it is likely that you – like us – groan at this question. Despite having worked in this area for many years, we haven't got very good at answering this in a 'party-appropriate' way. Maybe you say something vague about safeguarding, maybe you say something about children's rights or perhaps you go bold and mention the words 'exploitation' or 'violence'. Depending on who is asking the question, you might get a range of responses from ambivalence to macabre excitement. But what if instead we said 'I'm working to create societies where children can know love'? We imagine the partygoer might suddenly see someone they 'haven't seen for ages', make their excuses and leave. Love can seem a bit 'icky', but if there is one theme that threads across this book, and the matter we turn to now – values – then perhaps it is love. In this chapter, we draw on bell hooks's (2001) definition of love, which she notes is formed of six elements: care, commitment, trust, knowledge, responsibility and respect.

We don't often hear the word 'love' used when talking about children experiencing harm in their communities. Love is rarely discussed in assessments, during panels or as part of plans. Love can seem quite unfashionable, or even slightly perverse when we're talking about safeguarding. When children are involved in high-profile incidences of harm, newspaper articles rarely talk about them in ways that open up the opportunity for love. They favour instead titillating titles about 'gangs' and 'thugs'. But as we think about the work that moves us, the examples of practitioners that 'get it', the children who have shared their stories of friendship and what it's like when it 'works', love feels like the best explanation for what it is we are trying to do. CS is about creating societies where children can know love and we are doing that by trying to create systems that show it too.

In our journey to create safer communities, we have often led with our four-part framework, and it is these 'domains' that have provided the structure of this book. The four domains have outlined a clear and perhaps palatable set of measures which have supported a range of practitioners and those of differing professional persuasions to 'get on board' with the idea of CS. In writing this chapter, we thought about many of these examples. Examples that moved us in some way – they made us feel happy or sad or angry – and you can see these throughout the book. These feelings are rarely a result of aligning (or not) to the four domains (apart from perhaps Domain 2), but, as we will discuss, about values. However, what we have seen throughout this book is evidence that the domains are perhaps not always enough to strengthen against some of the more problematic practices and systemic issues that creep into or dominate the work of safeguarding. Author and activist bell hooks (2001) tells us that 'there can be no love without justice' (19). And so it is with this in mind that we explore the five values of CS.

We begin with an example that captures what – in some small way – it can look like to create a world where children know love, even in the darkest of times. This extract comes from an interview with a social worker. Here, she is talking about four boys involved in a peer assessment (for reasons that we won't outline here) and their relationship with a youth worker:

> 'I really felt like I got a sense of who these boys are, and I think there was a sense of love. Love came up as a theme as something that the boys are very interested in. It's a word they love using. Apparently, it's very cool to say "love, love, love" about a pair of trainers or about each other. But they'd had really deep and meaningful conversations with him [the youth worker] about what love means to them and about how love means responsibility and obligation, and they loved him [the youth worker] and they would tell him that on a regular, and one of them [the boys] had a tag and couldn't go to the youth centre to see him anymore, and he [the youth worker] missed him, so he'd go and see him at his house, and you really got a sense of who he [the boy] was.' (Interview with practitioner, Scale-Up)

When we are talking about children who 'are at risk', who might be experiencing 'significant harm' and might be being exploited or involved in the harm of others, it might be easy to lose sight of the need for finding a place within our systems for love. Stories of children involved in the types of harm that are part of this book are often dominated with ideas of risk and harm that rely on stereotypes. As Plowright (2022) notes, while these systems may talk a lot about 'care', the neoliberal focus on risk can foreclose the opportunity to create systems to accommodate and acknowledge emotions within them and make a place for love. In fact, they can themselves inflict harm comparable with that which they aim to stop. In an effort to mitigate against this harm, we have developed five values of CS, which we explore here.

The five values of Contextual Safeguarding

Those creating or working towards developing CS need to demonstrate that they are collaborative, ecological, rights-based, strengths-based and evidence-informed. We visit each of these now in turn.

Collaboration

CS requires collaboration between professionals, children, young people, families and communities to inform decisions about safety. There are two clear elements to this: collaboration with children and families, and collaboration between practitioners. It is the latter that seems to get more attention than the former. But as we saw in Lisa Bostock's chapter (Chapter 10), collaborating is more than just people coming together. Collaboration requires people to work critically and honestly to reflect together. This means being able to be honest about the varying intentions and aims of different groups by creating a culture and environment where partners can supportively critique one another to ensure that safeguarding (and not crime prevention) is the shared thread. As we saw in Lisa Bostock's chapter, too much emphasis is often placed on the inherent assumption that multi-agency partners can and should work together harmoniously to safeguard children. Yet, as we saw in Joanne Walker and Carlene Firmin's chapter (Chapter 5), partners often have differing values and intentions which do not always support collaboration.

While practitioners have been enthusiastic about collaborating with colleagues across organisational divides, the same cannot be said about collaborating with parents and young people. There are clear systemic barriers which prevent the opportunity to engage young people and parents. In Lisa Marie Thornhills's chapter (Chapter 9), we saw how the design of child protection systems (which focus on parenting) can responsibilise parents for the harm their children experience. Parents shared how these feelings of blame and shame prevented them from getting support and acted as a barrier to working with social workers. Similar themes were discussed by young people in Hannah Millar, Joanne Walker and Elsie Whittington's chapter (Chapter 8), who discussed the need for young people's rights to be upheld, supportive and trusting relationships and collaboration with practitioners. In Rachael Owens' chapter (Chapter 13), she talks about how this work requires working with practitioners who 'actually like adolescents' and dare we say perhaps love. While it might seem obvious, this has not always been the case. But where it is, we see the examples like those of Rob and Penny in Chapter 13. It's helpful here to draw on hooks's (2001) definition of love, which she notes is formed of six elements: care, commitment, trust, knowledge, responsibility and respect. The assumption of providing 'care' is not enough to have the privilege of collaboration. It is often the elements of trust, respect and commitment that young people and parents talk about as wanting in their experiences with services. True collaboration requires us to think more about ways we can embed these six elements into our work with children and families.

Ecological

The second value requires CS work to be ecological. This means that we need to understand and engage with the relationships between the contexts where young people experience harm and how these are driven by structural drivers. There is much talk about systemic approaches to social work and while social work practice can aim to acknowledge different ecological spheres (Bronfenbrenner, 1992), CS asks us to engage in practice which not only identifies but seeks to address harm in these broader contexts. CS was developed in some part as a counter narrative to the inherent individualist risk-adverse approaches of child protection which had been applied to children experiencing EFH. For many, the suggestion to think about peers and places was appealing. But the challenge is ensuring how we do so without just moving from labelling individual children as 'risky' to labelling their friends and communities as 'risky'. As we saw in Chapters 2 and 3, this is about recognising how issues of poverty, patriarchy, racism, ableism and so on shape how young people experience different places and how these structural elements also shape system responses. Doing this work, we have noticed that practitioners and areas asking for our help sometimes seem surprised when presenting us with a location assessment, only to be told that the assessment itself evidences racism inherent within the system. It is through these conversations with care and respect that we work together to shift the focus on to tackling these broader ecological challenges, even if that is sometimes only possible in small ways.

The pull of individual and behaviourist thinking is, however, strong. This is not about ignoring the agency of young people but understanding that the root of much of this harm is driven by these forces and not individual young people's choices. In Chapters 11 and 12, we saw how challenging it can be to think ecologically. What does it mean to change the social conditions of abuse? And if you can, how do we measure progress on a scale that can assure funders, commissioners and inspectors that things are 'working'. As we saw in Michelle Lefevre, Paula Skidmore and Carlene Firmin's chapter (Chapter 12), it is important not to attribute outcomes to CS without first ensuring that practice being evaluated is aligned to the domains and values. Individual approaches seem so intrinsic to UK child protection that we have often wondered if what we are doing is even possible. Examples from Delphine Peace (Chapter 6) and Vanessa Bradbury-Leather and Sue Rayment-McHugh's chapter (Chapter 7) remind us of the opportunities to consider systems beyond the UK. As Chapter 6 showed us, this might be possible where approaches to adolescent harm are more strongly positioned within jurisdictions where child welfare is prioritised. Chapter 7, however, cautions us of the potential challenges of implementing Eurocentric approaches to child protection in different contexts. This work would require recognition of the impact and legacy of British colonisation and would need to avoid repetition of destructive colonial practices.

Rights-based

There is sometimes an assumption made that safeguarding trumps rights. We see this play out in meetings where one partner (maybe a youth worker) is hesitant to discuss a matter in front of another partner (let's say the police). In these discussions, you may at some point hear someone declare that 'it's safeguarding' and therefore it's okay to pass this information on – it's the higher good that matters. When the apparent threat to a young person is so daunting, it can be easy to forget the need to protect certain rights. We have also seen though instances where sharing that little bit of information has undermined a trusted relationship that a young person has had with a youth worker – closing down any further relationship. Inherent within this tussle is the idea that in order to protect children, there are times where certain rights might be overruled – their right to privacy, for example. While the basic principle of CS is that all children have the right to safety, this does not undermine other rights – the right to have their views heard, the right to private family life, the right to association and so on. While the intention of CS has been about ensuring the safety of young people, as we saw in Carly Adams Elias, Lisa Marie Thornhill and Hannah Millar's chapter (Chapter 4), the use of CS, without recognition of rights, could undermine those rights and further harm young people. Safeguarding and rights do not always go hand in hand.

Rights and ethics can feel a bit scary. When we talk about the need to ensure young people have their rights protected, or when we talk about the times where the ethics of the work has been brought into question, it can feel uncomfortable. We can feel like we want to reject the conversation and continue safe in the knowledge what we are doing is 'safeguarding'. We ourselves have certainly been involved in research that we now ask ourselves 'was that ok?'; 'were they fully consenting?' While the temptation to ignore these questions is high, we know that to ensure our work is rights-based, we need to have spaces open to us to think, reflect and challenge ourselves and others on what this means. To be rights-based requires ongoing critical reflection and scrutiny of our own practice, a rights-informed ethical framework to guide us and partners that can support us in doing so together. Having these available to us would mean that when we start to talk about our concerns about mapping of children without their consent or ask ourselves about the meaningful participation of young people, this is not to judge piously who is most ethical but to engage in the process of learning and change.

Strengths-based

The fourth value is that the work needs to be strengths-based. The child protection system – in the UK at least – is inherently deficit-based. Practitioners are trained to assess risk and consider how to protect children from harm. In cases of EFH, the risk is often considered to be the ultimate form of harm: death or sexual assault. In her 'love ethic', hooks (2001) notes how (Western) societies' cultural obsession with death causes us to anxiously obsess over the need for security and safety through putting up (often physical) borders and boundaries against the other. This anxiety is felt throughout the child protection system. While there are many models and approaches which seek to build upon strengths, it is fair to say that this is not a dominant feature of the system. We have seen this throughout the chapters, whether it's concern over what friends a child has (as in Chapter 4), if parents are 'protective' (as in Chapter 9) or the measures used to assess success (as in Chapter 11). Yet as we saw in Chapters 2, 6 and 7, what we deem as safety and security is always viewed through the intersection of socially and culturally determined factors. For example, different groups and practices – through systems of power such as racism and sexism – are often viewed as 'riskier' than others. Instead of focusing only on risks, CS hopes to offer an avenue and language that supports practitioners to look for assets that exist and build upon these. How might a meeting change if we moved from asking 'what are we worried about' to 'what does this young person or group need?' Again, returning to a love ethic, it is often the children and adults in our communities that are best placed to do this. In Rachael Owens' chapter (Chapter 13), we saw how systems can become strengths-based and the benefits this can bring.

A theme across the values is that while the aim is for them to be applied to work with children, we also believe that they apply to the systems themselves. It is hard to draw upon young people's strengths when practitioners themselves are facing increasing scrutiny (Hood and Goldacre, 2021). Perhaps after reading the chapters of this book, you have not been overwhelmed by our focus on the strengths of the social care system. Many chapters have been overtly critical of practice. We do this not to criticise but through a will and hope that the system is capable of change. A key methodological feature of our approach is that we engage in 'embedded' approaches. This means we spend time with and alongside practitioners to understand their systems. This allows us to understand research in context.

It also allows us to identify and report findings in ways that are sensitive to the challenges and strengths of those places. We have steeled ourselves on a number of occasions when we have had to report back 'bad' things to practitioners and sites. But it is through love and kindness that we find a way for those critiques to be heard and understood. While increasingly neoliberal systems may encourage us to blame 'bad' individuals, we want to raise the importance of our collective belief in the need for change. The work to put this in practice and be strengths-based is a team activity. It requires practitioners and researchers to be supported with the time, space and psychological safety to be able to learn and develop – those things are scant resources in our current times.

Evidence-informed

The fifth and final value is that work needs to be evidence-informed. It needs to be rooted in the reality of young people's everyday lives. Perhaps it is no surprise that the quote shared at the start of this chapter was about the relationship between a youth worker and young people. Youth work and youth workers have a long history of being embedded in the communities and places that they serve in ways that allows them to understand the experiences of young people. It is through these relationships that workers can come to know what children love and need. As we saw in Lisa Bostock's chapter (Chapter 10), meetings focused on supporting children are often dominated by a focus on known 'facts' and 'intelligence'. Police data is often seen as the first and primary source of information. This focus can lead us to become preoccupied with the worst-case scenario. When we meet with teams trying to *do* CS, we often hear them say the 'one thing we need is an analyst'. Rarely do they state that the one thing they need is more youth workers. This is not because they don't want or need this, but often the shared knowledge that the funds available do not always value this type of resource. To ensure that responses to harm are evidence-informed, we need to increase opportunities for workers who are most likely to be better able to reflect the reality of young people's lives and find collective solutions. This requires moving out of the office, off the computer and into the places and spaces young people spend time.

Concluding thoughts

The four parts of this book have focused on the domains of CS. The domains set out a clear framework to think about *what* we are doing to respond to EFH. Rather than thinking about *what* we are doing, the values prompt us to think about *how* we are doing it. By foregrounding the values, we are sometimes asking you to go beyond or against the conventional practice framework. While there is a challenge that we risk becoming too prescriptive in our approach, placing ourselves in some hierarchy where we get to define what is or is not CS, it is the aim that these values create a space to reflect and ask questions of our practice. While the changes we are asking for may be daunting, we have already seen this happening across the country. What is needed to support this work, though, is funding and commissioning frameworks which focus on contexts and strive for social rather than individual change.

A final note about love. It is not possible to create the conditions where children can know love in systems where there is an absence of it. Over the last seven years, we have had the opportunity to witness practitioners across the country who are keen to champion CS and develop new and innovative approaches to adolescent harm. We have seen many where their work has exceeded expectations and we have seen examples where it has been unable to tilt the status quo. What often sets those that exceed apart from those that do not are working conditions where practitioners feel and show love for one another. It is often easy to see the care and affection that practitioners show for one another and, sadly, it is always easy to see when they don't. If we are not able to show those working in this field care, commitment, trust, knowledge, responsibility and respect, then it is unlikely that we will ever be able to do so for the children and families we are working with.

References

Aldridge, J., Medina-Ariz, J. and Ralphs, R. (2011). Counting gangs: Conceptual and validity problems with the Eurogang definition. In F.-A. Esbensen and C.L. Maxson (eds) *Youth Gangs in International Perspective: Results from the Eurogang Program of Research*, New York: Springer, pp 35–51.

Amnesty International (2018). *Trapped in the Matrix: Secrecy, Stigma and Bias in the Met's Gangs Database*, UK: Amnesty International.

Aussems, K., Muntinga, M., Addink, A. and Dedding, C. (2020). 'Call us by our name': quality of care and wellbeing from the perspective of girls in residential care facilities who are commercially and sexually exploited by 'loverboys', *Children and Youth Services Review*, 116, 105213.

Austin, A. (2018). Transgender and gender diverse children: considerations for affirmative social work practice, *Child and Adolescent Social Work Journal*, 35, 73–84.

Australian Institute of Health and Welfare (2021). *Child Protection Australia 2019–20*, Child Welfare Series No. 74. Cat. No. CWS 78, Canberra: AIHW.

Baltra-Ulloa, A.J. (2013). Why decolonized social work is more than cross-culturalism, in M. Gray, J. Coates, M. Yellow Bird and T. Hetherington (eds) *Decolonizing Social Work*, New York: Routledge, pp 87–104.

Barn, R., Di Rosa, R.T. and Kallinikaki, T. (2021). Unaccompanied minors in Greece and Italy: an exploration of the challenges for social work within tighter immigration and resource constraints in pandemic times, *Social Sciences*, 10(4), 134.

Barner, J.R., Okech, D. and Camp, M.A. (2018). 'One size does not fit all': a proposed ecological model for human trafficking intervention, *Journal of Evidence-Informed Social Work*, 15(2), 137–50.

Beckett, H. and Warrington, C. (2015). *Making Justice Work: Experiences of Criminal Justice for Children and Young People Affected by Sexual Exploitation as Victims and Witnesses*, Luton: University of Bedfordshire.

Beckett, H., Brodie, I., Factor, F., Melrose, M., Pearce, J.J., Pitts, J. et al (2013). *'It's Wrong – But You Get Used to It': A Qualitative Study of Gang-Associated Sexual Violence towards, and Exploitation of, Young People in England*, Luton: University of Bedfordshire.

Bennett, B. (2013). The importance of Aboriginal and Torres Strait Islander history for social work students and graduates, in B. Bennett, S. Green, S. Gilbert and D. Bessarab (eds) *Our Voices: Aboriginal and Torres Strait Islander Social Work*, Claremont, IIC: Palgrave Macmillan.

Bennet, D.L., Schluter, D.K., Melis, G., Bywaters, P., Barr, B., Wickham, S. and Taylor-Robinson, D. (2021). Child poverty and children entering care: a natural experiment using longitudinal area level data in England, 2015–2020, The Lancet. https://dx.doi.org/10.2139/ssrn.3972210

References

Berelowitz, S., Clifton, J., Firimin, C., Gulyurtlu, S. and Edwards, G. (2013). If only someone had listened, Office of the Children's Commissioner's Inquiry into Child Sexual Exploitation in Gangs and Groups, Final Report.

Bernard, C. (2019). Using an intersectional lens to examine the child sexual exploitation of black adolescents, in J. Pearce (ed) *Child Sexual Exploitation: Why Theory Matters*, Bristol: Policy Press, pp 193–209.

Bernard, C. (2020) *PSDP – Resources and Tools: Understanding the Lived Experiences of Black and Ethnic Minority Children and Families*, Totnes, Devon: Practice Supervisor Development Programme.

Bernard, C. and Harris, P. (2019). Serious case reviews: the lived experience of black children, *Child & Family Social Work*, 24(2), 256–63.

Billingham, L. and Irwin-Rogers, K. (2021). The terrifying abyss of insignificance: marginalisation, mattering and violence between young people, *Oñati Socio-Legal Series*, 11(5), 1222–49.

Blower, B., Dixon, D., Ellison, S., Ward, J., Thorley, K. and Gridley, N. (2017). *Step change: An Evaluation*, London: Department for Education.

Bostock, L. (2021). Contextual safeguarding study helps Bristol tackle CSE, Children and Young People Now, 42.

Bottoms, A. and Kemp, V. (2017). The relationship between youth justice and child welfare in England and Wales [online]. Available from: https://lawexplores.com/the-relationship-between-youth-justice-and-child-welfare-in-england-and-wales [Accessed 17 March 2022].

Bourdieu, P. (1984). *Distinction: A Social Critique of the Judgement of Taste*, Cambridge, Mass.: Harvard University Press.

Brandon, M., Sidebotham, P., Belderson, P., Cleaver, H., Dickens, D., Garstang, J., Harris, J., Sorensen, P. and Wate, R. (2020). Complexity and challenge: a triennial analysis of SCRs 2014–2017, Department for Education.

Brayley, H. (2014). Rapid evidence assessment: the sexual exploitation of boys and young men [online]. Available from: http://assets.mesmac.co.uk/images/Rapid-evidence-assessment-the-SE-of-BYM.pdf?mtime=20160108190046 [Accessed 8 September 2022].

Brodie, I., Latimer, K. and Firmin, C. (2020). *Peer Support Interventions for Safeguarding: A Scoping Review*, Luton: University of Bedfordshire.

Bronfenbrenner, U. (1992). *Ecological Systems Theory*, London: Jessica Kingsley.

Brown, K. (2019). Vulnerability and child sexual exploitation: towards an approach grounded in life experiences, *Critical Social Policy*, 39(4), 622–42.

Bruning, M.R. and Doek, J.E. (2021). Characteristics of an effective child protection system in the European and international contexts, *International Journal on Child Maltreatment: Research, Policy and Practice*, 4(3), 231–56.

Bryan, A., Hingley-Jones, H. and Ruch, G. (2016). Relationship-based practice revisited, *Journal of Social Work Practice*, 30(3), 229–33.

Bukowski, W., Laursen, B. and Rubin, K.H. (2019). *Handbook of Peer Interactions (Social, Emotional, and Personality Development in Context)*, New York: Guilford Press.

Bywaters, P., Kwhali, J., Brady, G., Sparks, T. and Bos, E. (2017). Out of sight, out of mind: ethnic inequalities in child protection and out-of-home care intervention rates, *British Journal of Social Work*, 47, 1884–902.

Bywaters, P., Brady, G., Bunting, L., Daniel, B., Featherstone, B., Jones, C., Morris, K., Scourfield, J., Sparks, T. and Webb, C. (2018). Inequalities in English child protection practice under austerity: a universal challenge?, *Child & Family Social Work*, 23, 53–61.

CAGE (2018). Separating Families: How PREVENT Seeks the Removal of Children, London: CAGE Advocacy UK.

Cameron, A., Lart, R., Bostock, L., Coomber, C. (2012). *Factors That Promote and Hinder Joint and Integrated Working across the Health and Social Care Interface*, London: SCIE.

Carden, C. (2017). 'As parents congregated at parties': responsibility and blame in media representations of violence and school closure in an Indigenous community, *Journal of Sociology*, 53(3), 592–606.

Cenat, J.M., McIntee, S., Mukunzi, J.N. and Noorishad, P. (2021). Overrepresentation of black children in the child welfare system: a systematic review to understand and better act, *Children and Youth Services Review*, 120, 1–16.

Chainey, S. and Tompson, L. (2008). *Crime Mapping Case Studies: Practice and Research*, New York: John Wiley & Sons.

Chard, A. (2015). *Troubled Lives. Tragic Consequences: A Thematic Review*, London: Tower Hamlets Children's Safeguarding Board.

Charmen, H. (2021). The politics of everyday life: motherhood [online]. Available from: www.newstatesman.com/politics/feminism/2021/03/politics-everyday-life-motherhood [Accessed 6 March 2023].

Child10 (nd). Global trends in child trafficking and sexual exploitation of children [online]. Available from: https://child10.org/about-child-trafficking/globaltrends [Accessed 27 April 2022].

Children and Young People Now (2018). Home Office announces £18m for youth projects to tackle serious violence [online]. Available from: www.cypnow.co.uk/news/article/home-office-announces-18m-for-youth-projects-to-tackle-serious-violence [Accessed 6 March 2023].

Children's Commissioner (2019a). Keeping kids safe: improving safeguarding responses to gang violence and criminal exploitation [online]. Available from: www.childrenscommissioner.gov.uk/report/keeping-kids-safe/ [Accessed 6 March 2023].

Children's Commissioner (2019b). The Stability Index 2019, overview report [online]. Available from: www.childrenscommissioner.gov.uk/publication/stability-index-2019/ [Accessed 22 June 2020].

Clapton, G. (2021). The tyranny of outcomes, *Practice*, 33(3), 223–31.

Clarke, K. and Yellow Bird, M. (2021). *Decolonizing Pathways to Integrative Healing in Social Work*, Abingdon: Routledge.

Clarke, R.V.G. (1997). *Situational Crime Prevention*, Monsey, NY: Criminal Justice Press.

Cockbain, E. and Tufail, W. (2020). Failing victims, fuelling hate: challenging the harms of the 'Muslim grooming gangs' narrative, *Race and Class*, 61(3), 3–32.

Commission on Race and Ethnic Disparities (2021). Independent report: foreword, introduction, and full recommendations [online]. Available from: www.gov.uk [Accessed 26 January 2022].

Connolly, M. (2004) A perspective on the origins of family group conferencing, American humane, FGDM issues in brief [online]. Available from: www.americanhumane.org/site/DocServer/fgdm_FGC_origins_New_Zealand.pdf?docID=1901 [Accessed 6 March 2023].

Cook, L. (2020). Evidence, accountability and legitimacy: the oversight of child welfare services, *Statistical Journal of the International Association of Official Statistics*, 36, 365–73.

Corney, T., Cooper, T., Shier, H. and Williamson, H. (2021). Youth participation: Adultism, human rights and professional youth work, *Children & Society*, 36(4), 677–90.

Cornish, D.B. and Clarke, R.V. (1987). Understanding crime displacement: an application of rational choice theory, *Criminology*, 25, 933–48.

Cossar, J., Brandon, M. and Jordan, P. (2016). 'You've got to trust her and she's got to trust you': children's views on participation in the child protection system, *Child & Family Social Work*, 21(1), 103–12.

Coulthard, G.S. (2014). *Red Skin, White Masks: Rejecting the Colonial Politics of Recognition*, Minnesota: University of Minnesota Press.

Council of Europe (2005). Council of Europe convention on action against trafficking in human beings (CETS No. 197).

Council of Europe (2007). Council of Europe convention on the protection of children against sexual exploitation and sexual abuse (CETS No. 201).

Council of Europe (2019). Human trafficking for the purpose of labour exploitation, Council of Europe [online]. Available from: www.coe.int/en/web/human-rights-intergovernmental-cooperation/human-trafficking-for-the-purpose-of-labour-exploitation [Accessed 6 March 2023].

Coy, M., Sharp-Jeffs, N. and Kelly, L. (2017). Key messages from research on child sexual exploitation [online]. Available from: www.wiganlscb.com/Docs/PDF/Professional/CSE/Key-messages-for-professionals-in-school-settings.pdf [Accessed 6 March 2023].

Cunneen, C. and Libesman, T. (2000). Postcolonial trauma: the contemporary removal of indigenous children and young people from their families in Australia, *Australian Journal of Social Issues*, 35(2), 99–115.

D'Addato, A. (2017). *Let Children Be Children: Lessons from the Field on the Protection and Integration of Refugee and Migrant Children in Europe*, Brussels: Eurochild and SOS Children's Villages International.

Darlington Council (2019). Community Safety Partnership [online]. Available from: www.darlington.gov.uk/your-council/policing/community-safety-partnership [Accessed 6 March 2023].

Davis, J. (2019). Where are the black girls in our CSA services, studies and statistics? [online]. Available from: www.communitycare.co.uk/2019/11/20/where-are-the-black-girls-in-our-services-studies-and-statistics-on-csa/ [Accessed 6 March 2023].

Davis, J. and Marsh, N. (2020). Boys to men: the cost of 'adultification' in safeguarding responses to black boys, *Critical and Radical Social Work*, 8(2), 255–9.

De Sousa Santos, B. (2007). *Another Knowledge Is Possible: Beyond Northern Epistemologies*, New York: Verso.

Degani, P., Pividori, C. and Bufo, M. (2015). *Trafficked and Exploited Minors between Vulnerability and Illegality*, Osservatorio Interventi Tratta.

Department for Education (2016). *Children in Need of Help of Protection*, London: National Audit Office.

Department for Education (2018). *Working Together to Safeguard Children*, London: HM Government.

Department for Education (2022). Children's Social Care Innovation Programme: insights and evaluation [online]. Available from: www.gov.uk/guidance/childrens-social-care-innovation-programme-insights-and-evaluation [Accessed 31 March 2022].

Desmeules, G. (2007). A sacred family circle: A family group conferencing model, in I. Brown et al (eds) *Putting a Human Face on Child Welfare: Voices from the Prairies*, Ottawa: Centre of Excellence for Child Welfare.

Dhumma, N. (2021). Fear and mistrust: young people and the police [online]. Available from: https://y-stop.org/news/fear-and-mistrust-young-people-and-police [Accessed 20 January 2022].

Dillon, J. (2019). *'Revolutionizing' Participation in Child Protection Proceedings*, Doctoral thesis, Liverpool: Liverpool John Moores University.

Dillon, J. (2021). 'Wishes and feelings': misunderstandings and missed opportunities for participation in child protection proceedings, *Child & Family Social Work*, 26(4), 664–76.

Dillon, J., Greenop, D. and Hills, M. (2016). Participation in child protection: a small-scale qualitative study. *Qualitative Social Work*, 15(1), 70–85.

Dimitrova, K., Ivanova, S. and Alexandrova, Y. (2015). *Child Trafficking among Vulnerable Roma Communities*, Sofia, Bulgaria: Centre for the Study of Democracy.

Doherty, J. (2022). *Safeguarding Practice Review: 'Carl and Max'*, LSCB: Croydon Safeguarding Children Partnership.

Drew, J. (2020). *Serious Case Review: Child C: A 14 Year Old Boy*, London: Waltham Forest Safeguarding Children's Board.

Dudgeon, P., Wright, M., Paradies, Y., Garvey, D. and Walker, I. (2010). The social, cultural and historical context of Aboriginal and Torres Strait Islander Australians, in P. Dudgeon, H. Milroy and R. Walker (2010) *Working Together: Aboriginal and Torres Strait Islander Mental Health and Wellbeing Principles and Practice*, Canberra: Australian Institute of Health and Welfare, pp 25–42.

Duffy Rice, J., Cheney-Rice, Z. and Ketteringham, E. (2020). Episode 23: Criminalizing mothers [online]. Available from: https://theappeal.org/justice-in-america-episode-23-criminalizing-mothers [Accessed 19 November 2021].

Duncan, K., Wakeham, A., Winder, B., Armitage, R., Roberts, L. and Blagden, N. (2020). The experiences of non-offending partners of individuals who have committed sexual offences: recommendations for practitioners and stakeholders [online]. Available from: https://huddersfield.box.com/s/1sumdnyq9yjkgwhw0axzvgt7e2rfgcih [Accessed 6 March 2023].

Elliott, G.C., Kao, S. and Grant, A. (2004). Mattering: empirical validation of a social-psychological concept, *Self and Identity*, 3(4), 339–54.

Elliott-Cooper, A. (2021). *Black Resistance to British Policing*, Manchester: Manchester University Press.

Epstein, R., Blake, J.J. and Gonzalez, T. (2017). *Girlhood Interrupted: The Erasure of Back Girls' Girlhood*, Center of Poverty and Inequality, Washington: Georgetown Law.

Eshalomi, F. (2020). Gang associated girls: supporting young women at risk [online]. Available from: www.london.gov.uk/sites/default/files/gang_associated_girls.pdf [Accessed 6 March 2023].

Factor, F.J. and Ackerley, E.L. (2019). Young people and police making 'Marginal Gains': climbing fells, building relationships and changing police safeguarding practice, *Journal of Children's Services*, 14(3), 217–27.

Family Matters Report (2017). Measuring trends to turn the tide on the over-representation of Aboriginal and Torres Strait Islander children in out-of-home care in Australia, Eltham: SNAICC [online]. Available from: www.familymatters.org.au/wp-content/uploads/2017/11/Family-Matters-Report-2017.pdf [Accessed 6 March 2023].

Fanon, F. (1986). *Black Skin, White Masks*, translated by Charles Lam Markmann, London: Pluto Press.

Featherstone, B. and Morris, K. (2021). Domestic abuse and child protection: Change Project case file audit report [online]. Available from: www.researchinpractice.org.uk/media/5926/case-file-audit-report-dva-change-project-291121_formatted-and-proofed.pdf [Accessed 6 March 2023].

Featherstone, B., White, S. and Morris, K. (2014). *Re-imagining Child Protection: Towards Humane Social Work with Families*, Bristol: Policy Press.

Featherstone, B., Gupta, A., Morris, K. and Warner, J. (2016). Let's stop feeding the risk monster: towards a social model of 'child protection', *Families, Relationships and Societies*, 7(1), 7–22.

Featherstone, B., Gupta, A., Morris, K. and White, S. (2018). *Protecting Children: A Social Model*, Bristol: Policy Press.

Featherstone, B., Firmin, C., Gupta, A., Morris, K. and Wroe, L. (2020). *The Social Model and Contextual Safeguarding: Key Messages for Practice*, Bedfordshire: University of Bedfordshire.

Fine, M., Freudenberg, N., Payne, Y., Perkins, T., Smith, T. and Wanzer, K. (2003). 'Anything can happen with police around': urban youth evaluate strategies of surveillance in public places, *Journal of Social Issues*, 59, 141–58.

Firmin, C. (2015). *Peer-on-Peer Abuse: Safeguarding Implications of Contextualising Abuse between Young People within Social Fields*, professional doctorate thesis, Luton: University of Bedfordshire.

Firmin, C. (2017). *Abuse between Young People: A Contextual Account*, Oxon: Routledge.

Firmin, C. (2019). From genograms to peer group mapping: introducing peer relationships into social work assessment and intervention, *Families, Relationships and Societies*, 8(2), 231–48.

Firmin, C. (2020). *Contextual Safeguarding and Child Protection: Re-writing the Rules*, London: Routledge.

Firmin, C. (2022). Green lights, speed bumps and cul-de-sacs: the road to Contextual Safeguarding (inaugural professorial lecture), Durham University [online]. Available from: www.youtube.com/watch?v=wWvKXSEI4Sg [Accessed 6 March 2023].

Firmin, C. and Knowles, R. (2020). *The Legal and Policy Framework for Contextual Safeguarding Approaches: A 2020 Update on the 2018 Legal Briefing*, Luton: Contextual Safeguarding Network.

Firmin, C. and Owens, R. (2022). Holding it together? Professional perspectives on the role of relationships when relocating young people due to extra-familial harm. *International Journal on Child Maltreatment: Research, Policy and Practice*, 1–25.

Firmin, C., and Rayment-McHugh, S. (2020). Two roads, one destination: community and organizational mechanisms for contextualizing child abuse prevention in Australia and the UK, *International Journal on Child Maltreatment: Research, Policy and Practice*, 3(2), 229–45.

Firmin, C., Curtis, G., Fritz, D., Olatain, P., Latchford, L., Lloyd, J. and Larasi, I. (2016). *Towards a Contextual Response to Peer-on-Peer Abuse*, Luton: University of Bedfordshire.

Firmin, C., Lloyd, J. and Walker, J. (2019a). Beyond referrals: levers for addressing harmful sexual behaviours between students at school in England, *International Journal of Qualitative Studies in Education*, 32, 1229–49.

Firmin, C., Wroe, L. and Lloyd, J. (2019b). *Safeguarding and Exploitation – Complex, Contextual and Holistic Approaches*, Darlington: Research in Practice.

Firmin, C., Wroe, L. and Skidmore, P. (2020). *A Sigh of Relief: A Summary of the Phase One Results from the Securing Safety Study*, Luton: University of Bedfordshire.

FitzSimons, A. and McCracken, K. (2020). *Children's Social Care Innovation Programme: Round 2 Final Report*, London: Department for Education.

Forin, R. and Healy, C. (2018). *Trafficking along Migration Routes to Europe: Bridging the Gap between Migration, Asylum and Anti-Trafficking*, Vienna: ICMPD.

Forrester, D. (2017). Outcomes in children's social care, *Journal of Children's Services*, 12(2–3), 144–57.

Forrester, D., Westlake, D., Killian, M., Antonopolou, V., Mccann, M., Thurnham, A., Thomas, R., Waits, C., Whittaker, C. and Hutchison, D. (2019). What is the relationship between worker skills and outcomes for families in child and family social work?, *The British Journal of Social Work*, 49, 2148–67.

FRA (2020). *Children in Migration in 2019*, Brussels: EU Agency for Fundamental Rights.

Franklin, A. and Smeaton, E. (2017). Recognising and responding to young people with learning disabilities who experience, or are at risk of, child sexual exploitation in the UK, *Children and Youth Services Review*, 73, 474–81.

Fraser, A., Ralphs, R. and Smithson, H. (2018). European youth gang policy in comparative context, *Children & Society*, 32(2), 156–65.

Freccero, J., Biswas, D., Whiting, A., Alrabe, K. and Seelinger, K.T. (2017). Sexual exploitation of unaccompanied migrant and refugee boys in Greece: approaches to prevention, *PLoS Medicine*, 14(11), e1002438.

Gibson, M. (2020). The shame and shaming of parents in the child protection process: findings from a case study of an English child protection service, *Families, Relationships and Societies*, 9(2), 217–33.

Gilbert, N. (1997). *Combatting Child Abuse: International Perspectives and Trends*, Oxford: Oxford University Press.

Giovannetti, M. (2017). Reception and protection policies for unaccompanied foreign minors in Italy, *Social Work & Society*, 15(2), 1–22.

Gorin, S. and Jobe, A. (2013). Young people who have been maltreated: different needs – different responses?, *British Journal of Social Work*, 43(7), 1330–46.

Gov.uk (2019/20). Explore education statistics [online]. Available from: https://explore-education-statistics.service.gov.uk/find-statistics/permanent-and-fixed-period-exclusions-in-england [Accessed 7 March 2023].

Gray, M., Coates, J., Yellow Bird, M. and Hetherington, T. (2013). *Decolonizing Social Work*, Farnham: Ashgate.

Gregulska, J.H., Makulec, C., Petreska, A., Safin, E. and Dominika Smetek, J. (2020). *Study on Reviewing the Functioning of Member States' National and Transnational Referral Mechanisms*, Brussels: European Commission.

Grunwald, K. and Thiersch, H. (2009). The concept of the 'lifeworld orientation' for social work and social care, *Journal of Social Work Practice*, 23(2), 131–46.

Hackett, S. (2004). *What Works for Children and Young People with Harmful Sexual Behaviours?*, Barkingside: Barnardo's.

Hallett, S. (2016). 'An uncomfortable comfortableness': 'Care', child protection and child sexual exploitation, *British Journal of Social Work*, 46(7), 2137–52.

Hamilton, C.J., Rodgers, A., Howard, K. and Warrington, C. (2019). From the ground up: young research advisors' perspectives on relationships between participation and protection, *Journal of Children's Services*, 14(3), 228–34.

Hamm, J.V. and Hoffman, A.S. (2016). Teachers' influence on students' peer relationships and peer ecologies, in T.A. Kindermann (eds) *Handbook of Social Influences in School Contexts*, Abingdon: Routledge, pp 218–39.

Hammond, I., Godoy, S., Kelly, M. and Bath, E. (2020). A transgender girl's experience: sexual exploitation and systems involvement, *International Journal of Human Rights in Healthcare*, 13(2), 185–96.

Hampson, M., Goldsmith, C. and Lefevre, M. (2021). Towards a framework for ethical innovation in children's social care, *Journal of Children's Services*, 16(3), 198–213.

Hanson, E. and Holmes, D. (2014). That difficult age: developing a more effective response to risks in adolescence, *Dartington: Research in Practice*.

Harris, J.P. (2014). *Co-determining the Outcomes that Matter with Young People Leaving Care: A Realist Approach*, Thesis, Luton: University of Bedfordshire.

Harrow Council (2018). *Community Safety, Violence Vulnerability and Exploitation Strategy*, London: Harrow Council.

Hennessey, R. (2011). *Relationship Skills in Social Work*, London: Sage.

Hickle, K., Lefevre, M., Luckock, B. and Ruch, G. (2017). *Piloting and Evaluating the 'See Me, Hear Me' Framework for Working with Child Sexual Exploitation*, London: Office of the Children's Commissioner.

Hill, N. (2018). *Serious Case Review: Chris*, London: Newham Children's Safeguarding Board.

Hirschi, T. (1969). *Causes of Delinquency*, Berkeley, CA: University of California Press.

HM Government (2018a). *Serious Violence Strategy*, London: Home Office.

HM Government (2018b). *Working Together to Safeguard Children*, London: Home Office.

Home Office (2011). *Cross-Government Definition of Domestic Violence – A Consultation*, London: Home Office.

Home Office (2018). *Criminal Exploitation of Children and Vulnerable Adults: County Lines Guidance*, London: Home Office.

Home Office (2020). *Group-Based Child Sexual Exploitation Characteristics of Offending*, London: Home Office.

Home Office (2021). Serious violence duty: draft guidance for responsible authorities (accessible version) [online]. Available from: www.gov.uk/government/publications/police-crime-sentencing-and-courts-bill-2021-draft-guidance/serious-violence-duty-draft-guidance-for-responsible-authorities-accessible-version#fn:2 [Accessed 6 March 2023].

Hood, R. (2019). What to measure in child protection?, *The British Journal of Social Work*, 49, 466–84.

Hood, R. and Goldacre, A. (2021). Exploring the impact of Ofsted inspections on performance in children's social care, *Children and Youth Services Review*, 129, 106188.

hooks, b. (2001). *All about Love: New Visions*, New York: Harper Perennial.

Human Rights and Equal Opportunities Commission (1997). *Bringing them Home Report: Report of the National Inquiry into the Separation of Aboriginal and Torres Strait Islander Children from their Families*, Sydney: Australian Human Rights Commission.

Hyslop, I. (2021). He Pāharakeke, He Rito Whakakīkinga Whāruarua, in *Reimagining Social Work in Aotearoa* [online]. Available from: https://reimaginingsocialwork.nz/2021/05/06/he-paharakeke-he-rito-whakakikinga-wharuarua [Accessed 31 January 2022].

Hyslop, I. (2022). *A Political History of Child Protection: Lessons for Reform from Aotearoa New Zealand*, Bristol: Bristol University Press.

Idahosa, G. and Bradbury, V. (2020). Challenging the way we know the world: overcoming paralysis and utilising discomfort through critical reflexive thought, *Acta Academia*, 52(1), 31–53.

Irwin-Rogers, K. (2019). Illicit drug markets, consumer capitalism and the rise of social media: a toxic trap for young people, *Critical Criminology*, 27, 591–610.

Isle of Wight Community Safety Partnership (2016). Isle of Wight Community Safety Partnership strategic plan 2016/17 [online]. Available from: www.iow.gov.uk/documentlibrary/download/community-safety-partnership-strategic-plan [Accessed 24 November 2021].

Ivec, M., Braithwaite, V. and Harris, N. (2012). 'Resetting the relationship' in Indigenous child protection: public hope and private realit, *Law & Policy*, 34(1), 80–103.

Johnston, A. and Akay, L. (2022). Radical safeguarding: a social justice workbook for safeguarding practitioners, Maslaha [online]. Available from: www.maslaha.org/Project/Radical-safeguarding [Accessed 6 March 2023].

Jordan, B. (2012). Individualisation, liberal freedom and social work in Europe, *Dialogue in Practice*, 1(14), 7–25.

Joseph Rowntree Foundation (2021). *UK Poverty 2020/21: The Leading Independent Report*, York: Joseph Rowntree Foundation.

Just For Kids Law (2021). Race, poverty and school exclusions [online]. Available from: https://londonchallengepovertyweek.org.uk/wp-content/uploads/2020/10/RacePovertyandSchoolExclusions_FV-1.pdf [Accessed 7 March 2023].

King, H., Crossley, S. and Smith, R. (2021). Responsibility, resilience and symbolic power, *The Sociological Review*, 69(5), 920–36.

La Valle, I., Holmes, L., Gill, C., Brown, R., Hart, D. and Barnard, M. (2016). *Improving Children's Social Care Services: Results of a Feasibility Study*, London: CAMHS Press.

Lansdown, G. and O'Kane, C. (2015). A toolkit for monitoring and evaluating children's participation: introduction, Booklet 1 [online]. Available from: https://resourcecentre.savethechildren.net/library/toolkitmonitoring-and-evaluatingchildrens-participation-introduction-booklet-1 [Accessed 7 March 2023].

Latimer, K., Adams Elias, C. and Firmin, C. (2020). *Opportunities for Peer Safeguarding Intervention: A Briefing Following Fieldwork with Safer London*, Luton: Contextual Safeguarding Network.

Lefevre, M. and Hickle, K. (2022). Learning to love and trust again: a relational approach to developmental trauma. In: Holmes, D. (ed) Safeguarding Young People: Risk, Rights, Relationships and Resilience, London: Jessica Kingsley, pp 159–76.

Lefevre, M., Hickle, K. and Luckock, B. (2019). 'Both/and' not 'either/or': reconciling rights to protection and participation in working with child sexual exploitation, *British Journal of Social Work*, 49(7), 1837–55.

Lewing, B., Doubell, L., Beevers, T. and Acquah, D. (2018). *Building Trusted Relationships for Vulnerable Children and Young People with Public Services*, London: Early Intervention Foundation.

Lewis, B., Pipe, C. and Bostock, L. (2022). Systemic social work and contextual safeguarding [online]. Available from: www.contextualsafeguarding.org.uk/media/nbtc2yui/cs-and-systemic-practice_08-03-22_final-1.pdf [Accessed 6 March 2023].

LGA (2019). *Councillor Guide to Tackling Modern Slavery*, London: Local Government Association.

Linklater, R. (2014). *Decolonizing Trauma Work: Indigenous Stories and Strategies*, Canada: Fernwood Publishing.

Lloyd, J. (2019). Why 'zero tolerance' doesn't work [online]. Available from: www.contextualsafeguarding.org.uk/blog/why-zero-tolerance-doesn-t-work [Accessed 6 March 2023].

Lloyd, J. and Firmin, C. (2020). No further action: contextualising social care decisions for children victimised in extra-familial settings, *Youth Justice*, 20, 79–92.

Losen, D., Hodson, C., Ee, J. and Martinez, T. (2014). Disturbing inequities: exploring the relationship between racial disparities in special education identification and discipline, *Journal of Applied Research on Children*, 5(2), 15.

Mabvurira, V. (2020). Making sense of African thought in social work practice in Zimbabwe: towards professional decolonisation, *International Social Work*, 63(4), 419–30.

Malthouse, K. and Oates, F. (2021). Child protection practice with Aboriginal and Torres Strait Islander children, families and communities, in B. Bennett (ed) *Aboriginal Fields of Practice*, London: Red Globe Press.

Māori Inquiry into Oranga Tamariki (2020). Ko Te Wā Whakawhiti: it's time for change: a Māori inquiry into Oranga Tamariki, Whānau Ora Commissioning Agency [online]. Available from: https://apo.org.au/sites/default/files/resource-files/2020-02/apo-nid274231_1.pdf [Accessed 6 March].

Mason, B. (1993). Towards positions of safe uncertainty, *Human Systems*, 4, 189–200.

Mason, W. (2019). 'No one learned': interpreting a drugs crackdown operation and its consequences through the 'lens' of social harm, *The British Journal of Criminology*, 60(2), 382–402.

Mason, W., Morris, K., Featherstone, B., Bunting, L., Davidson, G., McCartan, C. and Webb, C. (2021). Understanding out of home care rates in Northern Ireland: a thematic analysis of mixed methods case studies, *The British Journal of Social Work*, 51(7), 2645–64.

Massey, D. (2005). *For Space*, London: Sage Publications.

Matthews, S., Schiraldi, V. and Chester, L. (2018). Youth justice in Europe: experience of Germany, the Netherlands, and Croatia in providing developmentally appropriate responses to emerging adults in the criminal justice system, *Justice Evaluation Journal*, 1(1), 59–81.

Mayne, J. (2008). Contribution analysis: an approach to exploring cause and effect [online]. Available from: www.betterevaluation.org/en/resources/guides/contribution_analysis/ilac_brief [Accessed 25 April 2022].

McCann, E., Keogh, B., Doyle, L. and Coyne, I. (2019). The experiences of youth who identify as trans* in relation to health and social care needs: a scoping review, *Youth & Society*, 51(6), 840–64.

McKenzie, H.A., Varcoe, C., Browne, A.J. and Day, L. (2016). Disrupting the continuities among residential schools, the sixties scoop, and child welfare: an analysis of colonial and neocolonial discourses, *The International Indigenous Policy Journal*, 7(2).

McLeod, A. (2007). Whose agenda? Issues of power and relationship when listening to looked-after young people, *Child & Family Social Work*, 12(3), 278–86.

Measor, L. and Squires, P. (2017). *Young People and Community Safety: Inclusion, Risk, Tolerance and Disorder*, London: Routledge.

Megele, C. (2015). *Psychosocial and Relationship Based Practice*, London: Critical Publishing.

Melrose, M. and Pearce, J. (2013). *Critical Perspectives on Child Sexual Exploitation and Related Trafficking*, New York: Springer.

Merkel-Holguin, L., Fluke, J.D. and Krugman, R.D. (2019). *National Systems of Child Protection: Understanding the International Variability and Context for Developing Policy and Practice*, New York: Springer.

Metropolitan Police (2019). MPS Gang Violence Matrix (GVM) frequently asked questions (FAQs) [online]. Available from: www.met.police.uk/cy-GB/heddluoedd/metropolitan-police/areas/about-us/about-the-met/gangs-violence-matrix [Accessed 6 March 2023].

Milbourne, L. and Cushman, M. (2013). From the third sector to the big society: how changing UK government policies have eroded third sector trust, *VOLUNTAS: International Journal of Voluntary and Nonprofit Organizations*, 24, 485–508.

Muench, K., Diaz, C. and Wright, R. (2017). Children and parent participation in child protection conferences: a study in one English local authority. *Child Care in Practice*, 23(1), 49–63.

Muraya, D.N. and Fry, D. (2016). Aftercare services for child victims of sex trafficking: a systematic review of policy and practice, *Trauma, Violence, & Abuse*, 17(2), 204–20.

Nandy, A. (1988). *The Intimate Enemy: Loss and Recovery of Self under Colonialism*, Delhi; Oxford: Oxford University Press.

Neighbourhoods Project (2017). *Preventing Youth Sexual Violence and Abuse in Aurukun and West Cairns: Neighbourhoods Project Implementation and Evaluation Report*, Final Report to the Australian Department of the Prime Minister and Cabinet.

NHS Scotland (2018). *Child Poverty in Scotland: Health Impact and Health Inequalities*, Edinburgh: NHS Scotland.

O'Neill, K. (ed) (2007). *Getting It Right for Children: A Practitioners' Guide to Child Rights Programming*, London: Save the Children UK.

Okpokiri, C.G. (2017). *First-Generation Nigerian Immigrant Parents and Child Welfare Issues in Britain*, Doctoral thesis (PhD), Sussex: University of Sussex.

Okun, T. (1999). White supremacy culture, in *Dismantling Racism* [online]. Available from: www.whitesupremacyculture.info/uploads/4/3/5/7/43579015/okun_-_white_sup_culture_2020.pdf [Accessed 2 December 2021].

ONS (2020). Coronavirus (COVID-19) related deaths by occupation, England and Wales: deaths registered between 9 March and 25 May 2020 [online]. Available from: ons.gov.uk [Accessed 30 March 2022].

Ontario Human Rights Commission (2018). Interrupted childhoods: over-representation of indigenous and black children in Ontario child welfare report, Ontario Human Rights Commission [online]. Available from: https://cwrp.ca/sites/default/files/publications/en/interrupted_childhoods_over-representation_of_indigenous_and_black_children_in_ontario_child_welfare_accessible.pdf [Accessed 6 March 2023].

Ord, J., Carletti, M., Cooper, S., Dansac, C., Morciano, D., Siurala, L. and Taru, M. (2018). *The Impact of Youth Work in Europe: A Study of Five European Countries*, Helsinki: Humak University of Applied Sciences Publications.

OSCE (2019). *2018–2019 Report of the Special Representative and Co-ordinator for Combating Trafficking in Human Beings*, Brussels: Organization for Security and Co-Operation in Europe.

Osei-Hwedie, K. and Boateng, D.A. (2018). "Do not worry your head": the impossibility of indigenising social work education and practice in Africa, *Southern African Journal of Social Work and Social Development*, 30(3), 1–12.

Owens, R., Haresnape, S., Ashley, C., Bradbury, V. and Firmin, C. (2021). *Family Group Conferences and Contextual Safeguarding: Key Messages for Practice*, Luton: University of Bedfordshire.

Pain, R. (2000). Place, social relations and the fear of crime: a review, *Progress in Human Geography*, 24, 365–87.

Palmer, E. (2019). Trafficked children and child protection systems in the European Union, *European Journal of Social Work*, 22(4), 551–62.

Parton, N. (2010). "From dangerousness to risk": the growing importance of screening and surveillance systems for safeguarding and promoting the well-being of children in England, *Health, Risk & Society*, 12(1), 51–64.

Peace, D. and Wroe, L. (2022). *Contextual Safeguarding across Borders: Year One Scoping Review*, Durham: Contextual Safeguarding Network.

Pearce, J. (2007). Risk and resilience: a focus on sexually exploited young people, in B. Thom, R. Sales and J. Pearce (eds) *Growing Up with Risk*, Bristol: Policy Press, pp 203–18.

Pease, B., Vreugdenhil, A. and Stanford, S. (2018). *Critical Ethics of Care in Social Work: Transforming the Politics and Practices of Caring*, New York: Routledge.

Perera, J. (2021). *How Black Working-Class Youth Are Criminalised and Excluded in the English School System: A London Case Study*, London: Institute of Race Relations.

Pike, N., Langham, M. and Lloyd, S. (2019). *Parents' Experiences of the Children's Social Care System When a Child Is Sexually Exploited*, London: PACE.

Platt, L. and Warwick, R. (2020). Are some ethnic groups more vulnerable to COVID-19 than others? [online]. Available from: www.ifs.org.uk/inequality/wp-content/uploads/2020/04/Are-some-ethnic-groups-more-vulnerable-to-COVID-19-than-others-V2-IFS-Briefing-Note.pdf [Accessed 6 March 2023].

Plowright, R.C. (2022). The significance of love in relation to looked-after children and child sexual exploitation, *Critical and Radical Social Work*. DOI:10.1332/204986021X16523430934288

Plymouth (nd). Plymouth Safeguarding Children Partnership procedures [online]. Availabe from: www.proceduresonline.com/swcpp/plymouth/p_lscb_role_func.html [Accessed 6 March 2023].

Preston, O., Godar, R., Lefevre, M., Boddy, J. and Firmin, C. (2021). Considerations in the use of local and national data for evaluating innovation in children's social care, *Journal of Children's Services*, 16(3), 233–48.

Pruin, I. and Dünkel, F. (2015). Better in Europe? European responses to young adult offending, Transition to Adulthood Alliance.

Racher, A. and Brodie, I. (2020). Joining the dots? Tackling child exploitation during COVID-19, *Journal of Children's Services*, 15(4), 275–85.

Radford, L., Allnock, D. and Hynes, P. (2015). Preventing and responding to child sexual abuse and exploitation: evidence review, Child Protection Section Programme Division UNICEF Headquarters [online]. Available from: www.unicef.org/media/84081/file/Preventing-Responding-to-Child-Sexual-Abuse-Exploitation-Evidence-Review.pdf [Accessed 6 March 2023].

Rankopo, M. and Osei-Hwedie, K. (2011). Globalisation and cultural social work: African perspectives on indigenisation, *International Social Work*, 54(1), 137–47.

Rap, S.E. (2015). The participation of social services in youth justice systems in Europe, *European Journal of Social Work*, 18(5), 675–89.

RECLAIM (2020). *Listening to the Experts: Getting beyond the Headlines to Hear What Young People Want and Need to Stay Safe from Violent Crime*, Manchester: Manchester Reclaim.

Rose, G. (2021). Welcome to Tottenham, the Poetry Society [online]. Available from: https://poetrysociety.org.uk/poems/welcome-to-tottenham#:~:text=you're%20weak.-,Welcome%20to%20Tottenham.,can't%20be%20left%20alone [Accessed 8 April 2022].

Ruch, G., Turney D. and Ward, A. (2010). *Relationship Based Social Work: Getting to the Heart of Practice*. London: Jessica Kingsley.

Salmon, G. and Rapport, F. (2005). Multi-agency voices: a thematic analysis of multi-agency working practices within the setting of a child and adolescent mental health service, *Journal of Interprofessional Care*, 19(5), 429–43.

References

SAMHSA (2014). *SAMHSA's concept of trauma and guidance for a trauma-informed approach* [online]. Available from: https://ncsacw.acf.hhs.gov/userfiles/files/SAMHSA_Trauma.pdf [Accessed 7 March 2023].

Schmid, J. (2021). A reinterrogation of South African child welfare discourse: a case for decolonisation? *British Journal of Social Work*, 52(5), 1–18.

Schön, D.A. (1983). *The Reflective Practitioner: How Professionals Think in Action*, London: Temple Smith.

Seal, M. and Harris, P. (2016). *Responding to Youth Violence through Youth Work*, Bristol: Policy Press.

Sebba, J. with Luke, N., Rees, A. and McNeish, D. (2017). *Systemic Conditions for Innovation in Children's Social Care: Children's Social Care Innovation Programme: Thematic Report 4*, Oxford: Rees Centre.

Seddon, J. (2008). *Systems Thinking in the Public Sector*, Axminster: Triarchy Press.

Serin, H. (2021). Non-abusing mothers' agency after disclosure of the child's extra-familial sexual abuse, *European Journal of Women's Studies*, 28(4), 532–46.

Sethi, D., Bellis, M., Hughes, K., Gilbert, R., Mitis, F. and Galea, G. (2018). *European Report on Preventing Child Maltreatment*, Copenhagen: World Health Organization Regional Office for Europe.

Simon, G. and Salter, L. (2019). Transmaterial worlding: beyond human systems, *Murmurations: Journal of Transformative Systemic Practice*, 2(2), 1–17.

Simpson L.R. (2004). Anticolonial strategies for the recovery and maintenance of indigenous knowledge, *The American Indian Quarterly*, 28(3/4), 373–84.

Sloane, G., Notarianni, M. and Dachi, S., with Balci, M., Allen, P. and Hackney Contextual Safeguarding Team (2019) *Peer Group Mapping Guidance*, Luton: Contextual Safeguarding Network.

Smithson, H. and Jones, A. (2021). Co-creating youth justice practice with young people: Tackling power dynamics and enabling transformative action, *Children & Society*, 35(3), 348–62.

SPACE (2021). County lines: 'This parent-blaming response does nothing to protect exploited children' [online]. Available from: www.communitycare.co.uk/2021/12/09/county-lines-this-parent-blaming-response-does-nothing-to-protect-exploited-children/ [Accessed 7 March 2023].

Spradley, J.P. (1980). *Participant Observation*, New York: Holt, Rinehart and Winston.

Spratt, T., Nett, J., Bromfield, L., Hietamäki, J., Kindler, H. and Ponnert, L. (2015). Child protection in Europe: development of an international cross-comparison model to inform national policies and practices, *The British Journal of Social Work*, 45(5), 1508–25.

Stanley, N., Barter, C., Wood, M., Aghtaie, N., Larkins, C., Lanau, A. and Överlien, C. (2018). Pornography, sexual coercion and abuse and sexting in young people's intimate relationships: a European study, *Journal of interpersonal Violence*, 33(19), 2919–44.

Stein, N. (2007). Bullying, harassment and violence among students, *Radical Teacher*, 80, 30–5.

Suleman, M., Sonthalia, S., Webb, C., Tinson, A., Kane, M., Bunbury, S., Finch, D. and Bibby, J. (2021). *Unequal Pandemic, Fairer Recovery: The COVID-19 Impact Inquiry Report*, London: The Health Foundation.

Sutherland, E.H. (1947). *Principles of Criminology* (4th edn), Philadelphia, PA: J.B. Lippincott.

Talaga, T. (2018). *All Our Relations: Finding the Path Forward*, Canada: House of Anansi Press.

Temo, H. (2016). Tūhoe, Ngāti Tāwhaki, Ngāti Rongo, Te Mahurehure, oral teaching, personal communication with Vanessa Bradbury-Leather, July 2016.

Temple, A. (2020). *Excluded, Exploited, Forgotten: Childhood Criminal Exploitation and School Exclusions*, London: Just for Kids Law.

Thoburn, J., Lewis, A. and Shemmings, D. (1995). Family participation in child protection, *Child Abuse Review*, 4(3), 161–71.

Thom, B., Sales, R. and Pearce, J. (eds) (2007) *Growing up with Risk*, Bristol: Policy Press.

Thornhill, L.M. (2019). 'How would a child see it?' Exploring the impact when a parent downloads IIOC, PhD thesis, Luton: University of Bedfordshire.

Tidsall, E.K.M. (2017). Conceptualising children and young people's participation: examining vulnerability, social accountability and co-production, *International Journal of Human Rights*, 21(1), 59–75.

Tomaszewska, P. and Schuster, I. (2021). Prevalence of teen dating violence in Europe: a systematic review of studies since 2010, *New Directions for Child and Adolescent Development*, 178, 11–37.

Tower Hamlets (2021). Community Safety Partnership plan (2021–2024) [online]. Available from: www.towerhamlets.gov.uk/lgnl/community_and_living/community_safety__crime_preve/anti-social_behaviour/community_safety_partnership/csp-plan.aspx [Accessed 22 November 2021].

Truth and Reconciliation Commission of Canada (2015). *Canada's Residential Schools, Missing Children and Unmarked Burials*, vol 4, Gatineau: Truth and Reconciliation Commission of Canada.

Tuck, E. and Yang, K. (2012). Decolonization is not a metaphor, *Decolonization: Indigeneity, Education and Society*, 1(1), 1–40.

UNGA (2010). General Assembly of the United Nations (64th sess. 2009–2010), *Guidelines for the Alternative Care of Children*, New York: UNGA.

UNICEF (2008). *Child Trafficking in Europe: A Broad Vision to Put Children First*, New York: United Nations Publications.

United Nations Committee on the Rights of the Child (2009). *General Comment No. 12: The Right of the Child to Be Heard*, Geneva: United Nations.

van Bijleveld, G.G., Bunders-Aelen, J.F. and Dedding, C.W. (2020). Exploring the essence of enabling child participation within child protection services, *Child & Family Social Work*, 25(2), 286–93.

Villanueva, E. (2018). *Decolonizing Wealth: Indigenous Wisdom to Heal Divides and Restore Balance*, Oakland, CA: Berrett-Koehler Publishers.

Vinsky, J. (2018). The elephant in the room: addressing racial anxiety of white social workers in child welfare, Ontario Association of Children's Aid Societies [online]. Available from: www.oacas.org/2018/06/the-elephant-in-the-room-addressing-racial-anxiety-of-white-social-workers-in-child-welfare [Accessed 6 March 2023].

Violence and Vulnerability Unit (2018). County lines: a national summary and emerging best practice [online]. Available from: https://vvu-online.com/wp-content/uploads/2021/08/VVU-County-lines-national-summary-2018-1.pdf [Accessed 7 March 2023].

Wai (2021). He Pāharakeke, He Rito Whakakīkinga Whāruarua: Oranga Tamariki urgent inquiry, Waitangi Tribunal Report 2021, Legislation Direct [online]. Available from: https://forms.justice.govt.nz/search/Documents/WT/wt_DOC_171027305/He%20Paharakeke%20W.pdf [Accessed 6 March 2023].

Walker, S., Eketone, A. and Gibbs, A. (2006). An exploration of kaupapa Māori research, its principles, processes and applications, *International Journal of Social Research Methodology*, 9(4), 331–44.

Ward, H., Brown, R. and Westlake, D. (2012). *Safeguarding Babies and Very Young Children from Abuse and Neglect*, London: Jessica Kingsley.

Warrington, C. and Larkins, C. (2019). Children at the centre of safety: challenging the false juxtaposition of protection and participation, *Journal of Children's Services*, 14(3), 133–42.

Wever, C. and Zell, S. (2018). Re-working self-care: from individual to collective responsibility through a critical ethics of care, in B. Pease, A. Vreugdenhil and S. Stanford (eds) *Critical Ethics of Care in Social Work: Transforming the Politics and Practices of Caring*, New York: Routledge.

What Works for Children's Social Care (2021). Outcomes framework [online]. Available from: https://whatworks-csc.org.uk/research/outcomes-framework-for-research/ [Accessed 16 November 2021].

Whittington, E. (2019). Co-producing and navigating consent in participatory research with young people, *Journal of Children's Services*, 14(3), 205–16.

Wilkins, D. and Antonopoulou, V. (2020). Ofsted and children's services: what performance indicators and other factors are associated with better inspection results?, *The British Journal of Social Work*, 50, 850–67.

Williams, J., Scott, S. and Ludvigsen, A. (2017). *Safe Steps Case Innovation Project Evaluation Report*, London: Department for Education.

Williams, P. (2018). Being matrixed: The (over)policing of gang suspects in London, Stopwatch [online]. Available from: www.stop-watch.org/what-we-do/research/being-matrixed-the-overpolicing-of-gang-suspects-in-london/ [Accessed 6 March 2023].

Williams, P. and Clarke, B. (2016). *Dangerous Associations: Joint Enterprise, Gangs and Racism: An Analysis of the Process of Criminalisation of Black, Asian and Minority Ethnic Individuals*, London: Centre for Crime and Justice Studies.

Williams, P., Joseph-Salisbury, R., Harris, S. and White, L. (2021). A threat to public safety: policing, racism and the COVID-19 pandemic [online]. Available from: https://irr.org.uk/wp-content/uploads/2021/09/A-threat-to-public-safety-v3.pdf [Accessed 2 March 2023].

Williamson, H. (2020). Cornerstone challenges for European youth work and youth work in Europe: making the connections and bridging the gaps, 3rd European Youth Work Convention [online]. Available from: www.bonn-process.net/downloads/publications/38/8adbb3a39302dda6f7a37c739ba6515f/Challenges_for_Youth_Work_Howard_Williamson.pdf [Accessed 6 March 2023].

Wroe, L. (2019). Contextual safeguarding and 'county lines' [online]. Available from: www.contextualsafeguarding.org.uk/media/rqybrewm/contextual-safeguarding-and-county-lines-briefing_-wroe-oct-2019-final.pdf [Accessed 6 March 2023].

Wroe, L. (2020). Principles of contextual safeguarding, Contextual Safeguarding Network [online]. Available from: www.csnetwork.org.uk/en/blog/2020/principles-of-contextual-safeguarding [Accessed 6 March 2023].

Wroe, L. (2021). Young people and 'county lines': a contextual and social account, *Journal of Children's Services*, 16(1), 39–55.

Wroe, L. and Lloyd, J. (2020). Watching over or working with? Understanding social work innovation in response to extra-familial harm, *Social Sciences*, 9(37), 1–17.

Wroe, L. and Pearce, J.J. (2022). *Young People Negotiating Intra-and Extra Familial Harm and Safety: Social and Holistic Approaches*, London: Jessica Kingsley.

Young Foundation (2012). *Social Innovation Overview: A Deliverable of the Project: 'The Theoretical, Empirical and Policy Foundations for Building Social Innovation in Europe' (TEPSIE)*, European Commission – 7th Framework Programme, Brussels: European Commission, DG Research.

Young Researchers' Advisory Panel (2017). Introducing our new 'Participation as Protection' model! Safer Young Lives Research Centre, Blog, 9 November [online]. Available from: https://uniofbedssylrc.com/2021/11/09/young-researchers-advisory-panel-introducing-our-new-participation-as-protection-model/ [Accessed 6 March 2023].

Youth Justice Board and Ministry of Justice (2020/21). Youth justice statistics [online]. Available from: https://assets.publishing.service.gov.uk/government/uploads/system/uploads/attachment_data/file/1050107/Youth_Justice_Statistics_2020-21.pdf [Accessed 7 March 2023].

Zedner, L. (2007). Pre-crime and post-criminology?, *Theoretical Criminology*, 11, 261–81.

Index

References to figures appear in *italic* type; those in **bold** type refer to tables.

A

ableism 22, 39, 92, 99, 191
abuse, social conditions of 94, 132, 141, 142, 158
  and peer mapping and assessment 50, 55–6
  and structural and system drivers of EFH 38, 39, 41
  tackling 17–19
adolescents 3, 30, 48, 52, 95, 148, 161
  asylum-seeking 80, 82
  and contextual safeguarding beyond UK 78–88
  and CS approaches 37–41
  EFH emphasis in 82–3
  and inequalities in EFH experiences 18, 19, 21–9
  and love 190, 192, 195
  safety, and peer relationships 45–6
  victim/perpetrator binary of 83–4
  working with 83–4
  and youth work 85–6
adultification 24, 46, 91, 142
adultism, overcoming 108
antisocial behaviour (ASB) 50, 61, 69–73, 75, 87, 150, 168, 180
  location assessment 65
  peer mapping 178
  sanctions 64–5
Aotearoa New Zealand 88, 90, 95
asylum-seeking adolescents 80, 82
austerity, impact of 35
Australia 77, 88
Austria 80, 86
authoritative doubt, significance of 142

B

BAME (Black, Asian and Minority Ethnic) 23–4, 33–4, 90, 123
Bedfordshire, University of 110, 111, 134
Belgium 80, 81, 84
Beyond Referrals toolkit 29
Black children and young people 17, 18, 23–4, 32–4, 91
Bourdieu, P. 26, 27, 85
Bulgaria 81
business owners 40, 138

C

Canada 88
Child and Family Assessments 39, 48, 51, 169, 175

child criminal exploitation (CCE) 35–7, 63
  see also criminal exploitation
child poverty 21–2
  see also poverty
child protection processes
  language of 125–8, 130
  structure of 128–31
child sexual exploitation (CSE) 23–5, 36–7, 63, 68, 78–9, 80–3, 87, 133, 136, 148–9
  see also sexual exploitation
child welfare 46, 48–52, 55, 62, 75–6, 84, 87, 92, 137, 141, 192
Children Act (1989) 62
Children's Social Care Innovation Programme 148, 161, 174
civil society organisations 81, 87
collaboration 9–12, 20, 29, 80, 81, 190–1
  absence of 118
  collaborative relationship 53–4, 119
  and decolonising practice 94, 95, 97
  and parents as partners 122, 123, 126, 128, 130, 131
  and participation 105, 111, 118–19
  and peer mapping and assessment 51–7
  see also partnerships
collective capacity to safeguard 5–6, 8
collectivity 10, 11, 13, 85, 173, 194
  and decolonising practice 92, 93, 95, 98, *99*
  and peer mapping and assessment 44–5, 48
community guardians 41, 69, 70, 74, 95, 138, 140, 184, 186
community members 40–1, 69, 74, 76, 97
community safeguarding 61–2
  alignment possibility with CS 73–6, **75**
  and children's safeguarding 62
  and contextual safeguarding domains 65–7, **66**
  and extra-familial harm (EFH) 63–7
  legislative and governance arrangements for 62, *63*
  response, purpose of 71–3
  and roles, in CS system 68–73
  through Scale-up Project learning 67–8
context assessment triangles 4, *5*
context weighting 7–8, 21, 175
contextual safeguarding (CS)
  2020–22 and further for 8–10

216

Index

assessment triangles 4, *5, 6*
case studies on 178–86
challenges 2–3
conditions for 113–19
and decolonisation 94–7
foregrounding conditions 119–20
foundations of work of 2–8
framework of 3
levels of 4–5, 7
neighbourhood assessment triangle *153*, 154–7
rights for adopting 113
significance of 1–2
space for adopting 113–14
theory for 26–8
values of 9, 190–4
see also individual entries
contextual safeguarding across borders (CSAB) 77–8
and adolescents 83–4
and child protection interventions 85–6
and CS opportunities 82–7
extra-familial harm in European context 78–9
and partnerships 86–7
and trafficking in Europe 79–82
counter-radicalisation strategy 22
COVID-19 crisis 17–18, 25
Crime and Disorder Act (1998) 62, 150
crime and disorder framework 65–6, 69, 71–4, **75**, 76, 107, 150–1
criminal exploitation 2, 30, 35, 37, 64, 78, 107, 123, 126, 137, 140, 158, 165, 170
criminal justice 3, 11, 45–6, 50–1, 61, 66, 80, 83–4, 87, 168
criminalisation 18–20, 23, 28, 35, 37, 46, 50, 51, 80, 83, 106, 108, 142, 151
critical reflection 29, 100, 157, 192
critical reflexivity 98, *99*
critical thinking 19–21, 54, 89
Croatia 84
cultural competency training 93
culture
  of collective accountability and care 98
  in school environment 7
  and structural harm 33
  of trust 108
curiosity, in peer context 44, 51, 55, 56
Cyprus 81, 84

D

decolonising practice 88, 89–90, 100–1
  and collaboration 94, 95, 97
  and collectivity 92, 93, 95, 98, *99*
  and contextual safeguarding 94–7
  and ethics of care 92–100
  and history of colonialism 90–2
  path forward 97–100
  and racism 92, 95
  and relationality 93, 96, 98, *99*
  of social welfare 92–4
Department for Education 148, 161
disability
  rights movement 25
  social models of 24–5
Durham University 111, 134

E

ecological value 9, 29, 48, 51, 55, 123, 190, 192–3
engagement of young people, issues with 53–4
see also participation
Estonia 85
ethical peer assessment, creating conditions for 56–7
ethics of care 89–92, 96, 98
  and CS and decolonisation 94–100
  practising with *99*
  and social welfare decolonisation 92–4
Europe 77
  CS approach in 82–8
  CSE and trafficking in 79–82
  refugee and asylum-seeking young people in 77
  response to extra-familial harm 78–9
everybody's responsibility, safeguarding as 6–7
evidence-informed value 9, 194
exclusion 21, 23, 106–7, 108, 114
extra-familial harm (EFH) 3, 4, 5, 30–1
  addressal, through multi-agency meetings 133–4
  and adolescence 37–42
  in adolescence, as child protection issue 82–3
  European responses to 78–82
  everybody's responsibility 6–7
  and inequalities 21–6
  legislative framework domain in meetings of 137–8
  meetings 135–40
  outcome measurement domain in meetings of 139–40
  parents in protecting from 122–4
  partnership domain in meetings of 138–9
  practice examples of 31–7
  and social care 34
  target domain in meetings of 135–7
  vulnerability to 81–2
  see also risk, outside home

F

family group conferencing (FGC) 92–3, 94–5, 181
Finland 80, 81, 85, 86
First Nations Peoples 93, 95–6, 101
see also ethics of care

217

Fixed Penalty Notices (FPNs) 18
France 81, 84, 85
friendships 38, 44–6, 56, 136, 188

G

gangs 22–3, 63–4, 83, 126–7, 149, 155, 161, 188
  gang violence matrix 50
  and inequalities in EFH experiences 22, 23
  and parents as partners 122, 126
gender, and victimisation 24, 37
Germany 79, 80, 81, 84, 85, 86
Greece 80, 81, 84
group work and peer assessment 54–5
guardians/guardianships 38, 66, 154, 156, 157, 158, 171, 172
  community guardians 41, 69, 70, 74, 95, 138, 140, 184, 186
  guardianship capacity 4, 5, 6, 39–40, 41, 45, 48
  and relationships 148

H

habitus 27, 28
Hackney Children and Families Services 161–4
heteronormativity 92
high streets *see* streets
Holmes, L. 148
Home Office 63–4, 149
homophobia 22, 32, 92
hooks, b. 188, 189, 190, 193
hotspots, for harm 38, 95, 136, 162, 172
Hungary 80, 82
hypothesising, importance of 142–3

I

immigrant families 18, 80, 91
Indigenous knowings 93
Indigenous young people 77, 91
information sharing 6–7, 52, 74, 76, 81, 87, 114–15, 132, 141
Institute of Race Relations (IRR) 18
intersectionality 24, 25, 26, 39
interviews, and focus groups 109–10, **110**
Ireland 80, 84
Italy 80, 81, 84, 85

L

learning disabilities, youth people with 25
legislative frameworks 3, 23, 61–2, 63, 66, **66**, 72–6, **75**, 84, 96, 137–8
  see also community safeguarding; decolonising practice; Europe; extra-familial harm (EFH)
LGBTQ 24
lifeworld orientation 85
lived reality, understanding of 9

local areas 7, 10, 44, 55, 61, 65, 67–70, 109, 133, 166, 184
local residents 40, 69, 72
location assessment 20, 35, 40, 74, 136–7, 191
  and community safe partnerships (CSPs) 68–71
  and participation 109, 112, 113, 117
  and structural inequalities 33
London Borough of Hackney 133

M

Macpherson report 22
mattering, concept of 107
misogyny 30, 31, 32
multi-agency meetings 12, 36, 132, 141–3, 185
  data collection for study of 134
  EFH addressal through 133–4
  and EFH meetings 135–40
  implications of 143
  importance of 132–3
  participant profiles study of 135
  reflections on 141–3
  study analysis of 135
  study findings of 135–40
  and voices of young people 140
multi-agency partners 19, 22, 26, 38, 68, 70–1, 73–4, 173, 190
multi-agency system 33, 36, 68, 74, 87

N

National Lottery Community Fund 165
National Referral Mechanisms (NRMs) 79, 80, 138
neighbourhood assessment triangle 6, *153*, 154–7
Neighbourhood Survey 97
neighbourhoods 6, 11, 13, 26–7, 37–8, 40, 43, 134, 136, 143, 150
Netherlands, the 80, 81, 84
non-binary young people 37, 47
non-governmental organisations (NGOs) 87
non-offending parents (NOPs) 122
Norway 81–2

O

Ofsted ratings 148
organised criminal groups 35, 68
outcomes 147–8
  in children's social care 148–50
  in community safety 150–1
  for contextual safeguarding 151–7
  see also research and evaluation needs

P

parenting 39, 85, 121–4, 127, 129–31, 190
parents 121–2, 177

in protecting from EFH 122–4
research with 124–31
parks 1, 7–9, 19, 40–1, 43, 51, 94–5, 138, 168, 179, 180–1
participation 105–6
 analysis of 112–13
 and conditions to implement CS 119–20
 and CS conditions 113–19
 ethics and limitations for 111–12
 Scale-Up site consultation methods for 109–10
 study methodology of 109–13
 and young people and child protection system 106–8
 with Youth Research Advisory Panel 110–11
partners 4, 33, 43, 52, 72, 105, 108, 150, 168, 171, 191
 agencies 6–7, 137
 and chairs 142
 of child protection system 25, 27
 multi-agency partners 19, 22, 26, 38, 68–71, 73–4, 173, 190
 parents as *see* parents
 of police 23
 and rights 192
 safeguarding 52, 55
partnerships 3, 8, 9, 65–7, **66**, 69–70, 73–4, 75, 86–7, 115–16, 135, 138–9, 142–3
 child welfare focus in 76
 creative 41, 88
 lack of 81
 with local agencies 97, 161
 and relationships 117–18
 see also multi-agency meetings; parents; participation
patriarchy 19, 22, 24, 31, 151, 191
peer mapping and assessment 11, 20, 35, 44–5, 189
 and adolescent safety 45–6
 child welfare versus crime detection 50–2, 55
 collaboration for 118–19
 and community safety reimagining 69, 71, 74
 ethical 56–7
 framework *49*
 and group work 54–5
 and information sharing 115
 and participation 113, 114, 118–19
 and peer mapping and assessment 45, 48–50, 52
 research method for 47–9
 and safeguarding practices 46–7
 and social conditions of abuse 55–6
 study findings for 49–56
 trust versus surveillance 52–4, 55
peers paradox 46
plurality, engaging with *99*

Poland 80, 81
Police Reform and Social Responsibility Act (2011) 62
police/policing 18, 62, 64–5, 67–8, 80, 97, 194
 and Black young people 32
 and children's social care 134, 135, 137–8, 139, 141
 and criminal framework 35
 over-policing 107
 and peer assessment 50–1, 71
 and profiling 23
 in public space 8
 social care- supported actions 28
 undercovers 28
poverty 9, 77, 107, 143, 164, 175, 191
 and access to safety 40
 and contextual safeguarding beyond UK 85
 and COVID-19 crisis 17
 digital 25
 impact of 21–2
 and inequalities in EFH experiences 18–22, 28, 29
 and parents as partners 122, 123
 and structural and system drivers of EFH 30–2, 35–6, 40
Prevent programme 22
process change, significance of 161–2
professionals, inputs from 41

R

racism 9, 22–3, 77, 107, 191, 193
 and decolonising practice 92, 95
 and space 33
 and structural and system drivers of EFH 30–4
RAG rating 10, 135–9, 166
 case study for 166, 168
 system review for 166–9, *167*
reciprocity 92, 98, *99*
referrals 22, 36, 51, 124, 126, 136, 138–41, 164, 166, 168–9, 171
relationality 13, 39, 141
 and decolonising practice 93, 96, 98, *99*
 and participation 118, 119
relationships
 with professionals 115–16
 and relatability 117–18
 with social workers 116–17
 see also partners; partnerships
research and evaluation needs 160–1
 and safety measurement in contexts 170–3
 and system capabilities examination 165–70
 and whole-system change 161–5
resilience and responsibility 122
rights-based value 9, 191–2

risk, outside home 45, 78, 134, 139–40, 175
  case studies on 178–86
  and parents as partners 121–6, 129–31
  and participation 106–7, 109, 117–18, 120
  and structural and system drivers of EFH 30–2, 35
  see also extra-familial harm (EFH)
rules of child protection, rewriting 21–2, 25, 27, 28, 94

S

Safeguarding Children's Partnerships (2017) 62
Safer Steps programme 148–9
Safer Young Lives Research Centre (University of Bedfordshire) 110
safety, access to 40–1, *42*
safety mapping 4, 44, 109, 113
safety planning meetings 124, 130–1
sanction-based responses 45, 61, 64–5, 66, 73
Scale-Up Project 10, 11, 47, 157, 176, 177, 178
  and community safety reimagining 67–8
  and parents as partners 124, 126
  and participation 105, 119
  and structural and system drivers of EFH 32, 33, 35–6
Scandinavian countries 84
scenario-based activities, for participation 109
school assessment triangle 5
Serious Case Reviews study 22–3, 132
serious violence duty 63–4
sexism 77, 92, 95, 99, 175, 193
sexual abuse 9, 23, 78, 122
sexual exploitation 2, 30, 33, 37, 78–81, 111, 137, 165, 186
  see also child sexual exploitation (CSE)
shelters 82
social conditions
  of abuse 17–19, 38, 39, 41, 50, 55–6, 94, 132, 141, 142, 158
  of harm 55, 85–6, 123, 151–2, 158, 187
  and impact evaluation challenges 160, 166
  impacting harm 181–3, 187
  and outcome measurements 151, 152
  and peer mapping and assessment 44, 47
  significance of 3, 9, 11, 21, 67, 95, 123, 181, 183, 187
  and structural and system drivers of EFH 40, 43
social work services, significance of 84
social workers 2–5, 61, 132, 190
  and contextual safeguarding beyond UK 84, 85
  and decolonising practice 90, 93
  and parents as partners 126, 129

  and participation 108, 118–19
  and peer mapping and assessment 48, 51, 53–5
  relationship with 116–17
  and structural and system drivers of EFH 36, 38, 43
sociological theory (Bourdieu) 26–7
SPACE 107–8
Spain 80, 84
statutory system, tensions within 95–7
stigmatisation 27, 28, 121, 122
  see also parents
streets 2, 9, 20, 28, 30, 35, 38, 65, 66, 168, 179
strengths-based value 9, 193–4
structural barriers 77, 122, 123
structural disparity 17
structural inequalities 30
  and contextual safeguarding framework 26–8
  and critical thinking about context 19–21
  CS approaches to 37–42
  and extra-familial harm (EFH) 21–6
  naming, responding to 36–7
  naming and addressing, challenges in 32–4
  naming and addressing, impact of 34–6
  practice examples of 31–7
  and social conditions of abuse tackling 17–19
surveillance 27, 49, 56, 87, 95, 107–8, 119
  -based interventions 67
  in peer group context 52–4
Swansea Children's Services 153
Sweden 80, 81
Switzerland 84
symbolic violence 27–8
system review method, importance of 166–9
systemic barriers 122, 123, 190
systemic disparity 17
systemic harm 19, 21, 92, 94, 95

T

target 3, 11
  see also extra-familial harm (EFH); peer mapping and assessment; structural inequalities
Theory of Change (ToC) model 161–4, *163*, 170, 171, 173
trafficking 22, 78–83, 87
trans young people 27, 37
transparency 53, 54, 115, 148
trauma, impact of 126, 137, 140
trust 123, 180
  building, in peer group context 52–4, 55
  and collaboration 118
  as mutual 117
  negative impact on 116
  for young people 116

Index

U
United Nations Convention on the Right of the Child (UNCRC) 105–6

V
victimisation 64, 91, 124
  and gender 24, 37
  risk of 24, 50
victims 79–82, 87–8, 150
  and blame 91, 150
  and perpetrator, binary 23, 79, 83–4, 88
  and race and minorities 23–4
  secondary 122
Violence Reduction Units (VRUs) 64
voluntary and community sector (VCS) 87, 109
vulnerability 53, 77, 79–80, 97, 122, 137
  and community safety reimagining 67, 69, 73, 74
  to EFH 81–2, 86, 87
  and inequalities in experiences of EFH 22, 24, 25
  and structural and system drivers of EFH 32, 37, 40

W
Watching Over Working With resource 29
'Welcome to Tottenham' (poem) 30, 43
welfare 5–6, 62, 66, 69, 72–6, 136, 138–9, 168–9, 181, 183
welfare model 50–2, 55, 83
What Works for Children's Social Care 150
Working Together to Safeguard Children 22, 46–7, 123, 124, 148

Y
Youth Research Advisory Panel (YRAP) 105, 110–11
  consultative activities with **111**
  developing work and thinking through safeguarding *112*
youth workers 52, 54, 115, 117, 175, 180–1, 184, 189, 192, 194